AFRICAN AMERICANS IN PENNSYLVANIA

ABOVE GROUND AND UNDERGROUND

AN ILLUSTRATED GUIDE

African Americans in Pennsylvania
Above Ground and Underground: An Illustrated Guide

Text © 2001 by Charles L. Blockson
Photographs and artwork from the Charles L. Blockson
Afro-American Collection

ISBN 1-879441-85-3

LOC Control # 2001 130156

Published by

RB
BOOKS

Harrisburg, PA

Seitz & Seitz, Inc.
1010 North Third Street
Harrisburg, PA 17102
www.celebratePA.com

Designed by Klinginsmith & Company

Printed in China by Regent Publishing Services
St. Louis, MO 63123

AFRICAN AMERICANS IN PENNSYLVANIA

ABOVE GROUND AND UNDERGROUND

AN ILLUSTRATED GUIDE

MOTHER BETHEL
A.M.E. CHURCH

Founded on ground
purchased by Richard
Allen in 1787, this con-
gregation is the mother
church of the African
Methodist Episcopal
denomination. The
present structure,
erected 1889, replaces
three earlier churches
on this site.

CHARLES L. BLOCKSON

I have a deep sense of gratitude to those who helped me transform my years of research, endless notes, and travel, and particularly my vision, into this book. I thank my typist, Lisa Fitch, for her patience and extensive work. My editor, John Hope, worked long hours to craft my words into a much more readable text. Art Director Cheryl Klinginsmith, the designer of this book and jacket, has fulfilled my vision for an attractive presentation. I also appreciate Zohraz Kazanjian for his dedication and photographic skills. Martha Berg very carefully prepared the extensive index. And my publisher, Blair Seitz at RB Books, encouraged me, coordinated the team effort, and navigated the book through the press process. My sincere thanks to all of them.

Charles L. Blockson

Table of Contents

Introduction

For the past 30 years, I have traveled throughout Pennsylvania's 67 counties with an unquenchable desire to research and record the neglected history of African-Americans in our state.

My interest in the history of my people started with an incident when I was in school. The teacher was talking about Benjamin Franklin one day, and as I listened to her litany of Franklin's accomplishments, it struck me that all the historic achievements we had learned about were credited to white Americans. But I remembered discussions in my family, stories of Booker T. Washington, George Washington Carver, Joe Louis, Paul Robeson, and Jesse Owens.

When I asked the teacher to relate some notable contributions of black people, she betrayed no hint of uncertainty in her answer. "Negroes have no history," she declared. "They were born to serve white people."

I sat in stunned silence. For the first few moments after her response, I was dreadfully aware of the sea of white faces surrounding the three or four of us who were black in that classroom. I had never before been confronted with such flagrant prejudice.

Determined to help eliminate that ignorance, I've gone to cities and towns, to historical societies, to newspaper files, letters, books, and diaries whose pages contained some materials that I knew existed and others that I stumbled across by happy accident. Many of those materials are now part of the Charles L. Blockson Collection at Temple University in Philadelphia, which is a primary resource for documents and files on the Underground Railroad.

Two significant facts have emerged from my research. First, there was great diversity in the people and the roles they played in our history. And second, the exploitation of African-Americans by the dominant society was so sustained that a major theme of African-American life has been the struggle for equality and freedom from oppression.

The lives of African-Americans in Pennsylvania took on a dual character. Forced exclusion from the mainstream brought about the creation of separate institutions and lifestyles. But African-American citizens never stopped in their efforts to change the dominant white society.

The African presence in Pennsylvania can be traced to the late 1630s, when enslaved Africans served the Swedes, Dutch, Finns, and English. After the fall of the Dutch, the colony came into English hands. Among the early Quaker slaveholders was William Penn, the founder of the Commonwealth of Pennsylvania. Connected with the Penn family were slaves named Peter, Sam, Sue, Dorcas, Hesia, Yass, Jack, and Jack's wife, Parthenia.

Records indicate that the great majority of enslaved and free Africans throughout the period of slavery were located in the southeastern region of the commonwealth, in and around Philadelphia. There were many in Bucks, Chester, Montgomery, Lancaster, and York counties. Some years later, several persons of African descent came with the French when they settled in western Pennsylvania. And others could be traced wherever white people settled permanently.

Edward Turner, an early Pennsylvania historian, estimated the number of slaves to be 1,000 in 1700; 2,500 in 1725; and 6,000 in 1750, when slavery reached its peak in this colony.

In an effort to deter slaves from running away and to curb admixture with whites, repressive laws were enacted that restricted the slaves' freedom of movement and prohibited social intercourse with indentured servants. Both free and enslaved Africans were relegated to special courts and judges, and were punished with penalties different than those applied to whites.

Although a majority of early Pennsylvania's most prominent merchants and political figures were slaveholders, almost from the beginning of Penn's "peaceable kingdom" there were some feelings against slavery. As early as 1688, Francis Daniel Pastorius, a German lawyer, and others drafted their famous "Germantown Protest," which was followed by organization of the Pennsylvania Abolition Society. The society was founded by Quakers and others in 1775, partly in response to large problems raised by the increasing numbers of enslaved Africans recently freed but poorly prepared for freedom.

A 1780 law provided that no child born in Pennsylvania after its enactment should be a slave. It was the second abolition measure adopted by any state (a similar provision was put in the Vermont constitution in 1777).

One of the main elements in this book is the story of many of the Pennsylvania State Historical Markers that are related to African-American heritage. When one considers the number of historical landmarks and memorials in Pennsylvania, it is surprising that as recently as a decade ago, public memorialization had all but ignored the history of a very significant percentage of Pennsylvania's population. While progress has been made, African-American markers still are under-represented among the state's 1500+ markers.

The other main theme of this book is the Underground Railroad, a subject that has excited more admiration and curiosity than any other in American history. A border state between the north and south, Pennsylvania became an important refuge for runaway slaves. Nearly every county had some connection with the freedom network. Many religious institutions were connected with the clandestine activity, especially African-American churches.

Numerous escaping slaves who had planned to go to Canada felt safe from the clutches of slave hunters here and settled in crowded cities and sparsely populated rural areas. Many sites important to the Underground Railroad in Pennsylvania and elsewhere have been lost to development or deterioration. A number of important Underground Railroad stations were doomed by the secrecy that surrounded their existence during the 18th and 19th centuries.

My interest in the Underground Railroad certainly stems from my own family's association with it. When I was just 10 years old, sitting in the backyard of our Norristown home, my grandfather would tell me stories about our family.

"My father—your great-grandfather, James Blockson—was a slave over in Delaware," my grandfather said. "As a teenager he ran away underground and escaped to Canada." My grandfather knew little more about his father's flight to freedom because of the secrecy that surrounded the trip along the invisible rails of the Underground Railroad. Just as James Blockson kept the details of his journey secret, so did his cousin, Jacob Blockson, who escaped to Ontario in 1858. Jacob told William Still, the famous Underground Railroad agent in Philadelphia, the reason for his escape. "My master was about to be sold this fall," he said, "and I made up my mind that I did not want to be sold like a horse....I resolved to die sooner than I would be taken back."

Years later, I read Jacob Blockson's words in Still's classic book *The Underground Railroad* and saw the information about my family authenticated. After that, how could I not pursue my studies with the passion of someone whose family was a part of this great tradition? As interest in the Underground Railroad has grown and books and other materials have been published, former U.S. Rep. Peter Kostmayer, who represented Pennsylvania, raised the possibility of tracing the Underground Railroad, and asked me if I thought the project was feasible. In 1990, legislation was introduced in Congress by Representative Kostmayer and Senator Paul Simon of Illinois to study options for commemorating the Underground Railroad.

With the active support of delegations from several states, Congress enacted Public Law 101-628 on November 28, 1990, which directed the Secretary of the Interior through the National Park Service to conduct a study of alternatives for commemorating and interpreting the Underground Railroad. The first meeting of the Advisory Committee that I was asked to chair was held in Independence Hall in March 1993. President William Clinton signed the National Underground Railroad Network to Freedom law on July 21, 1998.

Several recent publications about the Underground Railroad in Pennsylvania have used maps and charts to illustrate Underground Railroad routes in the state. Although certain cities, towns, and villages were known to harbor runaway slaves, I believe it is misleading

Harriet Tubman

to indicate that these communities, often located in sparsely populated and densely wooded areas, were routes on the freedom network.

Slave hunters frequently watched specific cities and towns. Underground Railroad agents and conductors were known to change the direction of escape at a moment's notice. While a great amount of the evidence that made this study possible was collected by fieldwork over many years, I also have searched archives, libraries, and historical societies and have conducted oral interviews with people whose relatives were connected with the Underground Railroad.

My hope is that this lavishly illustrated book can help further interest in and appreciation for the rich multifaceted contributions of African-Americans in the Commonwealth of Pennsylvania. Ultimately, this is the story of people who risked everything, including their lives, for the chance to live free. Perhaps no one expressed their desires better than Harriet Tubman, the great Underground Railroad conductor, when she first crossed the Mason-Dixon line into Pennsylvania.

When Tubman escaped, she did not know what direction to go and had no compass to guide her. Her father taught her to recognize the star constellation we call the Big Dipper, known to slaves as the "Drinking Gourd." Harriet knew the words of the coded spiritual "Follow the Drinking Gourd."

*When the sun goes back
and the first quail calls
Follow the drinking gourd
The old man is a-waitin' for
to carry you to freedom
Follow the drinking gourd*

*Chorus
Follow the drinking gourd,
follow the drinking gourd
For the old man is a-waitin'
to carry you to freedom*

Follow the drinking gourd
The river bed makes a mighty fine road,
Dead trees to show you the way
And it's left foot, peg foot, traveling on
Follow the drinking gourd

The river ends between two hills
Follow the drinking gourd
There's another river on the other side
Follow the drinking gourd

I thought I heard the angels say
Follow the drinking gourd
The stars in the heavens
gonna show you the way
Follow the drinking gourd

The gourd's handle pointed to the North Star, which she called the "freedom star." Once she located the North Star, she knew in which direction freedom lay, and she began her journey.

When Harriet crossed the Mason-Dixon line in 1849, she said, "When I found that I had crossed the line, I looked at my hands to see if I was the same person. There was such a glory over everything. The sun came like gold through the trees and over the fields. I felt like I was in heaven. I was free; but there was nobody to welcome me to the land of freedom. I was a stranger in a strange land; and my home, after all, was down in Maryland; because my father, my mother, my brothers, my sisters and friends were there. But, I was free and they should be free. I would make my home in the North and bring them there. God helping me."

Charles L. Blockson
Philadelphia
June 2001

PHILADELPHIA COUNTY

CLIVEDEN
Former home of
Richard Allen

PHILADELPHIA

Mother Bethel
African Methodist
Episcopal Church

ORIGINALLY INHABITED BY NATIVE AMERICANS, AT DIFFERENT TIMES PHILADELPHIA WAS A POSSESSION OF THREE FOREIGN NATIONS-THE NETHERLANDS, SWEDEN, AND GREAT BRITAIN. ALL THREE OF THESE NATIONS HELD AFRICAN PEOPLE IN SLAVERY.

Nestled between the Schuylkill and Delaware Rivers, Philadelphia County began as a gateway to settlements throughout the state. Many settled in the port area. General information describes Philadelphia as a leading industrial center and tourist attraction. From its distant past, until the present, African-Americans left a prominent and poignant imprint on Philadelphia.

There is evidence that African-Americans were here as early as 1639. Many prominent Philadelphia merchants and religious and political figures were involved in the trade of African men, women, and children, despite the existence and legal acceptance of the "peculiar institution" of slavery in the "City of Brotherly Love."

Philadelphia once contained the largest free African-American community in the United States. These individuals created institutions for the purpose of collectively challenging slavery and racism and

Enslaved Africans were brought to Pennsylvania during the late 1630s among the Dutch, Swedes, and English.

championing the cause of universal application of "life, liberty and the pursuit of happiness." They proceeded to establish churches, schools, literary societies, fraternal organizations, and businesses.

Philadelphia – City Hall

The massive structure occupying four-and-one-half acres is one of the largest municipal buildings in the United States. John J. McArthur, Jr., designed the building. At the tower, rising more than 500 feet above the street, is a 26-ton statue of William Penn, the Quaker founder of Pennsylvania and Philadelphia. Penn believed in a "Just God" and an "Inner Light" of guidance and morality. He repudiated war and named his government a "Holy Experiment," proclaiming it a non-violent brotherhood.

Yet, Penn was a slaveholder. In 1700 Penn, eager to improve the moral conditions of his slaves and other enslaved Africans in his colony, sent to the Assembly a bill for the regulation of their marriage. However, the bill was defeated. When Penn returned to England in 1701, he liberated his slaves stating, "I give to...my blacks, their freedom as under my hand already."

This will, which was left with James Logan, Penn's secretary, was not carried out. Penn's last will contains no mention of his slaves. Logan and other administrators stated that they could not follow Penn's instructions because they were a "private matter."

Penn's original 1701 City Charter hangs in the Law Library Ceremonial Reception Room in City Hall.

Location: Broad and Market Streets

Philadelphia – First Protest Against Slavery – 1688

Led by Francis Daniel Pastorius and a small group of other German refugees and Quakers, the first protest against slavery in America occurred on April 18, 1688, in the former Thones Kunders house in Germantown. This group of men who had no previous acquaintance with the horrible institution of slavery was amazed to find it existing in William Penn's colony.

Though Pastorius was not a Quaker, he taught in a Quaker school in Germantown, and recent information indicates that he had

William Penn, founder of Pennsylvania, was a slave owner.

become a Quaker by the time he signed the Germantown Protest in 1688. As one of the few intellectuals in the province, he helped to shape the cultural life of early Philadelphia. Pastorius was also an author and owned a library of more than 250 books written in several languages.

Pastorius and three other men met at the Friends meeting-house in Germantown on April 18, 1688, and placed their signatures on this historic abolitionist document that stated the reasons why they were against slavery and the "traffic in men's bodies." Pastorius sent the protest document to Abington Meeting, which turned it down. It then was sent to Philadelphia Yearly Meeting, where it was dropped as "radical and untimely."

This "Germantown Protest" was but the first of a number of voices raised in Pennsylvania. It was followed by the writings of George Keith, John Woolman, Benjamin Lay, Anthony Benezet, Ralph Sandiford, Thomas Paine, and others. Following the anti-slavery example expressed in the wording of the Germantown Protest, proclamations against slavery were issued in several other colonies.

> **Location: Pennsylvania State Historical Marker at 5109 Germantown Avenue**

Philadelphia – Gloria Dei (Old Swedes') Church

Certified by the Philadelphia Historical Commission as the oldest original structure on its original site in Philadelphia, Gloria Dei (or Old Swedes' Church as it is commonly called) was first used for services in 1700. Its steep gable roof, square belfry, and small spire contribute to its Swedish character.

There were enslaved Africans in the region around the Delaware River before Pennsylvania was founded. They had arrived with the Dutch, Swedes, and the Finns. In April 1639, a Swedish ship, the *Vogel Grip*, returned from the Caribbean with a slave named Anthony and docked in Delaware, then known as New Sweden.

Anthony served as a slave under the Governor of New Sweden, John Printz, who moved his government from Fort Christina to Tinicum Island, the present site of the Philadelphia Airport.

Anthony holds the distinction of possibly being the first person of African descent in present day Pennsylvania. Immediately after William Penn arrived in his colony, there are records of slaves in Philadelphia and Chester counties between 1684 and1687.

Penn noticed that in his charter to The Free Society of Traders, one Swedish settler in South Philadelphia listed his Negro servant in a 1683 census.

Location: Delaware Avenue and Swan Street

Philadelphia – London Coffee House

The building was built in 1702 by Charles Reed, who obtained the land from William Penn's daughter, Letitia. In 1754, Major William Bradford, who then was publisher of the *Pennsylvania Journal*, successfully established a coffeehouse after the London style.

In the rear portion of the building, the *Pennsylvania Journal* was printed and sold. The front served as a meeting place for merchants, ship captains, judges, lawyers, city officials, and British Crown officers. When the coffeehouse was rented in 1780 to Gifford Dally, the written terms with John Pemberton, a Quaker, and its proprietor included a requirement that Dally "would exert his endeavors as a Christian to preserve decency and order in said house and to discourage the profanation of the sacred name of God, Almighty by cursing and swearing."

However, it was common practice of the day to sell enslaved Africans who recently arrived from slave ships a short distance from the London Coffeehouse. Slaves were crudely examined and

Slaves were paraded before buyers on a platform in front of the London Coffeehouse and also at an auction block at Water Street between Spruce and High Streets.

displayed upon a platform in front of the establishment. The building is now open to the public.

Location: Pennsylvania State Historical Marker at 2 South Front Streets

Philadelphia – Fort Mifflin

Designed in 1771 by Captain John Montressor, a British engineer, it was unfinished at the beginning of the Revolutionary War. "Mud Fort," its original name, has been called "one of the remaining examples of the oldest harbor defense fortification system in the United States."

When the British occupied Philadelphia, the fort had a garrison of 300 men and 20 cannons. The British abandoned "Mud Fort" when they evacuated Philadelphia. In 1795, the fort was renamed in honor of Thomas Mifflin, George Washington's *aide de camp* and Pennsylvania's first governor.

In 1800, a cargo of slaves used the fort as a hideaway until they received assistance from Philadelphia abolitionists and were sent to safety in other areas. During the War of 1812, when a British fleet established a blockade and threatened Philadelphia, a group of volunteers manned the fort.

African-American community leaders Richard Allen, Absalom Jones, and James Forten volunteered to defend the defenseless city. In August 1814, the British were marching from Washington D.C. towards Philadelphia. Once again, a group of African-Americans assembled at the junction of Gray's Ferry on the Schuylkill River dressed in colorful uniforms. Although the threatened invasion of Philadelphia did not occur, when the volunteers returned to the city, they were hailed as heroes.

Location: West bank of the Delaware River below the confluence of the Delaware and Schuylkill Rivers

Philadelphia – Mikveh Israel Cemetery

Mikveh Israel Cemetery is the oldest Jewish cemetery in Philadelphia. It is on land donated in 1740 by Nathan Levy. Buried here are Haym Solomon, the celebrated financier of the American Revolutionary War, and Rebecca Gratz, the inspiration for a character in Sir Walter Scott's Ivanhoe, and her brother Simon, co-founder of the Pennsylvania Academy of Fine Arts.

Also buried in this cemetery is a slave woman named Lucy Marks. The prominent Marks family owned Lucy Marks. Lucy took her owner's surname, as was the common practice during the period of slavery. According to Jewish historian Maxwell Whiteman, Lucy observed the traditions of Judaism and was a member of Congregation Mikveh Israel in the 1790s.

Upon her death in 1823, the family applied for the customary burial in the synagogue's cemetery. Some members of the congregation protested the burial of a servant in their cemetery. After a short delay and intense support from other members, Lucy was buried in an unmarked grave.

Rebecca Gratz, daughter of prominent merchant Michael Gratz, in attempting to have her non-Jewish mother buried in the same cemetery, used the fact of Lucy Marks' grave to illustrate that the cemetery had already received non-Jews.

Location: Spruce Street between Eighth and Ninth Streets

Philadelphia – General Lafayette Statue

The name Lafayette is familiar to most Americans; there are numerous buildings, streets, towns, cities, and educational institutions that bear his name. Along East River Drive (now Kelly Drive), near the Philadelphia Museum of Art, stand the statues of six foreign Revolutionary War heroes who fought for American Independence:

General Marquis de Lafayette

Major General Friedrich von Steuben, Naval Commander John Paul Jones, General Casimir Pulaski, General Richard Montgomery, General Nathaniel Greene, and General Marquis de Lafayette.

Lafayette (1757-1834) spent his long life in the interest of liberty. He fought in both the American and French Revolutions. His beliefs cost him his fortune and social position, but his actions won him the respect of Americans.

At a young age, Lafayette became a major general in George Washington's army. The British nicknamed him, "The Boy." During this period of the war years, he included among his friends several African-Americans. Perhaps the most celebrated of these was his favorite spy, James Armistead, a Virginia slave and soldier who served under Lafayette and who was with Lafayette when British General Cornwallis surrendered at Yorktown.

Hannah Till, an African-American woman cook for Washington and Lafayette during the war, lived at 182 South Fourth Street. When Lafayette returned to America in 1824, he presented her with a gift. She died in 1825. Lafayette vigorously opposed slavery and was a member of the Pennsylvania Abolition Society. It is said that one reason George Washington freed his slaves was because of Lafayette's urging.

Location: East River Drive (Kelly Drive) near the Philadelphia Museum of Art

Philadelphia – Anthony Benezet and the Free African School

Even before he became a Quaker, Anthony Benezet condemned slavery. He became colonial America's most prolific anti-slavery pamphleteer. In his first published work, he dismissed the charge that blacks were an inferior being.

"I might show from innumerable examples, how [slavery]

Anthony Benezet teaching African-American children in his Willing's Alley school.

introduces idleness, discourages marriage, corrupts the youth and ruins and debauches morals," Benezet wrote. He was a great believer in the education of African-Americans. The Willing's Alley Free African School was established by Anthony Benezet for African-American children.

The schoolhouse was a one-story, brick building approximately 32 feet by 18 feet in which Benezet also gave instruction to African-American adults in the evenings. In his will, he provided that after his wife's death, his estate should be used to hire religious minded persons to teach a number of Negro, Mulatto, and Indian children.

Richard Allen and Absalom Jones and a number of early African-American leaders of Philadelphia received their education as a result of this bequest. A small street in the Germantown section of the city honors Benezet's name.

Location: Between Chestnut and Walnut, Third and Fourth Streets

Philadelphia – Arch Street Meetinghouse and Olaudah Equiano

Olaudah Equiano (Gustavus Vassa) was captured as a slave from Nigeria in West Africa as a child and served under several masters in the Caribbean and America. He was owned for a short period by a wealthy Philadelphia Quaker merchant and slave dealer named Robert King, who belonged to Arch Street Meeting.

Because of Equiano's intelligence, King trained him to be a clerk. As he toiled to enrich his owner, he observed the misery of other slaves held in bondage. After gaining his freedom, he settled in London, England, where he wrote his classic book *The Interesting Narrative of the Life of Olaudah Equiano, or Gustavus Vassa* in 1789. In his narrative he said he had few illusions about the good life for a black freeman in America. His autobiography helped the British government abolish slavery in Great Britain. Even in Philadelphia, his narrative became a best seller. It has been ranked with the autobiographies of Benjamin Franklin and Frederick Douglass, who also vividly captured the historical tide.

Olaudah Equiano

Location: 320 Arch Street

Philadelphia – Head House Square

Originally known as the Old Market House, the Head House, beautifully restored, is the site of one of the oldest public market houses in the nation. An open-air market since 1745, Head House Square today provides an excellent look at the festive atmosphere where vendors of Old Philadelphia hawked and sold their wares.

African-American street and market vendors have a long and

interesting tradition at Head House Square. Here visitors purchased sea bass from the fish man, hominy from the hominy man, pies from the pie man, hot corn and pepper-pot soup from the pepper-pot woman, who called out, "Pepper-pot, all hot, all hot! Makee back strong! Makee live long! Come buy my Pepper pot!"

A typical gathering place for early vendors was the open market place at Head House Square.

Oystermen could also be seen offering their fare to hungry visitors in the square. Beautiful, exotic-looking, coffee and cream-complexion women of French and African descent, newly arrived from the Caribbean, dressed in richly French and West Indian fashion with colorful turbans upon their heads, escorted by wealthy French gentlemen, could be seen strolling through the square.

Location: Second and Pine Streets

Philadelphia – The Liberty Bell

The Liberty Bell, a historic symbol so reverently preserved as the noblest utterance of human rights and as the charter of freedom, was cast in London in 1751. The 2,080-pound bell arrived in Philadelphia the following year.

According to tradition, the bell got its familiar name "Liberty Bell" when it was rung at the adoption of the Declaration of

Independence on July 8, 1776. In later years, a small group of abolitionists known as the Friends of Freedom, founded in Boston, issued a series of publications entitled "The Liberty Bell" from 1839 to 1858. Inscribed in the 1839 issue of the pamphlet is a sonnet that reads, "Suggested by the inscription of the Philadelphia Liberty Bell." The crown of the bell is encircled with the words from Leviticus 35:10—"Proclaim liberty throughout all the land unto all the inhabitants thereof."

The Friends of Freedom associated with this publication were a number of distinguished anti-slavery and literary personalities such as Frederick Douglass, William Wells Brown, Lucretia Mott, Harriet Beecher Stowe, Elizabeth Barrett Browning, Henry David Thoreau, Lydia Maria Child, and William Lloyd Garrison.

Location: Fifth and Market Streets

Philadelphia – Stenton

Located in the Germantown section of the city, Stenton, built in 1728, was the former home of William Penn's secretary, James Logan. A Quaker, Logan was one of the most intellectual men in colonial America. His Georgian Colonial mansion housed America's finest private collection of books, which is now part of the collection of the Library Company of Philadelphia (Free Library of Philadelphia).

The house was occupied for a time in 1777 during the Revolutionary War by General George Washington and later by British General Sir William Howe, who made the home his headquarters for directing the Battle of Germantown.

On the historic home is a plaque honoring Logan's servant, an African-American woman by the name of Dinah. By her quick thought and presence of mind, Dinah saved the mansion from being burned by British soldiers in the winter of 1777.

According to family members many years later, two British

soldiers prepared to burn the mansion. When they went to the barn to get straw to set the fire, a British officer rode up with sword drawn and asked Dinah if she had seen any deserters. The wise old servant woman promptly replied that, "Two such have just gone to secrete themselves in the barn."

The officer rode to the barn and chased the "deserters" away, and Stenton was saved. The Logan family continued to live in the mansion for six generations until 1900. It is maintained by the National Society of Colonial Dames of America in the Commonwealth of Pennsylvania. A plaque was dedicated in honor of the black woman with this inscription: *In memory of Dinah, faithful, colored caretaker of Stenton, who by her quick thought and presence of mind, saved the mansion from being burned by the British soldiers in the winter of 1777.*

Although most historians in the past have said that Dinah was a slave, she had been freed by the Logans in the spring of 1776.

Born in England, Thomas Paine is known primarily for his radical ideas and because he signed the Declaration of Independence. A genuine lover of liberty, he spoke out emphatically against slavery.

Location: In Stenton Park on Windrim Avenue near 18th Street

Philadelphia – The Pennsylvania Abolition Society

Founded at the Sun Tavern in 1775 by Quakers and others as the Society for the Relief of Free Negroes Unlawfully Held in Bondage, the group was reorganized as the Pennsylvania Abolition Society in 1781. Listed among its members were such non-Quakers as Thomas Paine, Dr. Benjamin Rush, the Marquis de Lafayette, and Benjamin Franklin, who became its president.

In later years, noted anti-slavery advocates such as William Still, Robert Purvis, and Quaker Lucretia Mott were included among the society's members. Since its earliest years, the society has sponsored schools for African-Americans and has acted as a spur to urge the city and state to provide a decent education.

Today, the society continues to be an educational and civil rights organization connected with African-Americans.

Location: Pennsylvania State Historical Marker on Front Street below Chestnut Street

Dr. Benjamin Rush, member of the Continental Congress and a signer of the Declaration of Independence, was a brilliant social reformer and a friend of Philadelphia's African-American community.

Philadelphia – Thomas Paine and Independence Hall

Independence Hall and the Mall have been called the "most historic square mile in the United States." In the first floor Assembly room, delegates from all 13 colonies met on July 4, 1776, to approve the Declaration of Independence.

Many of the distinguished signers of that historic document were slave owners. Included among non-slave owners were Dr. Benjamin Rush and his friend Thomas Paine. Rush, who was America's foremost physician during that period, openly encouraged Richard Allen and other prominent African-American leaders to seek abolition of slavery, while writing against the horrid institution himself. Rush's influence with the African-American community was tremendous. It also was Rush who encouraged Thomas Paine to write his fiery pamphlet, suggesting the name "Common Sense," that called for immediate independence from Great Britain.

Paine was a genuine lover of liberty and bluntly attacked all forms of its abuse. His first published article in America, in the *Pennsylvania Journal and Weekly Advertiser*, March 8,

1775, was a scathing attack against slavery. He also wrote an article introducing Phillis Wheatley to the Philadelphia public.

Wheatley was brought as a child from Africa and sold on the docks of Boston. Before she was 20, she achieved some renown as a poet. She holds the distinguished honor of being the first African-American to publish a book in 1773. After receiving a copy of her book, General George Washington wrote her a letter of commendation.

When Paine died in 1809, in a shabby lodging house with no grieving friends present, he had accomplished more for human freedom than any of his contemporaries. He had no grave and his bones were lost, yet his published writings are read by people throughout the world.

Phillis Wheatley

Philadelphia – St. George's Methodist Church

Founded in 1767, St. George's Methodist Church is the oldest continuously used Methodist Church in the world. Richard Allen, who had purchased his freedom in Delaware, joined the Methodist Society at age 17 in 1777. Allen commenced traveling in 1783 as a circuit lay minister, conducting religious services in three states.

He returned to Philadelphia and joined the white congregation of St. George's Methodist Church. Allen was licensed to preach in 1784 and was permitted to hold services at 5:00 in the morning. Due to the increasing number of African-Americans who attended the church to hear Allen preach, tensions increased and white parishioners began to complain.

One Sunday morning, a white sexton met the African-American parishioners at the door and sent them to the gallery to sit in "Negro" pews. As Allen observed and heard considerable scuffling, he noticed that the trustees were pulling Absalom Jones and William White off their knees. When the prayer was over, the African-

The Rev. Richard Allen

American parishioners, led by Allen and Jones, withdrew from St. George's Church.

Location: 235 North Fourth Street

Philadelphia – Graff House

Jacob Graff, a bricklayer, built the original house in 1775. It was a small, brick dwelling with two rooms on each floor. The original house was razed in 1883. The present reconstructed house was built for the Bicentennial celebration as a recreation of the place where Thomas Jefferson resided during the summer of 1776.

Jefferson wrote the Declaration of Independence in rooms he rented from Jacob Graff. As chairman of the committee that drafted the Declaration of Independence Jefferson, a slave owner himself, wrote into his first draft a paragraph condemning human bondage in which he denounced George III for his propagation of slavery in the colonies.

But slavery was too profitable to the southern delegation and Jefferson's words were omitted from the final version of the Declaration as adopted by the Continental Congress of the United States on July 4, 1776. For freed and enslaved African-Americans, the principles of liberty and equality set forth in the Declaration were meaningless as long as they were not represented in the document.

Location: 7th and Market Streets

Philadelphia – Runaway Slave Newspaper Advertisements

Africans understandably were constantly seeking freedom by running away from their owners. The *American Weekly Mercury*, the first newspaper printed in Philadelphia in the year 1719, advertised in its second issue that a bright Mulatto by the name of Johnny had run away. The sale of black women slaves frequently appeared in this newspaper. Following are some ads as they appeared:

For Sale Female Slave
A very likely Negro woman to be sold, aged about 28 years. Fit for country or city business. She can card, spin, knit and milk; and any other country work. Whoever has a mind for the said Negro report to Andrew Bradford in Philadelphia.

Run away on the 4th instant, at night from James Leonard in Middlesex County, East New Jersey, a Negro man named Simon, aged 40 years, is well set fellow, about 5feet 10 inches high, has large eyes, and a foot 12inches long; he was bread and born in this country, talks good English, can read and write, is very slow in speech, can bleed and draw teeth, pretending to be a great doctor and very religious, and says he is a churchman, had on a dark grey broadcloth coat, with a good apparel, and peeked toe'd shoes. He took with him a black horse, about 13 hands and a half-high, a Star in forehead, branded with 2 on the near thigh or shoulder, and trots; also a black hunting saddle about half-worn. Whoever takes up and secures the said Negro, so that his Master may have him again shall have three pounds reward and reasonable charges, paid by James Leonard. Sept. 11, 1740

Run away on the 16th of July from Thomas Rutter, of this city a Negro Man, named Dick, commonly called "Preaching Dick," aged about 27 years.
      Thomas Rutter, Sept. 4, 1746

Location: 27-29 S. Second Street, corner of Black Horse Alley and Trotter Street (newspaper office)

This image of a runaway slave, represents one of the stereotype prints that were advertised in newspapers offering rewards for runaways.

Philadelphia – African Zoar Methodist Church

The 1787 walkout by Richard Allen, Absalom Jones, and other African-American members of St. George's United Methodist Church at Fourth and Race Streets led to the founding of African Zoar Methodist Church in 1794.

Although Allen and his congregants were welcomed at nearby St. Peter's Episcopal Church, they ultimately founded several other churches on their own. Led by the Reverend Harry Hosier and 15 men and women, the group originally worshipped from house to house and later occupied an abandoned butcher shop in the Campingtown section of Philadelphia before acquiring a permanent site in 1796.

An edifice was contracted on August 4 of that year and was dedicated by Bishop Francis Asbury and the Reverend John Dickins. It was the third Methodist structure built in Philadelphia.

The church served as the site of the first convention of Colored Local Preachers and Laymen, held August 23 to 27, 1852. It also served as a station on the Underground Railroad. In 1883, the congregation moved to 12th and Melon Streets.

> **Location: Pennsylvania State Historical Marker at the church's present site at 4th and Brown Streets**

Philadelphia – The Pennsylvania Hospital

Pennsylvania Hospital was founded in 1751 largely through the efforts of Benjamin Franklin and Dr. Thomas Bond. It was the first hospital in the nation; the first building was erected in 1755 and 1756. In later years, Dr. Benjamin Rush, who was called by his contemporaries the "greatest physician this country has produced," and who also earned the title "Father of American Psychiatry," was affiliated with Pennsylvania Hospital during the great Yellow Fever Plague of 1793.

It was also the year that refugees from Saint Dominique (Haiti) arrived during the hot summer fleeing the slave revolt on that island. Panic prevailed and within a month 17,000 persons had fled to other towns or into the country.

President George Washington retreated to Mount Vernon. Thomas Jefferson, likewise, fled the city. Corpses were thrown into coffins and buried at night. City officials ran the government from Germantown.

Mayor Mathew Clarkson, Stephen Girard, and Dr. Benjamin Rush called upon Richard Allen and Absalom Jones and the African-American community to volunteer to bury the dead. The yellow fever epidemic killed 5,000 people. The real heroes were the common people, along with Rush, Allen, Jones and Girard.

Location: Between Pine and Spruce Streets, 8th and 9th Streets

Philadelphia – St. Joseph's Catholic Church

Commonly called "Old St. Joseph's Church," it was founded in 1733 as the seat of the oldest Roman Catholic Church parish in Philadelphia. From the Revolutionary War era, St. Joseph's Church was closely connected to the French culture. Among the French freedom fighters who came to assist George Washington and his army and worship here were Marquis de Lafayette, the Conte de Rochambeau, and Admiral Francois de Grasse.

Less than a decade later, other French-speaking people arrived in Philadelphia from the Caribbean Island of Saint Dominique (now Haiti). They were fleeing a violent slave rebellion that broke out in 1791. Previously, the National Convention in Paris had declared that black slavery in all the colonies had been abolished. The decree was in vain. The wealthy planters of the colony opposed real equality and kept the French assembly from ratifying the treaty. Thus, a violent slave revolt occurred.

Throughout the early years of the 19th century, ships carrying hundreds of white refugees, their slaves, and free people of color arrived in Philadelphia and settled in the area of St. Joseph's Church and St. Mary's Catholic Church. Separate masses were conducted for white refugees and free persons of color, known as *gens de couleur*.
Because of the Pennsylvania Abolition Act of 1780, many wealthy owners freed their slaves, hired them as indentured servants, or moved to states where slaves were permitted.

Location: 321 Willings Alley

Philadelphia – Washington Square

As one of William Penn's five squares, Washington Square was originally called the Southeast Square. During the city's earlier years it served as a public burying ground or Potters Field. The name was later changed to Washington Square to honor George Washington.

Tradition also states that African-Americans and others called the Square "Congo Square." Slaves were brought to this square once a month before they were sold to buyers in Pennsylvania and elsewhere.

At "Congo Square," slaves and freed African-Americans could be seen praying, dancing, cooking traditional African foods, and conversing in various languages. The name "Congo" referred to the part of Africa now called "Zaire." A monument honoring "Unknown Soldiers of The Revolution" is located in this square. Many American and British soldiers' graves lie there, along with white and black victims of the yellow fever epidemic of 1793.

Location: Sixth to Seventh Streets, Walnut to Locust Streets

A Moses Williams silhouette

Philadelphia – Peale House

The Peale House honors Charles Willson Peale, a colonial American artist and portrait painter who painted a now-famous portrait of General George Washington in 1779. Peale's own slave, Moses Williams, who contributed to the development of the fine arts in this country, was an expert silhouette maker, one of the most popular and successful of his time.

Williams started out in the Peale establishment as an animal feeder. Promotion came later when Peale opened his museum in 1802 at Third and Lombard Streets. With the money Williams made from his silhouette proficiency, he was able to purchase his freedom.

As a free man, he began his family life when he married a white cook of the Peale house named Marie. This union was somewhat ironic in light of Marie's former contempt for Moses when he was a slave.

Location: 1811 Chestnut Street

Philadelphia – Rittenhouse Square

This scenic, tree-lined square was one of the original five squares planned by William Penn. In 1825 it was named for the famous astronomer and scientist David Rittenhouse, who was born in Germantown in 1732. Rittenhouse was known for his friendly relationships with African-Americans.

Listed among them were Benjamin Banneker, a self-taught, Maryland freeborn astronomer and scientist who published several important almanacs and made the first wooden striking clock in America.

At the age of 59, Banneker sent a copy of his almanac to Thomas Jefferson, then Secretary of State, along with a letter questioning Jefferson's contradictory views on slavery. Jefferson was sufficiently impressed with Banneker's work that he appointed him as a member of the commission to survey the new District of Columbia.

However, it was David Rittenhouse who provided Banneker with the highest recommendation when he wrote that he found Banneker's calculations sufficiently accurate for an almanac, and his total performance "extraordinary."

"Every instance of genius amongst the Negroes is worthy of attention," Rittenhouse went on to say, "because their oppressors seem to lay great stress on their supposed inferior mental abilities."

Location: 20th Street between Walnut and Locust Streets

Philadelphia – Free African Society

In 1787, the same year that Prince Hall, an African-American former Revolutionary War soldier, received formal approval for African Lodge No.1 in Boston, Richard Allen, Absalom Jones, Cyrus Bustill, and others were organizing the Free African Society in Philadelphia. The society was the first African-American organization in the United States formed on the basis of self-determination and self-reliance. It was conceived in struggle and born into existence for the specific purpose of uplifting Afircan-Americans out of the unjust circumstances they were forced into.

Right: The Rev. Absalom Jones

Out of the Society came the Free African Church of St. Thomas (Episcopal), with Absalom Jones as the rector, and Bethel Methodist Episcopal Church, with Richard Allen as the guiding light. The Free African Society contributed to the cost of providing social services for Philadelphia's African-American community such as caring for widows, burying the dead, providing adequate housing for local people, and helping escaping slaves on the Underground Railroad.

Location: **Pennsylvania State Historical Marker at Sixth and Lombard Streets**

Philadelphia – William Still

Abolitionist, writer, and businessman William Still was born in 1821, near Medford, Burlington County, New Jersey. Both of his parents were former slaves. His father, Levin, purchased his own freedom and changed his name from Steel to Still to protect his wife Sidney, who had escaped from slavery in Maryland. She changed her name to Clarity.

William Still was the youngest of 18 children. He arrived in Philadelphia in 1844, and three years later married Letitia George, who became the mother of his four children. During 1847, Still became an active abolitionist, taking a position as clerk in the

Underground Railroad chronicler William Still

Pennsylvania Anti-slavery Society and later serving as secretary of the Philadelphia Vigilance Committee.

In his classic book *The Underground Railroad*, published in 1872, Still provided his readers with numerous accounts of heroism of escapees and those who helped them flee from bondage at the risk of their own lives. He mentions several slaves who were boxed up and shipped to freedom to Philadelphia. Henry "Box" Brown, William Peel Jones, and Lear Green, a young woman, were shipped in a chest filled with straw from Baltimore, Md.

Still also described the ingenious escape of William and Ellen Craft, who traveled from Macon, Georgia, in 1848. They masqueraded as a master and slave, with Ellen portraying the master, aided by her light complexion and dressed in the top hat and well-cut suit of a planter. They contrived a bandage for a "toothache" and a sling for a "broken arm" to conceal her lack of a beard and her inability to write. The two traveled north with Ellen sleeping in first class accommodations in southern cities along their way until they reached Philadelphia and relative safety.

All of the above escapees received national acclaim for their daring escapes on the Underground Railroad.

Location: Pennsylvania State Historical Marker at Still's former home, 244 South 12th Street

Philadelphia – Cliveden

Quaker Benjamin Chew, Chief Justice of the Pennsylvania Supreme Court, built Cliveden, a large mansion and monument to American history, between 1763 and 1767. It is considered one of the finest Georgian homes in the nation. Cliveden figured most prominently in the Revolutionary War's Battle of Germantown, suffering heavy bombardment by the British.

Cliveden was also the home of Richard Allen and his family.

Allen was born in 1760, of a "pure African" father and Mulatto mother who were slaves. In need of money, Chew sold Cliveden to a Quaker family in Dover, Delaware, named Stokeley.

Tradition tells that Allen, who later became a bishop of the Bethel A.M.E. Church, helped to convert his master to the "ways of God." Stokeley permitted Allen and his brothers to hire out. Wisely, he saved his money, brought his freedom, and headed for Philadelphia.

Location: 6401 Germantown Avenue

Philadelphia – Christ Church

Christ Church, organized in 1695, is one of America's oldest and most historic churches. The present building, erected between 1727 and 1744, replaced the original structure constructed in 1695. George Washington, Thomas Jefferson, and Benjamin Franklin worshiped there. Five signers of the constitution were buried in Christ Church Burial Ground. The most noteworthy grave in the yard belongs to Benjamin Franklin.

Many years before any of the signers of the Declaration of Independence and the Constitution worshiped at the church, an amazing African-American woman known by the name of Alice, who was born in 1686 of slave parents in Philadelphia, vividly recalled the original wooden structure. The ceiling of it could be touched with her lifted hands. The bell, to call the people to worship, was hung in the crotch of a nearby tree. At the age of 10, Alice's slave owner then moved her to Dunk's Ferry, 17 miles up the Delaware River in Bucks County. She later collected tolls at Dunk's Ferry Bridge.

She is remembered riding on horseback, galloping to Christ Church at the age of 95. She vividly remembered William Penn, and

Benjamin Franklin's grave in Old Christ Church burial ground is one of several sites honoring his memory in Philadelphia.

Alice, a slave, used to come to Christ Church

Betsy Ross and seven signers of the Declaration of Independence occupied pews in Old Christ Church.

survived George Washington, the first President of the United States. Alice died at the age of 116 in Bristol, Bucks County.

The records of Christ Church showed that African-Americans were baptized, married, and were members of the congregation as early as 1717. There was a minister who had special charge of religious services for them.

Location: Second Street above Market Street

Philadelphia – Robert Morris House

John Reynolds built this imposing home in 1786 for Robert Morris financier of the American Revolution. A portion of Morris' wealth was acquired through the slave trade.

The commercial firm of Willings and Morris, brought hundreds of Africans to Philadelphia from 1754 to 1766, and sold them into slavery. John Inglis, another prominent Philadelphia merchant, who had a preoccupation with the slave trade, joined the firm of Willings and Morris and later became a full-fledged partner.

Built in Flemish bond of alternating red stretcher and black header brick, the Morris House is now a private residence and not open to the public.

Location: 225 S. Eighth Street

Philadelphia – Independence Hall

Probably more people visit Independence Hall than any other historic site in Philadelphia. This venerable historic building sits on a plot of land that is now called Independence National Historic Park.

When the first Constitutional Convention met here in 1787, delegates from northern states contended that slaves were property and

Robert Morris

thus should not be counted when apportioning representation. A compromise—the first of many that slavery would bring about—was reached:

Representatives and direct taxes shall be apportioned among the several states...according to their respective numbers, which shall be determined by adding to the whole numbers of free persons...three-fifths of all other persons.

These "other persons" were slaves. The slave trade was extended for 20 years in Article 10, Section 9 of the new Constitution. Article 4, Section 2 provided for the return of runaway slaves:

No person held to service or labour in one state, under the laws thereof, escaping into another, shall...be discharged from such service of labour, but shall be delivered up on claim of the party to whom such service of labour may be due.

The Fugitive Slave Law of 1793 further strengthened this extradition of fugitive slaves.

Independence Day, celebrated on July 4 each year, is the birthday of the United States of America. During the decades of the 1840s, 1850s, and 1860s, most African-Americans and some white abolitionists did not honor this day. They celebrated instead British West Indies Emancipation, when the slave trade was abolished on August 1, 1833.

Location: Fifth Street between Chestnut and Market Streets

Philadelphia – John Bartram House and Gardens

John Bartram was a Quaker botanist. He sired 11 children and planted thousands of trees and shrubs during Philadelphia's colonial period. In 1728, Bartram founded the first botanical garden in America in Pennsylvania.

His collection of native plants was probably the finest in the nation and he was one of the first botanists to produce a hybrid. In 1758, his fellow Quakers branded Bartram a heretic for denying the divinity of Christ and had him "read out of meeting."

Denounced and shunned by members of Darby Friends Meeting, Bartram was given a year to recant, but steadfastly refused. Nevertheless, he occasionally attended the meetinghouse even after his expulsion, but was not permitted to speak.

In 1731, Bartram built a two-and-a-half story Georgian colonial structure of rough stone. Its naïve and unusual interpretation of classical elements gives the house a peculiar charm. Rare and exotic plants brought from distant lands are in profusion in the Bartram gardens. Assisting Bartram and his children in transplanting and nourishing the plants was a freed slave named Harvey, who also ran the farm.

Visitors were often shocked to find Harvey eating at the same table with the Bartram family. Bartram's Garden is perhaps the first historical preservation project in America. He also helped to found the American Philosophical Society.

Location: 54th Street and Lindbergh Boulevard

Philadelphia – Mother Bethel African Methodist Episcopal Church

Mother Bethel sits on the oldest parcel of land continuously owned by African-Americans. In 1787, when the Free African Society voted to establish an Episcopal Church, Richard Allen declined to be its pastor because he wanted to remain a Methodist.

In 1791, Allen purchased a frame blacksmith shop and with a

Mother Bethel A.M.E. Church was a major station on the Underground Railroad.

team of horses moved it to a vacant lot he owned at Sixth and Lombard Streets. In July 1794, the congregation dedicated the converted wooden framed church and named it Bethel. In November of the same year, the Reverend Allen issued a declaration of independence from the leadership of St. George's Methodist Episcopal Church, using for the first time the name African Methodist Episcopal Church. Familiarly known as "Mother Bethel," the current building was constructed in 1889 in the same location. Stained glass windows feature both religious and Masonic themes. The shrine of the church contains the tomb of Bishop Richard Allen. The Richard Allen Museum housed in the lower level of the church contains 19th century artifacts such as the original pulpit constructed and used by Bishop Allen.

> **Location: Pennsylvania State Historical Marker at 419 Richard Allen Avenue, 6th and Lombard Streets**

Philadelphia – St. Thomas African Episcopal Church

The Reverend Absalom Jones organized St. Thomas, America's first African Episcopal Church, in 1792. It was an outgrowth of the Free African Society.

Jones was born a slave in Sussex County, Delaware, in 1746. As a child, he learned to read, and with the pennies he managed to save, he bought a speller. In 1761, a clerk taught him to write and permitted him to study in night school. He brought his freedom in 1784.

Over time, Jones became a friend of Richard Allen, and together they founded the Free African Society in 1787. During the Yellow Fever epidemic at the end of the century, the ministers Jones and Allen, along with other African-Americans, stayed in Philadelphia burying the dead while others fled. They were praised for their bravery.

Heroically, the African-American church members nursed the sick and buried the dead, performing those unpleasant and dangerous services voluntarily or for only little monetary reward.

In 1804, led by Jones, the church organized a day school for young people and in 1809 it set up a society for the suppression of vice.

Location: Pennsylvania State Historical Marker at the church's original location on 5th Street south of St. James Place (present location at 6361 Lancaster Avenue).

Philadelphia – Fraunces Tavern

President George Washington's personal cook, "Black Sam" Fraunces, established this tavern in 1790, when he came with the president to Philadelphia, then the nation's capital. Fraunces modeled the establishment after another tavern he owned in New York City, which was recognized as one of colonial America's finest. Washington was a regular customer there whenever he was in New York.

According to documented information, Fraunces' daughter Phoebe, who was George Washington's housekeeper, saved his life while Washington was eating in her father's tavern in New York City. She learned that one of the general's bodyguards, Thomas Hickey, was a British agent who had poisoned a dish of peas, and she warned Washington. Hickey was hanged June 28, 1776, with a large crowd looking on.

Location: Pennsylvania State Historical Marker at former establishment address, 310 South 2nd Street

Samuel Fraunces was a true patriot, helping the Revolution with food and money and serving as George Washington's personal cook during Washington's presidency.

James Forten, Sr.

Philadelphia – James Forten Sr.

James Forten was born free and served as a gunpowder boy during the American Revolution under Stephen Decatur, U.S. Naval Commander. He later established a very successful business manufacturing sails and invented an apparatus for managing sails.

The business, located at 95 Wharf Street in Philadelphia, employed both black and white craftsmen. Through his success as a sail maker, Forten was estimated to have amassed a fortune exceeding $100,000, an enormous sum for any man to accumulate in the 19th century. He was a key African-American abolitionist and was active in politics.

Forten was one of the founders of the Free African Society in 1787 and was instrumental in founding the American Reform Society. When British troops threatened the security of Philadelphia during the War of 1812, Forten and the Reverend Absalom Jones organized 2,000 black men to erect defenses at Gray's Ferry along the Schuylkill River, at the southern edge of the city.

The men joined forces again to solicit many of the 1,700 black subscribers for William Lloyd Garrison's anti-slavery newspaper, *The Liberator*. Forten played an integral role in the organization of the first Negro Convention in Philadelphia in 1830 and was its chairman.

> **Location: Pennsylvania State Historical Marker at 336 Lombard Street**

Philadelphia – Charlotte Forten

Charlotte Forten, granddaughter of James Forten, described the emotions surrounding a runaway slave trial in 1859. In her *Journal of Charlotte Forten,* she mentions Robert Purvis, her uncle through marriage.

Monday, April 4-Heard today that there has been another fugitive arrested. There is to be a trial. God, grant that this poor man may be released from the clutches of the slave hunters. Mr. Purvis has gone down. We wait anxiously to hear the results of the trial. How long? Oh, how long shall such a state of things as this last?

 Saturday, April 23-Daniel has left us and we hear with joy that he is safe in Canada. Oh, Stars and Stripes, that wave so proudly over mockery of freedom, what is your protection?

Charlotte Forten was educated at home and in Salem, Massachusetts. The journal that she began writing in her school years became an important historic document. She was familiar with anti-slavery leaders such as Frederick Douglass, Lucretia Mott, John Greenleaf Whittier, and others. She volunteered to go to St. Helena, South Carolina, after the Civil War, to teach newly emancipated slaves. She returned to Philadelphia in 1864.

Charlotte Forten

Location: Her father's house at 336 Lombard Street

Philadelphia – Girard College

Stephen Girard, a Frenchman, founded Girard College in 1848. He lived in Philadelphia and through successful trade in the Caribbean Islands and other parts of the world became one of the richest Americans of his time.

 At his death in 1831, he bequeathed a large sum of money toward establishment of Girard College. The stipulations in his will stated that the College was for "poor white boys only," and that a high wall should be built around it.

 The will sparked one of the longest cases in Philadelphia's legal history. Even though the school is situated in the midst of Philadelphia's African-American community, the city adhered to the stipulations for 100 years, until noted African-American lawyer Raymond Pace Alexander challenged it.

 Raymond Pace Alexander was the first African-American to serve on the Philadelphia Common Pleas Court. He charged the city with discrimination at Girard College in the 1930s. The case was not

Stephen Girard

won until the mid-1960s, when another African-American attorney, Cecil B. Moore, led hundreds of protesters to the college in May 1965. In August that same year, the Reverend Martin Luther King Jr., the nationally known civil rights leader, joined the protest march. The case was won when the United States Supreme Court decided against the legality of Girard's will. Both African-American boys and girls attend the school today.

Location: Pennsylvania State Historical Marker at Corinthian and Girard Avenues

Philadelphia – First African Baptist Church

Originally located at 10th and Vine streets, this church is one of the oldest African-American Baptist churches in the nation. The first pastor, the Reverend Henry Cunningham, helped secure the first location and served until 1813. The Reverend John King and the Reverend James Burrows, an enslaved African whose freedom was secured by two members of the congregation, Samuel Bivins and his cousin, followed him.

In 1896, Dr. William Creditt became pastor, and it was during his tenure that the First African Baptist Church became one of the outstanding religious institutions in the world. Under Creditt's guidance, the church organized the Mutual Aid Insurance Society, the first insurance company to serve black Philadelphians. The society was later moved to 10th and Cherry Streets, where Creditt founded the Cherry Building and Loan Association, as well as the Downingtown Industrial School, formerly the Downingtown Industrial and Agricultural School. The cornerstone for the church's current building was laid in 1906.

Location: Pennsylvania State Historical Marker at 16th and Christian Streets

Philadelphia – First African Baptist Church Cemetery

This was where the First African Baptist Church congregation buried its dead between 1824 and 1842. The site was excavated during the mid-1980s to make way for the Vine Street Expressway, and it was confirmed that the group retained ancient African burial customs here in Philadelphia. The remains were re-interred in Eden Cemetery in Delaware County.

> **Location: Pennsylvania State Historical Marker at 8th and Vine Streets**

Philadelphia – First African Presbyterian Church

John Gloucester, who is largely responsible for making Presbyterianism appealing to African-Americans, established the First African Presbyterian Church. Gloucester was an enslaved African of Dr. Gideon Blackburn.

Blackburn tutored him in religious thought and eventually freed him so he could serve as a missionary. The two migrated to Philadelphia, with Gloucester ultimately purchasing land at 7th and Bainbridge Streets that became the church's first site.

> **Location: Pennsylvania State Historical Marker at 42nd Street and Girard Avenue**

Philadelphia – Robert Purvis

Born free in Charleston, South Carolina, in 1810, Robert Purvis came to Philadelphia at an early age with his wealthy, white

Despite having English, African, and Jewish ancestors, wealthy abolitionist Robert Purvis preferred to live as an African-American.

father, William, and his mother Harriet, who was of African, English, and Jewish ancestry.

Recent research reveals that both of Purvis' parents owned and traded slaves in South Carolina before arriving in Philadelphia, where they became involved in the abolitionist movement. They sent their sons, Robert, Joseph, and William, to the Clarkson School, sponsored by the Pennsylvania Abolition Society.

While attending Amherst College in New England, Purvis met William Lloyd Garrison, whose writings influenced him to devote his life to the liberation of African-Americans.

He was active in the Colored Convention Movement in 1830 and served as vice president and corresponding secretary in 1833. The first united effort of importance on the part of free African-Americans was the convention movement that began in Philadelphia in 1831 and met annually for the next five years.

In 1838, the so-called Reform Constitution of Pennsylvania disenfranchised African-Americans. In response, Purvis published *Appeal of Forty Thousand Citizens Threatened with Disfranchisement to the People of Pennsylvania*. He and other African-Americans flooded the state legislature with appeals, memorials, and petitions, and won some supporters for their cause.

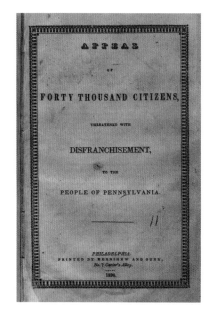

Robert Purvis' Appeal

Three years after they were deprived of their right to vote, African-Americans held the first state convention in Pittsburgh in August 1841, with 147 delegates present.

Between 1841 and 1847, they organized an association they called the Citizens Union of the Commonwealth of Pennsylvania, with a stated purpose to "obtain for colored people of the State all the Rights and Immunities of Citizenship." In 1870, African-Americans in Pennsylvania were once again granted the right to vote after the brutal years of the Civil War and a series of amendments to the U.S. Constitution that restored the franchise that was taken from them.

Purvis was active in many anti-slavery societies; he was a charter member of the Pennsylvania Anti-Slavery Society, President of The Philadelphia Underground Railroad, and Chairman of the

Philadelphia Vigilance Committee. Purvis refused to pay taxes when African-American children were excluded from the public schools in Byberry in 1853. After Purvis moved to Bucks County, his large farm at Byberry became an important station of the Underground Railroad. He protested racial discrimination by the War Department during the Civil War, although he supported African-American enlistment in the Union Army. Robert Purvis died in 1898 at 1601 Mt. Vernon Street. After his mother's death, her home at 270 Lombard Street became an important station on the Underground Railroad.

Location: Pennsylvania State Historical Marker at 1601 Mt. Vernon Street

Philadelphia – Pennsylvania Hall

Built in 1838 by abolitionists as a rallying place, Pennsylvania Hall was burned to the ground on May 17, 1838, one day after the

Planned to be the center of abolitionist activity in the state, three days after Pennsylvania Hall opened, it was destroyed by a mob while Philadelphia police looked on.

first anti-slavery meeting was held there. Mob violence was at its height in Philadelphia, and the hall was just one of the structures burned by white supporters of slavery. Others were the Shelter for Colored Orphans, 13th and Callowhill Streets, and an African-American church at 7th and Bainbridge Streets.

> Location: Pennsylvania State Historical Marker at 6th and Haines Streets

Philadelphia – A.M.E. Book Concern

As early as 1820, the African Methodist Episcopal Church in America founded publishing companies in various cities. Founded in 1836, the A.M.E. Book Concern served as an outlet for members of the African Episcopal Church, and published many important historical works by African-American authors, including protests against slavery and appeals to support black businesses.

In 1839, the Baltimore A.M.E. Conference adopted resolutions to raise two cents per month from each member for the Book Concern to aid the Preachers Fund. In 1852, the Book Concern moved to Philadelphia from Pittsburgh. In 1855, it received its charter from the State of Pennsylvania.

In 1866, the Reverend Elisha Weaver, of the A.M.E. Book Concern, published an appeal to the African-American community to support the purchase of Liberty Hall when the building became available. The three-story building was a meeting place for members of the African-American community, who generally were denied the right of mixing with white people at political and social gatherings.

Wealthy African-American businessmen such as Stephen Smith, William Whipper, and William Still led the way in purchasing the building. Two prominent people of the A.M.E. Book Concern were Bishop Benjamin T. Tanner and Henry McNeal Turner, who was appointed by President Abraham Lincoln to serve as chaplain to the first regiment of U.S. Colored Troops during the Civil War.

Location: Pennsylvania State Historical Marker at 631 Pine Street

Philadelphia – Abraham Lincoln's Monument

An enthusiastic crowd of 50,000 people witnessed the dedication in 1871 of sculptor Randolph Rogers' monument of President Abraham Lincoln.

The bronze statute resting on a granite base stands 9' 6" high. Rogers' rendering of Lincoln shows the president, seated with quill in hand, holding the Emancipation Proclamation in the other hand, gazing at the horizon and contemplating the gravity of the moment. The historic document was signed January 1, 1863. It expressly permitted those slave states or part of them fighting on the Union side to keep their slaves.

Another purpose of the Emancipation Proclamation is found near the end of the document:

"Negroes of suitable condition will be received into the armed services of the United States to Garrison Forts, positions, stations and to man vessels of all sorts in said service."

Lincoln favored colonization for African-Americans and several hundred former slaves were shipped to Haiti, where their plight soon became desperate. A warship was sent for them, and they were resettled in Arlington, Virginia. The Emancipation Proclamation also permitted certain states such as West Virginia, Maryland, and certain parishes in Louisiana

Randolph Rogers' bronze tribute to Abraham Lincoln is in Philadelphia's Fairmount Park.

to continue to hold slaves in bondage. Tennessee was omitted in hope that it would return to the Union. Seven counties of Virginia and the cities of Norfolk and Portsmouth also were permitted to continue to hold slaves in bondage.

Dedicated six years after Lincoln's death, the statue was at its location for 130 years until it was moved in 2001 less than 60 feet from its original spot due to modern traffic safety concerns.

Location: Kelly and Sedgely Drives

Philadelphia – Belmont Mansion Historic House

Located in the Fairmount Park section of Philadelphia, Belmont Mansion Historic House is the former home of Judge Richard Peters. Peters and his family were closely connected with United States District Court Judge William Lewis, who entertained both George Washington and Thomas Jefferson in his large home, Strawberry Mansion, which also is located in Fairmount Park.

Both Judge Lewis and Judge Peters privately supported the abolition of slavery. However, because of their political positions, they were unable to become public. During the era of the Underground Railroad, members of the Peters family, according to recent documentation, sheltered escaping slaves in a tunnel area at Belmont Mansion, which became a natural safe house for escaping slaves seeking freedom on the Underground Railroad.

For many years, the Peters family servant, a former slave named Cornelia West, known as "Old Cornelia," and her daughter, lived at Belmont. Belmont Mansion Historic House is now owned and operated by American Women's Heritage Society, Inc. an African-American organization.

Location: 2000 Belmont Mansion Drive

Philadelphia – Franklin Institute Science Museum and Fels Planetarium

This imposing building is named for Benjamin Franklin, a multi-talented personality during the Colonial and Revolutionary era. It is one of several sites honoring the memory of Franklin in the Philadelphia area.

On the subject of African-Americans, Franklin's attitude was at first ambivalent, even though he owned slaves as a young man. Though he printed some anti-slavery works during his early printing career, he did not show any great concern about the institution itself.

In 1764, his political opponents openly accused Franklin of keeping black paramours. He seems to have made no attempt to deny it. As an elder statesman, he joined the Pennsylvania Abolition Society in 1787, serving as president of the society in 1789.

Shortly before his death, he sent a petition to Congress, which he signed, asking the members to exert the full extent of the power vested in them by the Constitution in discouraging the traffic of human species. If Franklin were living today, he would probably be proud of the fact that an African-American scientist, Derrick Pitts holds the official title of Senior Program Developer-Chief Astronomer at the Franklin Institute.

Location: 20th Street and Benjamin Franklin Parkway

Philadelphia – Benjamin Banneker Institute

Founded in 1854, this institute adopted its name from a one-room schoolhouse named in honor of African-American astronomer and scientist Benjamin Banneker. During the 1700s, he published an almanac for the States of Pennsylvania, Delaware, Maryland, and Virginia. The Banneker Institute that later became a prominent African-American literary society was originally located in Central Hall on Walnut Street above Sixth Street.

During the 1930s and 1940s, a large portion of the Institute's book and archival collection was donated to the Historical Society of Pennsylvania located at 1300 Locust Street. Philadelphia members of this institute also operated the Banneker House, a well-known resort for African-Americans located a short distance from the beach at Cape May, New Jersey, due to the policy of segregation at the seashore. Accommodations at the newly renovated house in 1858 were $6 per week for room and board.

Location: Pennsylvania State Historical Marker at 409 South 11th Street

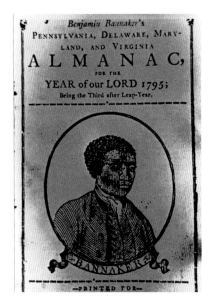

Benjamin Banneker's Almanac

Philadelphia – Philadelphia Female Anti-Slavery Society

Quaker abolitionist Lucretia Mott organized this group of 60 black and white women dedicated to the elimination of slavery on December 9, 1833. African-American members included Grace and Sarah Douglass, as well as James Forten's three daughters, Sarah, Harriet, and Marguerite. White members included Mary Grew, Sarah Pugh, Elizabeth Neall, and Abby Kimber.

Location: Pennsylvania State Historical Marker at former office at 107 N. 5th Street

Philadelphia – Germantown, Birthplace of Louisa May Alcott

Until recent years, few people knew that the author of the American classic novel *Little Women*, Louisa May Alcott, was born in Germantown. Her family moved to Concord, Massachusetts, when she was a child.

Her father, Amos Bronson Alcott (1799-1881), a writer and leader of the Transcendentalist Movement, had a great impact on his time. He married Abby May, a member of a well-known New England family, who was an abolitionist. In 1830, Bronson Alcott received an invitation to teach in a Philadelphia school at 222 S. 8th Street.

Alcott and his family moved to 5425 Germantown Avenue (Pine Place). He opened a school and accepted several African-American students. He was made principal of the lower school that would become part of Germantown Academy. After his progressive school failed, he moved his family to Massachusetts, where he became friends with Ralph Waldo Emerson, Henry David Thoreau, and John Brown, and was connected with the Underground Railroad. Louisa May Alcott's book *Little Women* enshrined her forever in Germantown annals.

Location: 5425 Germantown Avenue

Philadelphia – William S. Whipper

William Whipper was an early advocate of non-violent resistance who petitioned for the freedom of African-Americans in Philadelphia. He was born free and lived in a station on the Underground Railroad in Columbia, Pennsylvania. As one of the nation's first African-American capitalists, he was co-owner of a lumberyard and was a partner in both coal and railroad boxcar businesses.

In addition to these accomplishments, Whipper was co-founder of the Reading Room Society, edited a magazine, and served as treasurer of the Philadelphia Building and Loan Association, founded in 1869.

Location: Pennsylvania State Historical Marker at 919 Lombard Street

Jacob C. White, Jr.

Stephen Smith

Philadelphia – Jacob C. White, Jr.

Jacob C. White, Jr., was Philadelphia's only African-American principal and teacher when he was appointed principal of Robert Vaux Elementary School in 1864. He had also served as agent for Haitian emigration. After retiring from education, White served as chairman of the board of Frederick Douglass Hospital.

Location: Pennsylvania State Historical Marker at 1032 Lombard Street

Philadelphia – Stephen Smith

During his lifetime, Stephen Smith was one of the wealthiest African-Americans in the United States. He was born in Columbia, Pennsylvania, and went on to build an empire that included the Smith, Whipper and Company Lumber and Coal Yard. He was a leading agent on the Underground Railroad when he lived in Columbia.

In 1867, he donated property and cash worth $250,000 for the establishment of a home for the aged and infirm. The home, which bears his name, was dedicated two years before Smith's death and still operates today.

Location: Pennsylvania State Historical Marker at his former home address, 1050 Belmont Avenue

Philadelphia – Grand United Order of Odd Fellows

The first African-American Odd Fellows Lodge in Pennsylvania and the third in the nation was established as Unity Lodge No. 711 on May 14, 1844, by Peter Ogden. In 1908, the head-quarters of the Odd Fellows was erected in Philadelphia, and the group's national publication, *The Odd Fellows' Journal*, was published here.

Peter Ogden

Philadelphia - Institute for Colored Youth

One of the first high schools to prepare black youth for skilled trades and teaching, the Institute for Colored Youth later evolved into Cheyney University. The institute's predecessor was a farm school on the outskirts of Philadelphia that was established in 1852 with bequests from two Quakers— $10,000 from Richard Humphrey and $18,000 from Jonathan Zane.

Shortly after opening, students—all young males— rebelled because of stringent rules and the farm labor required of them. The school closed and the farm was sold. Twenty years later, in 1852, a new school, the Institute for Colored Youth, was built and gained an excellent reputation thanks to Mrs. Fanny Jackson Coppin, who served as principal from 1869 to 1902.

In 1902, the school was relocated to Cheyney, Pennsylvania, and ultimately became a state teachers college and then state university.

INSTITUTE FOR COLORED YOUTH

Begun as a farm school. In 1852 it became one of the first schools to train Blacks for skilled jobs. It gained recognition here under Fanny J. Coppin, principal, 1869-1902. Relocated, it later became Cheyney University.

PENNSYLVANIA HISTORICAL AND MUSEUM COMMISSION 1991

State Historical marker at the former Institute for Colored Youth

Philadelphia – Knights of Pythias

This prestigious organization was created in 1907 and paid death benefits to members through a mortuary department. Membership increased under the leadership of Grand Chancellor B.G. Collier. Prominent supporters included James H. Irvin and Dr. John P. Turner.

The Universal Negro Improvement Association (UNIA) became one of the largest mass movements among people of African descent in the world, stressing themes of black nationalism, racial pride, and the return of African-Americans to Africa.

Location: Pennsylvania State Historical Marker at former address, 19th and Addison Streets

Philadelphia – The Johnson House

The Johnson House built in 1768 by German Quaker Derick Jansen, has an interesting history. Jansen, a tanner by trade, anglicized his name to Johnson. He built the house for his son, John.

This house figured prominently in the Battle of Germantown of October 4, 1777, and bullets and cannonballs left their mark on three doors. During the 1850s, the Johnson family was part of the American Anti-Slavery Society and operated their home as a station on the Underground Railroad.

According to family tradition, escaping slaves were sheltered in the basement and attic; they also were hidden in smaller buildings on the property. The Johnson family often sent their Underground Railroad passengers to the next station in Plymouth Meeting, a predominantly Quaker village, where Johnson's wife's family operated a station along with the Corson family. The Johnson House has been preserved as it appeared when it sheltered escaping slaves during the era of the Underground Railroad.

The Johnson House

Location: Pennsylvania State Historical Marker at 6306 Germantown Avenue

Philadelphia – Marian Anderson Historical Society

Located at 762 South Marian Anderson Way is the former residence of the internationally known contralto Marian Anderson, affectionately called "The Lady from Philadelphia." A tall woman of grace and dignity, Marian Anderson was born February 27, 1897, at 1833 Webster Street, and lived for many years with her mother and sisters in a Martin Street home where the historical society is now located.

Her formal voice training began about the age of 15. Along with 300 other young people, she entered a competition and won first prize. This led to a concert tour and appearance with the New York Philharmonic Orchestra.

Her continental debut was made in Germany in 1939. That same year, Howard University sought to bring her to perform at Constitution Hall in Washington, D.C. The request was denied by the Daughters of the American Revolution (DAR), who owned the hall, because she was black.

Right: Famed contralto Marian Anderson was the first African-American to perform at the Metropolitan Opera in New York City.

Eleanor Roosevelt, who sat on the board of the DAR, resigned her membership in protest over this decision and other prominent women followed suit. Mrs. Roosevelt then arranged a concert for Anderson at the Lincoln Memorial that was attended by 75,000 people, with millions more listening to a radio broadcast of the event. Four years later the DAR invited Anderson to take part in a concert for China Relief at Constitution Hall. She accepted.

Marian Anderson owed much of her success to a strong heritage of self-confidence and independence. Achievement and development of one's talents were expected in the Anderson family. After her death in 1993, Philadelphia officials established the Marian Anderson Annual Award in her honor. Recently, the city's Historical Commission established The Marian Anderson Village with the assistance of Blanche Burton-Lyles, a concert pianist and founder of the Marian Anderson Historical Society. The Marian Anderson Historical Society is open by appointment only.

(A Pennsylvania State Historical Marker has been placed at Marian Anderson's Church, Union Baptist Church, 1910 Fitzwater Street.)

Location: 762 South Marian Anderson Way

Philadelphia – St. Peter Claver's Roman Catholic Church

St. Peter Claver's Roman Catholic Church is Philadelphia's first Roman Catholic Church for African-Americans. It was named in honor of a humanitarian whose efforts on behalf of African emancipation won him the title "Apostle of the Slave Trade."

St. Peter Claver, born of African descent in 1580, was a native of Verdu, Catalonia, Spain. He was ordained a priest in 1616. In the port city of New Granada in South America (now Colombia), he began his life work of ministry to slaves newly arriving from Africa. For more than 30 years, Claver provided spiritual assistance to people suffering from the brutal institution of slavery. He assisted those who were condemned to death and comforted those who were lepers. Pope Leo XIII canonized him in 1888 and made him the patron of missions to people of African descent.

This church began in Philadelphia in the 1880s, when Saint Katharine Drexel provided funds and helped to find priests in the Holy Ghost Order who would be exclusively devoted to African-American Catholics, who were generally not welcome in most white Philadelphia Catholic churches.

During the 1920s, the church hosted performances of various African-American literary and dramatic groups. On Sunday, July 30, 2000, the last mass was held at St. Peter Claver's church. The reason cited by the Archdiocese of Philadelphia for closing the church was the dwindling membership.

> **Location: Pennsylvania State Historical Marker at 1200 Lombard Street**

Philadelphia – The Union League of Philadelphia

Two Philadelphians, George Henry Boker, a playwright and poet, and John Innes Clark Hare, a jurist, founded the Union League in 1862. Its purpose was to support President Abraham Lincoln and the Union Army. It contributed $100,000 to that cause during the Civil War and distributed literature.

The Union League also was instrumental in recruiting African-American volunteers during the war. The League participated in the organization of Camp William Penn, the all African-American camp once located at LaMott, in Montgomery County, a few miles north of Center City Philadelphia. After the war, the League aided officials of the Freedmen's Bureau in Washington, D.C., in developing a strong Republican political organization to elect African-American legislators in the South.

The noted educator and founder of Tuskegee Institute Booker T. Washington was invited to deliver a lecture at the League on February 12, 1899, but a snow storm prevented his train from arriving that day. In 1972, William Coleman, President Gerald Ford's Transportation Secretary, became the first African-American member. In 1986, the Union League allowed women to join.

Location: Broad Street south of City Hall

Philadelphia – African American Museum in Philadelphia

The African American Museum in Philadelphia opened its doors in 1976, during the nation's Bicentennial celebration. African-American architect Theodore V. Cam designed the building. It was the first African-American historical museum in the nation built from the ground up.

In 1981, the museum mounted an imposing exhibition entitled "Of Color, Humanities and Statehood: The Black Experience in Pennsylvania Over Three Centuries 1681-1981." The exhibition won national, state, and local history awards. The achievements of people of African descent are documented through historical artifacts, books, paintings, sculpture, multimedia presentations, and photographs. This museum also houses a first class book and gift shop.

Location: 701 Arch Street

Philadelphia – W.E.B. Dubois Marker

W.E.B. Dubois

A scholar, educator, author, poet, historian, sociologist, and activist, Dr. William Edward Burghart Dubois (1868-1963) was perhaps the greatest African-American intellectual of the 20th century. He was born in Great Barrington, Massachusetts, and received degrees from Fisk University, Harvard University, and the University of Berlin in Germany.

In 1909 Dubois became a founding member of the National Association for the Advancement of Colored People (NAACP). The young, dapper, and urbane man arrived in Philadelphia in 1896 and was given a temporary post as Assistant in Sociology at the University of Pennsylvania to conduct a study of the African-American community of the city's seventh ward. It was the first scientific study of its kind.

Distinctively, *The Philadelphia Negro* focuses on all aspects of African-American life—migration, church, education, family, crime, population, statistics, and social conditions. *The Philadelphia Negro* was published in 1899, and has been called the most comprehensive landmark sociological inquiry ever written by an American sociologist. While conducting his study, Dubois and his wife lived in the College Settlement House at 617 Carver (now Rodman) Street.

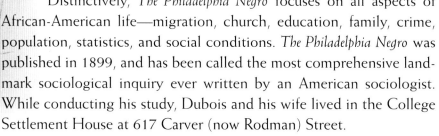

Location: Pennsylvania State Historical Marker at Sixth and Rodman Streets

Philadelphia – Paul Robeson's Last Residence

Scholar, athlete, lawyer, actor, singer, linguist, activist, and humanitarian Paul Robeson was born in Princeton, New Jersey, on April 9, 1898, the son of a minister. On the maternal side of his family, Robeson's ancestors included Cyrus Bustill, who operated a baker's shop during the American Revolutionary War.

As a scholarship student at Rutgers University, Robeson

excelled academically and athletically, graduating Phi Beta Kappa and earning 12 letters in baseball, basketball, and track. He twice was named an All-America football player. He earned a law degree at Columbia University.

After encountering a great deal of racial prejudice, Robeson turned to entertainment as a career, singing at first, and then pursuing the stage. He built a stellar career as an actor and concert artist whose voice and name were loved and respected throughout the world.

From the beginning of his career he accepted the responsibility of working for civil rights and civil liberties as one of the most talented people of his race. From the 1940s, Robeson took an increasingly militant stand on civil and human rights for workers and oppressed minorities. He was one of America's most outspoken critics of racism after World War II.

During the cold war, because of his steadfast defense of the Soviet Union, Robeson was seized upon by the media, the U.S. government, and the followers of Republican Sen. Joseph McCarthy, who accused him of being a member of the Communist Party, tarnishing his name and remarkable achievements. Robeson never was a member of the Communist Party, however.

In 1946, he led a crusade against lynching in Washington, D.C. That same year he appeared before a California legislative committee as co-chairman of the National Committee to Win Peace. Three times he swore before congressional committees that he was not then and never had been a member of the Communist Party, describing himself as an "anti-fascist." In later years he refused to answer when asked if he was a member of the Communist Party.

In 1956, after Robeson appeared before the House Un-American Activities Committee, the State Department revoked his passport, prohibiting him from traveling abroad. He suffered continuous persecution and was roundly criticized by conservatives. His name was deleted from books, and church ministers and concert hall and theater officials were threatened if they invited Robeson to perform.

His book, *Here I Stand*, which was published in London, was banned in the U.S. and no commercial bookseller would display it. It sold out overseas within six weeks of publication and earned laudatory reviews throughout Europe. In 1958, the same year that *Here I Stand* was published, the U.S. Supreme Court ruled that the affidavit that Robeson had refused to sign in 1950 was not valid grounds for denial of a passport and he was given the right to travel abroad again.

Robeson survived the hysteria of the McCarthy period and resumed his illustrious career until he moved to Philadelphia in 1966 to live in retirement in the home of his sister, Marian Forsythe, for 10 years until his death on January 23, 1976.

Location: Pennsylvania State Historical Marker at 4951 Walnut Street

Philadelphia – Church of the Advocate

This renowned Gothic Revival church with picturesque stained glass windows was built between 1887 and 1897. Located in North Philadelphia, the church served a growing African-American community after 1930.

Under the leadership of its African-American Episcopalian priest Father Paul Washington, it became a center for controversial causes. In the 1960s and 1970s, the Church of the Advocate played host to major Black Power conferences.

Father Washington has been referred to as a man of "deep compassion to humanity" based upon a profound understanding of the Christian faith. In 1974, the first 11 women Episcopalian priests were ordained at the Church of the Advocate.

Today, the Church of the Advocate is the headquarters for The Arts Sanctuary, a literary organization for local writers and artists who invite national lecturers to speak and perform. The church has been designated as a national historic landmark.

Location: Pennsylvania State Historical Marker at 18th and Diamond Streets

Philadelphia – The All Wars Memorial To Colored Soldiers and Sailors

Commissioned in 1927 by the State of Pennsylvania through its sole African-American legislator, Samuel Beecher Hart, this memorial was created by Swiss sculptor J. Otto Schweizer, who lived in Philadelphia, as a tribute to African-American war heroes. The imposing bronze and granite monument was originally relegated to a remote location in Fairmount Park on West Lansdowne Drive.

The Philadelphia Arts Jury and the Committee to Restore and Relocate lobbied elected officials to move the monument. It was relocated to its current location in November 1994. The memorial's design includes an 18-foot column. Columbia is depicted offering a laurel wreath to 12, life-sized figures encircling the column. The story of African-Americans' service in the armed forces is one of the neglected aspects of American history.

Location: 20th Street and Benjamin Franklin Parkway

Philadelphia – Julian Francis Abele

Born on April 29, 1881, in South Philadelphia, Julian Abele was educated at the Institute for Colored Youth. In 1902, he was the first African-American to be graduated from the University of Pennsylvania School of Architecture. He also was the first black to have an impact on the design of large buildings in the United States.

Much of Abele's professional career was spent with the architectural firm of Horace Trumbauer. He became an assistant to Trumbauer's chief designer, Frank Seeburger, whom he replaced when Seeburger left the firm in 1906. When Trumbauer died in 1938, Abele and William O. Frank continued the firm as "The Office of Horace Trumbauer."

Although many clients never knew that Abele was the chief designer for Trumbauer, he was responsible for designing several buildings at Duke University, the Philadelphia Museum of Art, and the Free Library of Philadelphia on Logan Circle. He was also a pianist and spoke French fluently.

> Location: Pennsylvania State Historical Marker at the Philadelphia Art Museum, 26th Street and Benjamin Franklin Parkway

Philadelphia – Robert Mara Adger

Born in Charleston, South Carolina, Robert Adger was one of 13 children. His mother, Mary Ann Morong, was a full-blooded Native American. In 1848, he moved to Philadelphia with his family, receiving his early education at the Bird School.

As a teenager, he worked in his father Robert's furniture store. Adger later used the business skills he developed working with his father as director of the Philadelphia Building and Loan Association, one of the first African-American mortgage companies. His success was achieved during a period of intense racial discrimination in the city, which forced 38% of black skilled artisans to give up their trades.

Adger joined the Black Enlistment Committee to assist in the recruitment of black soldiers for the Union Army. He was convinced that conditions would deteriorate even more for blacks if the Confederacy won the Civil War.

In 1860, Adger organized the Fraternal Society, a group of refugees from South Carolina interested in gaining equal rights. Adger and other members of the Fraternal Society worked collectively with other black social-political groups. In 1865, Adger was a delegate to

Julian Francis Abele

the first state conference in Harrisburg to discuss the creation of a Pennsylvania Equal Rights League.

He later organized the Afro-American Historical Society, which contained his personal collection of rare books and pamphlets of African-Americans and the anti-slavery movement. He died of a heart attack on June 10, 1910. Funeral services were held at 1115 Lombard Street, Adger's last residence, and he was buried in the Merion Cemetery in Merion, Pennsylvania.

Location: Pennsylvania State Historical Marker at 823 South Street

Sadie Alexander

Philadelphia – Sadie T. M. Alexander

Sadie Alexander was the first African-American woman to earn a Ph.D. in economics, to be awarded a law degree by the University of Pennsylvania, and to practice law in Pennsylvania. Born in Philadelphia on January 2, 1898, she received her early education in Washington, D.C., where she attended the M Street High School and was greatly influenced by Dr. Carter G. Woodson.

She received her college education at the University of Pennsylvania, where she was awarded a Bachelor of Science in Education (1918), a Master of Arts in economics (1919), and a Ph.D. in economics for her dissertation "The Standard of Living Among One Hundred Negro Migrant Families in Philadelphia," in 1921.

Alexander was a member of the first black sorority at the University of Pennsylvania, Gamma Chapter of the Delta Sigma Theta Sorority. In 1921, she was elected first president of the National Grand Chapter. She married Raymond Pace Alexander in 1923, who later became a judge and received his own national recognition, and continued her education. After earning her law degree in 1927, Alexander was admitted to the Pennsylvania Bar and began her practice.

She held the post of Assistant City Solicitor from 1928 to 1930, and again from 1934 to 1938. She played leadership roles in many national civic organizations, including the National Urban League, Lawyers' Committee on Civil Rights, National Association for the Advancement of Colored People, and a host of others.

Location: Pennsylvania State Historical Marker at 700 Westview Street, on corner near Sherman Road

Philadelphia – Pearl Bailey

Born in Newport News, Virginia, on March 29, 1918, Pearl Bailey moved with her parents to Philadelphia, attending the Joseph Singerly School and William Penn High School. She started her career at 15, when she entered an amateur night contest at the Pearl Theater in Philadelphia and won a two-week engagement. She also won a second contest, at the Apollo Theater in New York.

Bailey performed with Noble Sissle's band as a specialty dancer and chorus girl in Philadelphia nightclubs. She was a vocalist for Edgar Hayes, Cooti Williams, and the Sunset Royal Band. Around 1944, she made her debut as a soloist at the Village Vanguard in New York. She also lived for a time in Pottsville, Pennsylvania, performing as a star of the nightclub scene.

By 1946, Bailey was appearing on Broadway in *St. Louis Woman*. The following year, she made her film debut in *Variety Girl*. Her earlier film career included *Carmen Jones*, *That Certain Feeling*, *St. Louis Blues*, *Porgy and Bess*, and *All The Fine Young Cannibals*. In 1968, she published her autobiography, *The Raw Pearl*. In 1978, at age 66, Bailey completed a bachelor's degree in theology at Georgetown University in Washington, D.C.

> Location: Pennsylvania State Historical Marker at 1946 N. 23rd Street

Ebenezer Don Carlos Bassett

Philadelphia – Ebenezer Don Carlos Bassett

Born in Litchfield, Connecticut, Ebenezer Bassett received his education at Connecticut State Normal School, Yale College, and the University of Pennsylvania. He was employed as a high school principal in New Haven, Connecticut, and Philadelphia.

In 1869, President Ulysses S. Grant appointed Bassett to the post of Minister Resident of the United States to Haiti, the first diplomatic appointment of an African-American by the federal government. In 1879, he served as Consul General of Haiti in New York. He returned to Haiti in 1888. Upon returning to the United States, Bassett published the *Handbook of Haiti* in 1892.

He was primarily known and respected within the African-American community in the U.S. as an outstanding educator and diplomat. His last years were spent in Philadelphia with his family in their 29th Street home.

> Location: Pennsylvania State Historical Marker at 2121 N. 29th Street

Philadelphia – Robert Bogle

Robert Bogle was the originator of the catering profession and the first African-American in Philadelphia to gain prominence in the field, which was one of the first businesses in which Philadelphia's African-Americans achieved affluence. As a leading caterer, his specialties were meat pies and soups.

He also performed as master of ceremonies at weddings and funerals for his wealthy clientele. One of these clients, Nicholas Biddle, head of the first bank in the United States, wrote a verse in Bogle's honor in 1829 entitled, "An Ode to Bogle."

Bogle united the vocations of caterer and undertaker frequently, officiating at a funeral in the afternoon and a party in the evening, presenting on all occasions the same gravity of demeanor. No party, no ball, no large, formal dinner was truly a social event unless it was under his direction.

Robert Bogle

Location: Pennsylvania State Historical Marker at 112 S. 8th Street

Philadelphia – David Bustill Bowser

David Bowser was a self-taught African-American artist who began his career as a sign painter in Philadelphia. His early paintings included landscapes, portraits, emblems, and banners for local organizations such as a firemen's group. His most noted works include portraits of President Abraham Lincoln and abolitionist John Brown.

Bowser was actively involved in the anti-slavery movement, and during the Civil War designed regimental flags for the Union's colored troops.

Location: Pennsylvania State Historical Marker at 841 N. 4th Street

David Bustill Bowser

Philadelphia – Cyrus Bustill

Born into slavery in Burlington, New Jersey, Cyrus Bustill later bought his freedom. He perfected the art of baking and opened a bakery in Philadelphia. Next door, his wife Elizabeth, and one of their eight children, Grace, opened a millinery store.

During the American Revolution, Bustill risked his life to take bread to George Washington's starving troops at Valley Forge. It was said that Bustill received a silver piece from Washington. He was one of the founders of the Free African Society in 1787.

Although he was a Quaker, Bustill contributed funds for the construction of St. Thomas African Episcopal Church. When he retired from baking, Bustill opened a school for black children in his home at Third and Green Streets.

He was buried in a family plot at his farm, Edge Hill. Paul L. Robeson was a great-great-great grandson of this patriot.

Location: Pennsylvania State Historical Marker at
210 Arch Street

Octavius V. Catto

Philadelphia – Octavius V. Catto

Octavius Catto was a member of the first graduating class at the Institute for Colored Youth and later taught there. He was commissioned a major in the National Guard during the Civil War.

Actively involved in organizing black voters in Philadelphia, he was assassinated while rallying African-American support for the Republican Party during the 1871 elections. The U.S. Marines were called in after the assassination to prevent race riots. The militia at the Armory, Broad and Race Streets, guarded Catto's body, and he was buried with full military honors in one of the largest funerals ever held in Philadelphia.

Location: Pennsylvania State Historical Marker at
812 South Street

Philadelphia – John W. "Trane" Coltrane

Born in Hamlet, North Carolina, into a religious and musical family, John Coltrane became a major pioneer and innovator in the modern jazz movement. His father played the violin and sang; his mother was a church pianist.

At an early age, he was exposed to religious music in the A.M.E. Zion Church, where both his grandfathers were ministers. He began clarinet study at age 12 and began learning to play the alto saxophone a year later.

Coltrane moved with his family in 1944 to Philadelphia, where he began his professional career as a saxophonist and composer. He formed his own group in 1960 and incorporated African-American, African, and Indian elements into his music to create a style that had a great impact on jazz musicians. He played with Eddie Vinson, Dizzy Gillespie, Thelonius Monk, Miles Davis, McCoy Tyner, Jimmy Garrison, Jimmy Oliver, the Heath Brothers, Lee Morgan, Philly Joe Jones, and many other greats.

He died July 17, 1967, of liver cancer, at age 40. Coltrane's early death only added to his legendary reputation as a musical genius. Mary Alexander, his favorite cousin, founded The John W. Coltrane Cultural Society, Inc., to continue to promote and preserve Coltrane's musical legacy.

Location: Pennsylvania State Historical Marker at former
home address and current site of The John W. Coltrane
Cultural Society, 1511 N. 33rd Street

Philadelphia – Father Divine

Father Divine, who once identified himself as the Rev. Major J. Divine, is one of the most fascinating religious figures of the 20th century. His followers knew him as the "Prince of Peace" and "Everlasting Father." A brilliant organizer, he demanded complete loyalty of his large congregation, which included blacks and whites.

While living in New York's Harlem, he began attracting white followers from upper, middle, and poor economic levels. Sometime later his Peace Mission Movement grew nationwide and acquired a vast amount of real estate holdings, including a number of hotels and restaurants.

In 1953 Father Divine moved to Woodmont, a large estate in Gladwyn, Montgomery County, which became the center of his movement and a place of pilgrimage. He died September 10, 1965, and was buried in a "Shrine to Life" on his estate.

In addition to Woodmont, his area properties included the Divine Lorraine Hotel in North Philadelphia and the Divine Tracy Hotel in West Philadelphia.

Crystal Bird Fauset

Location: **Pennsylvania State Historical Marker at Divine Lorraine Hotel, northeast corner of Broad Street and Ridge Avenue**

Philadelphia – Crystal Bird Fauset

Crystal Fauset was the first American woman to be elected to a state House of Representatives and the first African-American woman elected to the Pennsylvania State Legislature (1938). She was a graduate of Cheyney State Teachers College and the wife of Dr. Arthur Huff Fauset. Through her friendship with Eleanor Roosevelt, Fauset became a member of President Franklin Roosevelt's "Black Cabinet," advising on matters pertaining to African-Americans.

On January 29, 1955, she was awarded her second Commonwealth of Pennsylvania Meritorious Service Medal. She died on March 25, 1965.

Location: Pennsylvania State Historical Marker at 5403 Vine Street

Philadelphia – Jessie Redmon Fauset

Jessie Fauset, one of the most prolific writers of the Harlem Renaissance movement, was one of the first African-American women to be recognized publicly as an accomplished writer. The daughter of an old Philadelphia family, she was educated in the city's public schools and went on to earn a B.A. at Cornell University (1905), and M.A. from the University of Pennsylvania, and to study at the Sorbonne in France.

She was literary editor of *The Crisis*, the journal of the National Association for the Advancement of Colored People, taught French and Latin at the high school level, and attended the Second Pan-African Congress in London, Brussels, and Paris in 1921, writing two important articles on the event. Fauset's novels included *There Is Confusion* (1924), *Plum Bun* (1929), *The Chinaberry Tree* (1931), and *Comedy: American Style* (1933).

Location: Pennsylvania State Historical Marker at 1853 N. 17th Street

Philadelphia – Meta V. Warrick Fuller

Born in Philadelphia, Meta Fuller was known as an "impressionist realist." She received early artistic training in the city, and also studied and exhibited in Paris, where her work drew praise from the

Jessie Redmon Fauset

Meta Fuller's sculpting was noted for its realistic style and concern for racial subjects.

great French sculptor and painter Auguste Rodin.

Proud of her African heritage, she discovered during genealogical research that her great-great grandmother was an African princess who was brought to Philadelphia on a slave ship and sold to a wealthy family. As a member of the Women's Peace Party, Fuller participated in the suffrage movement.

She was the sister of Dr. William H. Warrick, a prominent physician in the city's Germantown section, and the wife of Dr. Solomon Fuller.

Location: Pennsylvania State Historical Marker at 1013 Rodman Street

Elizabeth Taylor Greenfield worked tirelessly for the anti-slavery movement and Underground Railroad in Philadelphia.

Philadelphia – Elizabeth Taylor Greenfield

Elizabeth Taylor Greenfield was the first African-American singer to appear in a command performance before English royalty, a concert given at Buckingham Palace in 1854 for the Queen of England. Born a slave in Mississippi in 1809, she was brought to Philadelphia at an early age by a Quaker woman named Greenfield, who reared her as a free person. She raised money to support the Underground Railroad.

She received voice, piano, and guitar lessons as a child, and was recognized for having an unusual vocal range of three-and-one-quarter octaves. Greenfield performed extensively throughout the United States, England, and Canada, and music critics who heard her rich, clear voice named her the "Black Swan."

Location: Pennsylvania State Historical Marker at 1013 Rodman Street

Philadelphia – Frances Ellen Watkins Harper

Born free in Baltimore, Maryland, in 1825, Frances Harper was the first African-American woman instructor in vocational education at the African Methodist Episcopal Union seminary near Columbus, Ohio, where she taught domestic science. This remarkable self-educated woman was referred to as the "Brown Muse," and was described as a "petite, dignified, woman whose sharp black eyes and attractive face reveal her sensitive nature."

Forced into exile by an 1853 Maryland law forbidding free blacks to enter the state, she pledged herself to the anti-slavery movement. Harper came to Philadelphia and lived in an Underground Railroad station. William Still wrote that she was "one of the most liberal contributors as well as one of the ablest advocates for the Underground Railroad and the slave."

As a lecturer for the anti-slavery movement, Harper was so effective that the Pennsylvania Anti-Slavery Society hired her. Because of her popularity as a spellbinding orator, Harper spoke from a podium in more than eight states, usually daily but sometimes two or three times a day.

She married Fenton Harper and they had one child. After her husband's death, she continued her anti-slavery activities as a lecturer, poet, and writer. She sympathized with John Brown as he prepared for his ill-fated raid on Harpers Ferry in 1859, and later spent two weeks with Brown's wife prior to his execution.

After the Civil War, Harper lectured as a temperance reformer and appeared at women suffrage conventions, even though most of these organizations were made up mostly of white women. She was a role model for feminists of her day.

She was superintendent of the colored branch of the Philadelphia and

Frances Ellen Watkins Harper

79

Pennsylvania chapters of the Woman's Christian Temperance Union. She also was an active member of the National Council of Women, The American Women's Suffrage Association, and the American Association for Education of Colored Youth.

She moved to her Bainbridge Street home in 1870 with her daughter. In 1893, Harper, with her colleagues Fannie Barrier Williams, Anna Julia Cooper, Fannie Jackson Coppin, Sarah J. Earley, and Hallie Q. Brown, charged an international gathering of women at the World's Congress of Representative Women in Chicago with indifference to the needs and concerns of African-American women. As a result, she was active in the establishment of the National Association of Colored Women and became its Vice President.

She died in 1911. Her contributions as a writer and poet were numerous and include her famous poems *The Slave Mother and Bury Me in a Free Land*.

Location: Pennsylvania State Historical Marker at her former home, 1006 Bainbridge Street

Philadelphia – Christian Street YMCA

This was the first African-American YMCA in the nation to be contained in its own building and remains an important institution in Philadelphia's African-American community. It was completed in January 1914 with assistance from the Rosenwald Fund, the Reverend Henry L. Phillips, and other prominent individuals.

Over the years, the Christian Street YMCA has provided recreational and educational opportunities for many, and has been a social center and meeting place for a host of African-American organizations.

Location: Pennsylvania State Historical Marker at 1724 Christian Street

Philadelphia – Frederick Douglass Memorial Hospital

This was the first African-American hospital in Philadelphia and the first hospital to be staffed wholly by African-Americans. It was founded in 1895 by Dr. Nathaniel Mossell, one of the first black graduates of the medical school of the University of Pennsylvania. The hospital was a primary training center for African-American doctors, nurses, and pharmacists in a period when racial discrimination limited their opportunities in the medical profession.

Location: Pennsylvania State Historical Marker at 1522 Lombard Street

Philadelphia – The Dunbar Theatre

This early modern theater was where African-Americans performed and were entertained when segregation prevailed. Two African-Americans who went on to become theatrical impresarios, E. C. Brown and Andrew Stevens, erected it.

The Dunbar Theatre, which was later renamed the Lincoln Theater, introduced the Lafayette Players to the public. The group's premier stars were Cleo Desmond, the creator of "Madame X," and Andrew Bishop. From the 1920s to the 1940s, the theater hosted luminaries such as Duke Ellington, Louise Beavers, Willie Bryant, Lena Horne, Don Redman, Ethel Waters, Cab Calloway, Paul Robeson, and many more.

Location: Pennsylvania State Historical Marker at Broad and Lombard Streets

State Historical Marker at Freedom Theatre

Philadelphia – Freedom Theatre

Cited by the John F. Kennedy Center for the Performing Arts in Washington, D.C., as one of the six best black theaters in the United States, Freedom Theater is one of the oldest African-American theaters in Pennsylvania. John Allen founded it in 1966, and since that time has provided a nationally acclaimed program of theatrical and performing arts training for youth and adults, as well as community service.

Freedom Theater offers professional instruction in acting, dancing, singing, and theater production. Located in the former home of Heritage House, founded by Dr. Eugene Waymon Jones in 1949, the theater has presented African-American classics such as *A Raisin in the Sun* by Lorraine Hansberry, *Day of Absence* by Douglass Turner Ward, and *Zooman And The Sign* by Philadelphian Charles Fuller, a Pulitzer Prize winner.

Location: 1346 N. Broad Street

Philadelphia – Mercy Hospital

This institution provided training and employment to black medical professionals. It was founded in 1907 by Dr. Henry M. Minton, and in 1948 merged with Frederick Douglass Memorial Hospital, becoming known as Mercy-Douglass Hospital. Its location prior to its closing was 51st Street and Woodland Avenue.

Location: Pennsylvania State Historical Marker at former hospital address, 17th and Fitzwater Streets

Philadelphia – Standard Theatre

This vaudeville-style theater was the showplace for leading

black entertainers of the 1920s, including Bessie Smith, Duke Ellington, Louis Armstrong, and the comedy team Bito and Ashes. It was owned and operated by John T. Gibson, know as the "little giant of black theatricals." The Standard was where many young performers began their careers, including Ethel Waters.

The theater, which attracted both African-American and white audiences, closed in 1931 as a result of the Depression.

Location: Pennsylvania State Historical Marker at former address 1126 South Street

Philadelphia – Tindley Temple

The Reverend Charles Albert Tindley founded this church in 1902 as the East Calvary Methodist Church; it was later renamed in his honor. The Reverend Tindley was born a slave in Berlin, Maryland, and worked as a hod carrier and brick mason before coming to Philadelphia in 1870 to study for the ministry.

He became known as a composer of gospel songs, including the soul-stirring "We Shall Overcome," and was instrumental in helping migrants from the south who had settled in Philadelphia. This tradition survives today, as Tindley Temple continues to provide free meals and clothing to the needy.

Location: Pennsylvania State Historical Marker at 762 S. Broad Street

Philadelphia – Union Local 274 American Federation of Musicians

Chartered in 1935, Local 274 was established as a separate union for African-American musicians in Philadelphia because the existing union, Local 77, did not admit black musicians. Born through the efforts of Frank T. Fairfax Sr., Raymond L. Smith, Charlie Gaines Sr., Harry Marsh Sr., and other black musical leaders, the union provided African-Americans the opportunity to participate in the American labor movement during a period when most black workers were non-union due to racial discrimination.

Until its demise in 1971, Local 274 was the most democratic musician's union in the city, admitting musicians of all ethnic groups. Its presidents included George "Doc" Hyder, James "Jimmy" Shorter, Charles "Charlie" Gaines Sr., and James Euclid "Jimmy" Adams. Membership rolls included many prominent musicians such as Dizzy Gillespie, John Coltrane, Nina Simone, Beryl Booker, Clara Ward, Philly Joe Jones, and Bootsie Barnes.

Local 274 also held the distinction of being the nation's last black musician's union in the American Federation of Musicians. When the Civil Rights Act of 1964 was passed, the Federation abolished dual unionism based on race, and the number of black unions dwindled from 50 to 1. Local 274 refused to merge with Local 77. The membership felt the union would lose its autonomy and ability to function as a social and cultural institution. Consequently, in 1971, the American Federation of Musicians cancelled Local 274's charter.

Local 274 appealed the AFM's decision, but it was upheld in court. Today, the Philadelphia Clef Club of the Performing Arts, Inc., an outgrowth of the union founded by Local 274's last president, Jimmy Adams, preserves and promotes African-American music.

Location: Former address, 912 S. Broad Street

Philadelphia – Berean Institute

Berean Institute was founded in 1899 by the Reverend Dr. Matthew Anderson to provide African-Americans training in skilled trades, training to which other institutions denied them access due to racial discrimination. The Reverend Anderson was a native of Pennsylvania and had been educated at Iberia and Oberlin Colleges in Ohio, Princeton University, and the School of Theology at Yale University.

Chartered by the Commonwealth of Pennsylvania in 1904, Berean has expanded its curriculum over the years to meet students' changing demands. Today the Institute is fully integrated.

> Location: Pennsylvania State Historical Marker at
> 1901 W. Girard Avenue

Philadelphia – Citizens and Southern Bank

Major R.R. Wright Sr., an educator, politician, and editor, organized the third African-American bank in Philadelphia in 1931. Named for a bank in Georgia, Citizens and Southern survived the Great Depression and was one of the few banks allowed to re-open immediately after the "Bank Holiday" declared in March 1933 by President Franklin Roosevelt.

The institution later became interracial and operated branch offices at 19th and Chestnut Streets and 55th Street and Chester Avenue, in addition to the main office at 19th and South Streets.

> Location: Pennsylvania State Historical Marker at former
> address at 1849 South Street

Philadelphia – Jack and Jill of America Foundation

Established in 1938 by 11 African-American mothers of middle class families to provide activities for their children, Jack and Jill of America was a dramatic response to racial segregation. Today, the organization founded by a group led by Marion Turner Stubbs and

Lela Jones operates more than 187 chapters throughout the country, with more than 7,000 participating families.

The Philadelphia chapter has sponsored many national service projects, has raised funds for rheumatic fever research, and is a regular contributor to social service organizations, including the United Negro College Fund, the National Foundation for Infantile Paralysis, and the NAACP Legal Defense Fund.

> **Location: Pennsylvania State Historical Marker at former meeting address, 1605 Christian Street**

Philadelphia – Opportunities Industrialization Centers (OIC)

The Reverend Dr. Leon H. Sullivan of Zion Baptist Church founded OIC in 1964 as a community-based, self-help program to motivate young men and women whose formal education had ceased to learn marketable job skills and enter the world of work. The first training center, in an abandoned jail at 19th and Oxford Streets, was dedicated by Sullivan and his fellow ministers with the slogan "We help ourselves" on January 24, 1964, before a crowd of more than 8,000.

Born out of the civil rights movement of the 1950s and 1960s, OIC continues to assist African-Americans and other groups disadvantaged by racial prejudice, providing comprehensive employment and training through a network of branches throughout the United States and abroad.

> **Location: Pennsylvania State Historical Marker at initial address, 19th and Oxford Streets**

State Historical Marker at the first OIC location

Philadelphia – The Pyramid Club

Founded in the mid-1930s, this club provided the African-

American community many of the social and cultural activities otherwise denied by a segregated city and thus was the epitome of Philadelphia's black elite. Among the prominent African-Americans who visited and were connected with Pyramid Club members were Adam Clayton Powell Jr., Mary McLeod Bethune, Duke Ellington, Josephine Baker, and Langston Hughes. The Club's first president was Dr. Walter F. Jerrick.

Location: Pennsylvania State Historical Marker at
1517 W. Girard Avenue

Philadelphia – Universal Negro Improvement Association (UNIA)

UNIA became one of the largest mass movements among people of African descent in the world. Stressing themes of black nationalism, racial pride, and the return of African-Americans to Africa to establish a "unified empire," the organization was founded by Marcus Garvey in 1911. Thousands were attracted to Garvey's ideas, and within months, 30 UNIA branches were established.

Location: Pennsylvania State Historical Marker at
1609-11 W. Cecil B. Moore Boulevard

Marcus Garvey

Philadelphia – The Philadelphia *Tribune*

The Philadelphia *Tribune* is the oldest continually-published African-American newspaper in the United States. It was founded by Christopher Perry in 1884 as a forum for his quest to improve employment and working conditions for Philadelphia's black workers.

The first edition, a single, hand-printed page, was published at 725 Sansom Street. Through the years, the pages of the *Tribune* have urged black representation and participation in city government, in addition to opposing discrimination, graft, and prejudice in politics. Today, the paper continues to be the voice of the city's African-American community.

> Location: Pennsylvania State Historical Marker at
> 520-26 S. 16th Street

Philadelphia – Prince Hall Grand Lodge

Philadelphia's first African-American Masonic Lodge was established in 1797 under Worshipful Master Absalom Jones, Senior Warden Richard Allen, and First Treasurer James Forten, and grew out of the same self-determination movement that created the first African-American church. Members contributed one shilling a month toward assistance for the sick, burials, and the support of widows and orphans.

The lodge's original location was in the Olde City section of Philadelphia, on Lombard Street between Fifth and Sixth. (Old maps list the address as 155 Lombard Street.) The first black fraternal order in the city was the African Lodge of Free Masons, organized under the charter of the Reverend Prince Hall.

Grand Master Hall soon chartered other lodges in the city in

State Historical Marker at Prince Hall Grand Lodge

the early 1800s. These organizations provided leadership and were rallying points for African-Americans demonstrating collective commitment to their own progress. Today, many lodges hold meetings at the Prince Hall Grand Lodge.

Location: Pennsylvania State Historical Marker at 4301 N. Broad Street

Philadelphia – African-American Baseball in Philadelphia

The Pythians and Excelsiors baseball clubs, formally organized in Philadelphia in 1867, are thought to be the first African-American teams in the United States. That same year, the newly formed National Association for Baseball Players, also located in Philadelphia, passed a resolution barring the participation of African-American clubs.

Although the Pythians and Excelsiors were the first organized clubs, African-Americans may have participated in the game well before the Civil War, for it was known as a popular pastime in this country after 1839. The first African-American playing on an otherwise all-white team in Pennsylvania was Bud Fowler, who reportedly played second base with a New Castle team in 1872.

In 1885, the first colored baseball team composed of paid players was organized in Babylon, New York. From that humble beginning Colored or Negro baseball grew and grew. The best known and the most powerful African-American baseball team in Philadelphia sports history was the Hilldale Club, founded by Edward Bolden and later purchased by John M. Drew, a wealthy Darby, Pennsylvania, African-American businessman.

Eastern Colored League Champions from 1923 to 1925, Hilldale won the World Series 1925. The Philadelphia Stars from 1933-52, won the Negro National League in 1933-48, and many of their games took place on this site.

Legendary Josh Gibson of the Homestead Grays, who was said to have been the greatest right-hand hitter of all time, hit numerous home runs here.

Location: Pennsylvania State Historical Marker at Belmont and Parkside Avenues

Philadelphia – Francis "Frank" Johnson

After gaining early experience in a black military band during the War of 1812, Frank Johnson built a reputation during the 1800s as a composer, bandleader, fiddler, bugler, French horn player, and orchestra director. His musical ability so impressed General Lafayette during a performance at Philadelphia's Chestnut Street Theatre in 1825 that the general sponsored a European tour for him.

It was during the tour that Johnson was invited to play for Queen Victoria, who presented him with a silver bugle after his performance. When he died, the bugle was buried with him.

Location: Pennsylvania State Historical Marker at former home address, 536 Pine Street

Frank Johnson

Philadelphia – Alain Leroy Locke

The first African-American to be named a Rhodes scholar and to receive a Doctorate in Philosophy, Alain Locke was the only child of Pliny Ishmael and Mary Hawkins Locke. Born in Philadelphia on September 13, 1885, he spent most of his professional life at Howard University as a professor of philosophy and was co-founder of the Howard University Players. Also known as a critic and chronicler of the Harlem Renaissance, Locke edited *The New Negro* (1925).

Location: Pennsylvania State Historical Marker at former home, 2221 S. 5th Street

Dr. Alain Locke

Philadelphia – Gertrude E.H. Bustill Mossell

Gertrude Mossell was an author whose articles appeared in numerous publications, including the *Christian Recorder, Philadelphia Press, Philadelphia Times, Philadelphia Inquirer, New York Freeman, Indianapolis World* and *New York Age*. In 1894, she wrote *The Work of the Afro-American Woman*.

Born in Philadelphia on July 3, 1855, she was the daughter of Charles H. and Emily Bustill, who were originally members of the Society of Friends, but later joined the Old School Presbyterian Church. She was the aunt of Paul Robeson, whose mother, Maria Louisa Bustill, was her sister.

Mossell was educated in the Philadelphia public schools, the Institute for Colored Youth, and the Robert Vaux Consolidated Grammar School. In 1893, she married Dr. Nathaniel F. Mossell, a physician who founded the Frederick Douglass Memorial Hospital and Training School, and helped him raise $30,000 for the institution. Mossell also organized the Philadelphia branch of the National Afro-American Council and was active in many other organizations.

Location: Former home address, 1423 Lombard Street

Philadelphia – Henry L. Phillips

The Reverend Henry Phillips, a native of the West Indies, became the first African-American rector of the Church of the Crucifixion in 1877. Under his leadership, the Church of the Crucifixion sponsored several funds for the poor, including the Progressive Workingmen's Club, the parish's first charitable organization, which was established in 1878 with Phillips as president. His other philanthropic work included the establishment of a home for crippled children, support of mission work in the African-American community, and work in prisons.

Location: 620 S. 8th Street

Philadelphia – Billie Holiday

An internationally recognized singer during the 1940s and 1950s, Billie Holiday was born in Philadelphia on April 7, 1915. Named Eleanora Fagan by her parents, Sadie Fagan and Clarence Holiday, an early jazz guitarist and banjoist, she was taken to Baltimore shortly after her birth. Exposed to music as a child, she was mentored by her idols, Bessie Smith and Louis Armstrong.

Holiday debuted professionally in New York at age 18, and made her recording debut with Benny Goodman in 1933, which was arranged by John Hammond, a well-known agent and jazz critic of the time. While Goodman recorded with Holiday, Hammond was unable to persuade him to hire her to sing with his band because of the racial climate in the country.

During the 1930s, she sang with many top musicians, including Teddy Wilson, Count Basie, and Artie Shaw.

Two of her greatest and commercially successful recordings were "Fine and Mellow" (1939) and "Strange Fruit"(1939), the latter of which was a protest against lynching of African-Americans in the south, and against racial discrimination throughout the nation. When she returned to Philadelphia as a performer, Holiday resided at the Douglass Hotel.

Location: Pennsylvania State Historical Marker at former address of the Douglass Hotel, 1409 Lombard Street

Philadelphia – Henry Ossawa Tanner

The most celebrated African-American realist-romantic is Henry Ossawa Tanner (1859-1937) who, although a native of Pittsburgh, spent the greatest part of his adult life in France, where he died. Tanner commenced his studies at the Pennsylvania Academy of the Fine Arts, where his principal teachers were the now famous Thomas Eakins and Thomas Hovenden.

Tanner's work included biblical landscapes and genre subjects; his early efforts portrayed the ordinary lives of African-Americans, exemplified by two noted works, "The Banjo Lesson" and "The Thankful Poor." His awards include Philadelphia's Walter Lippincott Award and the Second Medal from the San Francisco Exposition of 1915.

Among the museums where Tanner's work is on display are the Metropolitan Museum of Art in New York and the Philadelphia Museum of Art. Tanner is the first African-American to have his work on permanent display at the White House in Washington, D.C. His religious paintings are among his best-known works and include "Daniel in the Lion's Den" and "Christ Learning to Read."

Henry Ossawa Tanner was the first African-American to win a prize at the Paris Salon.

Location: Pennsylvania State Historical Marker at 2908 W. Diamond Street

Philadelphia – Laura Wheeler Waring

The works of Laura Waring, which include portraits of many distinguished African-Americans, have been exhibited in notable galleries, including the Philadelphia Museum of Art. She was born in Hartford, Connecticut, and educated at the Arsenal Grade School as well as Hartford High School.

In 1906, she moved to Philadelphia and enrolled at the Pennsylvania Academy of the Fine Arts, where she studied for six years. She was awarded a Cresson Travel Scholarship in 1914, which she used to study in Europe.

Upon completion of her studies, Waring was invited to direct the art and music departments at Cheyney State Teachers College. It was during her tenure at Cheyney that Waring painted some of her most outstanding portraits and landscapes.

Location: Pennsylvania State Historical Marker at former home address, 756 N. 43rd Street

Philadelphia – Reverend Jehu Jones Historical Marker

The Rev. Jehu Jones was the first African-American Lutheran minister in the United States. With the help of his congregation, Jones founded St. Paul's Evangelical Lutheran Church, the nation's first African-American Lutheran Church in 1834. The congregation worshipped at this site with Jones until 1839.

Location: Pennsylvania State Historical Marker at 310 South Quince Street

Philadelphia – Jean Pierre Burr

Jean Pierre Burr, the illegitimate son of Aaron Burr, was a barber by trade at his home, which served as an important station on Philadelphia's Underground Railroad network. Burr hid runaway slaves in his attic and cellar and a deep hole in his backyard.

A fair-skinned African-American, Burr sometimes passed as a white man. He led escapees through side streets and alleys to the South Street bridge over the Delaware River before passing them on to other conductors.

Location: Fifth and Spruce Streets

Philadelphia – Thomas J. Dorsey - Prominent Caterer and Entrepreneur

Born a slave in Maryland in 1812, Thomas J. Dorsey became one of the wealthiest and most influential African-Americans in Philadelphia. In 1836, Dorsey and his three brothers had run away from their owner, Thomas Soller, of Plantation Liberty in Frederick County, Maryland. Soller's father (who most likely also was the Dorsey brothers' father) had promised the three their freedom upon his death, but Thomas Soller refused to honor his father's promise.

The Costly brothers, as they were called during that period, escaped from the plantation and traveled along an Underground Railroad route to Pennsylvania. In Philadelphia, the brothers were introduced to Robert Purvis, the well-known African-American anti-slavery leader. Purvis hid the brothers in his mother's home at Ninth and Lombard Streets until it was safe for them to move farther north.

Thomas, the youngest, elected to stay in Philadelphia, while Purvis and his brother Joseph transported Basil, Charles, and William to Robert Purvis' large farm in Byberry, Bucks County. For obvious reasons, the brothers adopted the name Dorsey, but a jealous brother-in-law who visited them betrayed them.

Their former owner promptly engaged a slave hunter to reclaim his property. Thomas had been captured in Philadelphia and taken to Baltimore. However, a group of abolitionists in Philadelphia collected $1,000 to pay for his freedom. After a lengthy hearing in Doylestown, Bucks County, Judge John Fox agreed to dismiss the case on a technicality—that the prosecution did not prove that Maryland was a slave state—and the Dorsey brothers were granted their freedom.

In his later years, Robert Purvis said of the Dorsey case: "I have always considered it the most interesting case of my long and eventful life."

Thomas Dorsey married a free woman, Louise Tobias, from Pennsylvania, and sired several children. By 1838, his name appeared in a pamphlet entitled, *"A Register of Trades of the Colored People in the City of Philadelphia and Districts,"* conducting a boot and shoemaking business at 36 N. Sixth Street. He later established himself as the most prominent of Philadelphia's high-stature caterers, with an establishment located at 1231 Locust Street.

The 1875 directory listed Dorsey as one of the wealthiest African-Americans in Philadelphia. Dorsey and his family lived in a style appropriate to his position and wealth. Included among the friends invited to Dorsey's large home and business establishment at 1231 Locust Street were Frederick Douglass and Senator Charles Sumner.

Dorsey also was an agent on the Underground Railroad, working with other agents and conductors such as Mifflin Wistar Gibbs, and often traveling across the Delaware River to receive escapees who had been transported to Camden, NJ, by friendly sea captains who were connected with the freedom network.

Gibbs became a pioneer in California and British Columbia. When he settled in Little Rock, Arkansas, in 1871, he became the first African-American elected a municipal judge. He later became a U.S. consul in Madagascar.

At his death in 1876, Dorsey willed his vast estate to his wife Louise; upon her death the properties were divided among his three children, William, Mary Louise, and Sarah. William became an artist and a noted collector of books and documents pertaining to people of African descent.

Location: Restaurant and home, 1231 Locust Street

Thomas Dorsey

MONTGOMERY AND BUCKS COUNTIES

Pennsbury
Manor

LA MOTT
Camp William Penn

VALLEY FORGE
NATIONAL PARK

Patriot Monument
of African Descent

MONTGOMERY AND BUCKS COUNTIES ARE THE IMMEDIATE NEIGHBORS NORTH OF PHILADELPHIA. RICH IN HISTORY, THEY HAVE BEEN HOME TO GENERATIONS OF AFRICAN-AMERICANS AND THE STAGE OF EARLY ANTI-SLAVERY ACTIVITY. MOST OF THE FIRST SETTLERS IN THESE COUNTIES AFTER THE NATIVE AMERICANS WERE ANGLICANS AND QUAKERS. OTHER GROUPS STARTED TO COME INTO MONTGOMERY AND BUCKS COUNTIES IN THE EARLY PART OF THE 18TH CENTURY.

In 1790, the first United States census listed only 118 slaves in Montgomery County. By 1810, the county had only three slaves still in bondage. Slavery was never popular in this county. Most of the landowners were comparatively small farmers who hired a small number of workers. Many settlers opposed slavery in the early 18th century. Some Quakers permitted slave holding. Mennonites believed that slave holding was a shocking departure from Christianity, and the Schwenkfelders and other sectarian groups held the same point of view.

Bucks County, one of the three original counties of Pennsylvania, was more conservative than Montgomery County. It has been the home of African-Americans as both slaves and freed persons since its founding in 1682. William Penn, the Quaker founder of the commonwealth and a slave owner, had an estate in the county at Pennsbury.

By 1780, the first public registry of slaves in Bucks County listed a slave population of 580. Because of the Pennsylvania Act of Gradual Emancipation passed in that year, the number of slaves began to drop. In 1790, it was reported that there were 261 slaves in the county.

Despite early efforts to use laws on behalf of African-Americans, whites in Bucks County would, through the mid-19th century, still remain largely opposed to equal rights for African-Americans. All of these difficulties were a mere prelude to the Underground Railroad, when escaping slaves underwent their most severe ordeals.

Benjamin Lay

Montgomery County – Benjamin Lay and Abington Friends Meetinghouse

Benjamin Lay was born to a Quaker family in England in 1677. He arrived in Philadelphia in 1732 and took up residence in a cave near Abington. Dwarfish (he was only about four feet tall), Lay was also hunch-backed, eccentric, and a vegetarian.

Lay was one of the sternest opponents of slave-holding in the 18th century. While a resident of Abington in 1737, he wrote a 271-page book entitled *All Slave Keepers that Keep the Innocent in Bondage, Apostates Pretending to Lay Claim to the Pure and Holy Christian Religion*, that was published by Benjamin Franklin.

Lay was known for dramatic incidents. One freezing winter Sunday, he lay down in the snow in front of the Friends Meetinghouse so the worshippers would immediately confront him upon their departure. On another occasion, he took his sword and ran it through his coat. When he removed it, the blade was soaked with blood (it had punctured a filled bag concealed beneath his clothes). He shouted, "Thus shall God shed the blood of those persons who enslave their fellow creatures."

Lay died in 1759; his personal library continued nearly 200 volumes for he was a noted scholar as well as a sharp-tongued idealist.

Location: 520 Meetinghouse Road

Montgomery County – Millgrove – The Home of John James Audubon

Millgrove, the home of youthful painter and ornithologist John James Audubon, dates from the middle of the 18th century. William Penn's son John, the last provincial governor of Pennsylvania, brought the property in 1776 and sold it to Audubon's father, a wealthy French naval officer, planter, and slave trader.

Audubon was born in Haiti, April 26, 1785. His mother was a Creole of Haiti. She was killed during the slave revolt on that island and Audubon escaped with his father to France.

Educated in Paris where his artistic talents were developed, he came to America in his teens and began his collection of birds, roaming the countryside around Millgrove, remaining in the woods for days at a time, sketching, hunting, and trapping. It was there that he met his future wife, Lucy Blackwell.

The couple moved to Henderson, Kentucky, in 1818. He purchased for the sum of $2,400, from William Pate, two Mulatto slaves named Lewis and Anderson. At this time, Audubon owned a grist and lumber mill; his business failed and he filed for bankruptcy. He later moved to Cincinnati, Ohio.

Because of his mother's racial identity, there has long been speculation that Audubon had ancestors of African descent. In 1838, the folio edition of *Birds of America* was completed and Audubon became an internationally known personality and acquired some wealth. The National Audubon Society honors his name.

Millgrove was purchased by Dr. Samuel Wetherill, a Quaker paint manufacturer, who made it an Underground Railroad station, sheltering escapees from the Corson family in Plymouth Meeting.

Location: Audubon and Pawlings Roads

Montgomery County – Bryn Mawr – Historic 1704 Harriton House

Tucked in a wooded area on Gulph Road, a short distance from Bryn Mawr College, is Harriton, a large but unpretentious house that has stood since 1704 on a tract that Rowland Ellis, the property owner, called Bryn Mawr Harriton. It is the former home of Charles Thompson, who was secretary of the Continental Congress.

Perhaps the most unusual aspect of this unique place is its connection with African-American history. The area has a record of slave holding as evidenced by a survey revealing that there were 108 slaves residing in Montgomery County upon its official establishment in 1784.

Richard Harrison, the original owner of Harriton, was a slave owner and tobacco planter. For a number of years, slaves cultivated tobacco on much of the land located along Gulph Road. According to local tradition, several of the slaves attempted to murder the Harrison family by poisoning a pitcher of hot chocolate to be served during breakfast.

However, while grace was being said, there was a knock on the door and as one of the members of the family rose to answer it, a cup of the chocolate was spilled. The family cat lapped it up and shortly died. The slaves who were responsible confessed their guilt and were severely punished.

Location: 500 Harriton Road

Montgomery County – Glenside – Cremona Morrey's Former Home

Located in Glenside, Cheltenham Township, is a large two-story, stone house that is one of the first in the state of Pennsylvania to be owned by an African-American family. According to documented records, Humphrey Morrey, who acquired more than 700 acres in other properties, owned the original land grant of 200 acres.

When Humphrey died in 1715, his son Richard inherited the vast estate. He freed his own slaves and provided land for them. After he deserted his wife, Richard fathered five children by a woman of African descent named Cremona. Colonial law prohibited Richard Morrey from formally marrying Cremona; nevertheless, she inherited the house and property when he died in 1753 or 1754.

A deed dated 1746, executed by Richard Morrey, gives 198 acres to Cremona Morrey, a "Negress." She later married John Frey, a freed man of African descent, and they had two children—Joseph and a daughter named Cremona after her mother. When the mother died in 1772, she willed her property to her husband John.

A dispute transpired between Frey and Cremona's children. The property was held in trust until the death of John Frey, when the proceeds were divided among his former wife's children. Cremona Frey, the daughter, married John Montier, a freed person of African descent, after whom a street and graveyard were named. The former graveyard was located on Limekiln Pike, next to the present Knights of Columbus building.

The area where Cremona's former home is located was changed to Edge Hill in 1838; its original name was Guineatown after an area in Africa where the slaves originally came from. The town is known as Glenside today.

Several large estates were built on Cremona Morrey's property, including Gray Towers, now part of Beaver College (now known as Arcadia University). Cremona's former home is a private residence today.

Location: Humphrey Merry Way

The Morrey Home

Valley Forge Monument honoring Revolutionary War "Patriots of African Decent"

Montgomery County – Valley Forge – Valley Forge National Park

Soldiers of African descent were fighting side-by-side with their white comrades in most of the units of the continental army by the summer of 1778. Hardly a ship sailed in the continental navy without an African-American gunner, officer's helper, or seaman.

Custer, an African-American shipwright from the Southwark section of Philadelphia, served in the navy. He participated in a raid on Tory pirates near Billingsport in 1778, where he cut off the head of one of the pirates and proudly brought the grizzly trophy back to Philadelphia and placed it on display in a Sansom Street tavern.

From the earliest battles at Lexington and Concord, in the spring of 1775, to victory eight years later at Yorktown, African-Americans fought bravely. The bravery of soldiers of African descent was especially impressive in Valley Forge during the harsh winter and poor provisions.

In 1776, the Continental Congress had given permission to free African-Americans to enlist in the army and General James M. Varnum was sent to Rhode Island to recruit African-Americans for service. These men later became known as the First Rhode Island Regiment.

On April 18, 1993, the Valley Forge Alumnae Chapter of the Delta Sigma Theta sorority, an African-American organization, dedicated a large stone monument, standing 9'6" tall and 6' wide, in honor of "Patriots of African Descent, Who Served, Suffered and Sacrificed during the Valley Forge Encampment, 1777-1778."

Location: Pennsylvania State Historical Marker 150 yards east of Washington Memorial Chapel, two miles off Pennsylvania Turnpike, Pa. Rte. 23 (Interchange 24)

Montgomery County – Swedesburg – Leah Hector's Grave at Old Swedes' Church

Built in the 1760s by the Swedish settlers, Old Swedes', or Christ Church as it is sometime called, has a cemetery where Leah Hector is buried in an unmarked grave. She was the wife of Revolutionary War hero Edward (Ned) Hector whose parents were baptized in Christ Church in Philadelphia.

Leah Hector was a former slave who died at the age of 107 on March 4, 1882. An account at the time of her death said, "She was an amazing woman who, for the past hundred years, prepared her own kindling wood." She was tall, gaunt, and double-jointed. Her mind was sharp and she could recall many events in United States history, particularly the time she saw General George Washington. She remembered that her mistress paid $300 for her.

At the time of her death, Leah Hector was a resident of the Montgomery County Alms House.

Location: River Road, Swedesburg, and Upper Merion Township, near Bridgeport

Montgomery County – Conshohocken – Edward (Ned) Hector's Marker

Edward (Ned) Hector was an African-American patriot of the Revolutionary War who served in the Battle of Brandywine in September 1777 as a private in Captain Hercules Courtney's Company/ Third Pennsylvania Artillery Continental Line. He saved the day for the American forces.

Hector died in 1834, at the age of 90, and the following obituary, which appeared in two Norristown newspapers, recalled his heroism and saved Hector's name from obscurity. In a condensed form it reads:

Edward Hector, a colored man and veteran of the Revolution, exhibited an example of patriotism and bravery which deserves to be recorded. At the Battle of Brandywine, he had charge of the ammunition wagon attached to Col. Proctor's regiment and when the American army was obliged to retreat, an order was given—to abandon the wagon to the enemy. The heroic reply of the deceased was uttered in the spirit of the Revolution: The enemy shall not have my team. I will save the horses or perish myself. He instantly started on his way and proceeded. Amid the confusion of the surrounding scene, he calmly gathered up arms which had been left on the field by retreating soldiers, and safely retired with wagon, team, and all in the face of the victorious foe.

Hector's grave lies in Upper Merion Township. A Pennsylvania State Historical Marker is located on the former site of his cabin and a street honors his name.

Location: Fayette and Hector Streets

Montgomery County – Plymouth Meeting – The Maulsby House

Plymouth Meeting is a quiet, country town with large, old homes and stately trees. It continues to resist the change of centuries. Plymouth Meeting once played an important role in a turbulent period of American history.

While abolitionists thundered in protest and wily slave hunters scanned Philadelphia and surrounding area newspapers for descriptions of runaway slaves from the South, Plymouth Meeting calmly functioned as the nearest point of the Underground Railroad to Philadelphia.

Samuel Maulsby's home was an important safe house. As early as 1820, Maulsby had spoken openly against slavery along with Allen Corson and his brother Joseph. His large stone house welcomed local and national anti-slavery personalities, including Lucretia Mott, Benjamin Lundy, Abby Kelley, and William Wells Brown.

The Maulsby Home

This site was also a center of activity during the Abolition movement. Many local and national anti-slavery lecturers visited or stayed in the home. Meetings also were held here.

So well known was Maulsby's home that slave hunters and anti-abolitionists threatened to burn it down. Yet today the nearly 280-year-old structure still stands virtually unchanged. The Irish-born artist Thomas Hovenden, who married Helen Corson, lived in this house for several years. It now is a private residence.

The Plymouth Friends Meetinghouse located directly across Germantown Pike is another important historic site. It was used as a house of worship since about 1708. During the Battle of Germantown, it served as a hospital and campsite for Washington's army.

Location: Germantown Pike (Old U.S. 422) and Butler Pike

Montgomery County – Plymouth Meeting – Abolition Hall

Abolition Hall was built in 1856 as a meeting place for those advocating the abolition of slavery. It was also a refuge for escaping slaves making their way north to freedom.

George Corson, of the noted Quaker and abolitionist Corson family of Plymouth Meeting, built it, and it comfortably accommodated 150 persons. There members could carry on their work without disturbance.

So strong was the faith of this Quaker community that runaway slaves were passed from other Underground Railroad stations at night in closed covered wagons to the Corson family. Abolition Hall also served as the studio for the noted American artist Thomas Hovenden, who married into the Corson family. Here he painted his well-known work "John Brown's Last Moment." The original painting is owned by the Metropolitan Museum of Art in New York City. A Pennsylvania State Historical Marker stands on the site today.

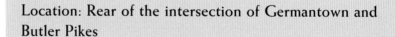

Location: Rear of the intersection of Germantown and Butler Pikes

Quaker abolitionist Lucretia Mott

Montgomery County – Elkins Park – Lucretia C. Mott's "Roadside" Home Historical Marker

Only a gatehouse remains to mark the existence of "Roadside," the home of Lucretia and James Mott dating from 1857. A Pennsylvania State Historical Marker standing on the site of her former home reads: *Nearby stood "Roadside," the home of the ardent Quaker, Lucretia C. Mott (1793-1880).* Roadside was also a station on the Underground Railroad.

Mott was a diminutive woman who never weighed more than 100 pounds. Her most notable work was in connection with anti-slav-

Roadside

ery, women's rights, temperance, and peace. In their large home, the Motts entertained many persons, famous and obscure, American and foreign, dedicated to the anti-slavery movement, including William Lloyd Garrison, Anna E. Dickinson, Frederick Douglass, John Greenleaf Whittier, Lucy Stone, British actress Frances Kemble, and the widow of John Brown, the noted abolitionist who was hanged at Harper's Ferry. Roadside was demolished in 1913.

Location: U.S. Rte. 611 north of Cheltenham Avenue

Montgomery County – LaMott – Camp William Penn

The history of LaMott is closely tied to the lives of Lucretia Mott and her family. The neighborhood is named for her and the village of LaMott is located in Cheltenham Township; it also stands as an important landmark in American and African-American history.

During the Civil War, the land on which LaMott now rests became the Union Army's first recruiting and training center for African-American soldiers. Eleven thousand recruits were trained there on land provided by Lucretia Mott and her family.

The Union Army did not accept African-Americans as soldiers until 1863. Camp William Penn, as it was then called, originally occupied 13 acres with long rows of framed barracks, mess halls, guardhouses, officer quarters, and a chapel. The camp was self-contained to prevent African-American soldiers from entering Philadelphia, a short distance away.

At first, African-American soldiers used a segregated drill manual with the title page reading, "For United States Colored Soldiers." Frederick Douglass, the noted abolitionist and African-American lecturer, was instrumental in recruiting volunteers for the formation of colored regiments.

Two Pennsylvania State Historical Markers were erected in LaMott to honor the United States Colored Regiments who were mustered into the army at Camp William Penn. Three medals of honor were awarded to soldiers who trained at this camp. A small museum located near the corner of Sycamore and Willow Avenues also honors the 11 regiments who trained at Camp William Penn.

Location: 7322 Sycamore Avenue

Montgomery County – LaMott – Harriet Tubman Speaks to Soldiers at Camp William Penn

Harriet Tubman, the celebrated conductor on the Underground Railroad, was familiar with the Philadelphia area. Born a slave in Dorchester, Maryland, as a woman in her 20s she set off one dark summer night and made it to Philadelphia, penniless and a "stranger in a strange land."

In Philadelphia, she found employment and later began returning to the South, seeking passengers for her underground train. Dark of skin, medium in height, with a broad face, topped often with a colorful kerchief, she developed extraordinary physical endurance and mental fortitude.

John Brown so admired Harriet's character and prowess that he nicknamed her "General Tubman." She had planned to join John Brown on his ill-fated attack on Harper's Ferry, but became ill. Like her friend Frederick Douglass, Harriet traveled to Camp William Penn to inspire the soldiers of the 24th Regiment. Many of the soldiers, former slaves themselves, were thrilled to have this nationally known woman to speak to them.

The Christian Recorder, an African-American newspaper, reported about Harriet, "It was the first time we had the pleasure of hearing her. She seems to be very well known by the community at large, as the great Underground Railroad woman, and had done a good part to many of her fellow creatures in that direction." The article continued, "During her lecture, which she gave in her own homespun language, she received considerable applause from the soldiers. She gave thrilling accounts of her trials in the South, during these past three years among the contrabands and the colored soldiers."

During the war in South Carolina, Harriet served as a spy nurse and led a group of men in a raid against Confederate soldiers.

Location: Cheltenham Avenue and Sycamore Street

Montgomery County – Norristown – The First Baptist Church

A decision to form a Baptist congregation in December 1832 led to the First Baptist Church of Norristown. It was the only white church in the county (aside from some Quaker and Unitarian

Camp William Penn

institutions) open to anti-slavery lectures.

The Reverend Samuel Aaron, the pastor between 1841 and 1844, represented the more radical wing of the anti-slavery movement. His home in Bucks County was a station on the Underground Railroad. An eloquent orator himself, Aaron invited celebrated abolitionists such as William Lloyd Garrison, Frederick Douglass, Lucretia Mott, J. Miller McKim, Mary Grew, and others to speak.

Henry "Box" Brown who made his famous escape through the Underground Railroad in a box, spoke in the church. These fiery abolitionists strengthened the anti-slavery sentiment in the community.

At the same time, they incited violent opposition from the pro-slavery segment of Norristown, which threatened to burn the church to the ground. One night, a mob threatened Lucretia Mott and Frederick Douglass when a rumor started that Mott and Douglass left the church arm-in-arm, which was considered an assault on white motherhood.

A Philadelphia Underground Railroad agent stands behind the box in which Henry "Box" Brown traveled to freedom.

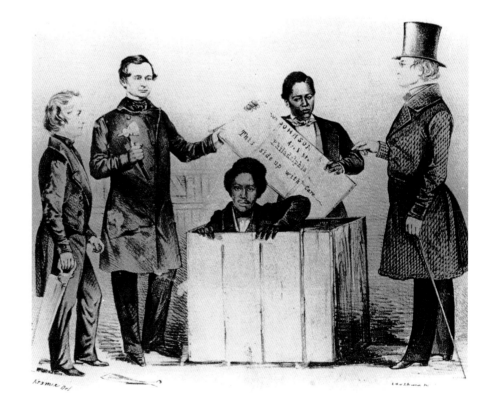

Mott and Douglass were rescued by members of the anti-slavery element of the community and by Benjamin F. Hancock, father of famous Civil War general Winfield Scott Hancock, who grew up in Norristown.

Once located on the corner of Swede and Airy Streets, where a large county office building stands today, in 1971 First Baptist Church moved.

Location: Burnside Avenue, West Norriton Twp.

Montgomery County – Norristown – The Soldiers and Sailors Monument

In the tree-lined public square in front of the county courthouse, between Main and Swede Streets, there stands a marble and bronze monument with the following inscription: *"Erected by the citizens of Montgomery County September 17, 1869. In honor of our brave soldiers and sailors who fell while defending the Union during the Great Rebellion, AD 1861-1865."*

Included with the names of their white comrades on the rear, lower portion of monument is a section dedicated to the United States Colored Troops, honoring the following who gave their all for their nation:

E. Wilmore, Sergeant Robert Brown– 8th Regiment, Embrose Jackson – 41st Regiment, Daniel Davis – 45th Regiment, William Van Lear – 127th Regiment, James Wilson – 137 Regiment, Isaac Hopkins and George Price – 54th Massachusetts Volunteers, Albanus Fisher– Sergeant, of Norristown, who survived the conflict, served with the 54th Regiment.

Some of the county's white citizens did not want the names of African-Americans included on the monument.

Location: Corner of Main and Swede Streets

James Bland

Montgomery County – Bala Cynwyd – James Bland's Grave

"Oh, Dem Golden Slippers," the theme song of the Philadelphia Mummers Parade, was written by African-American songwriter and minstrel performer James Bland. He wrote more than 600 songs including "Carry Me Back to Old Virginny," official state song of Virginia.

Bland was a celebrity during the later part of the 19th century, winning acclaim in America and Europe, and for a short period he earned a large sum of money annually. Bland, whose father was one of America's first African-American college graduates, was born in New York in 1854. He was graduated from Howard University and served as a page on the floor of the United States House of Representatives. After poverty and toil in beer gardens and clubs, he lived a lonely life in Philadelphia, where he died penniless in 1911. Upon his death, there was no money for even a modest funeral or grave marker.

An overdue tribute to Bland, as late as July 1941, was given by Governor William H. Tuck and the Lions Club of Virginia. They accorded Bland an honorary burial in Merion Memorial Park, in Bala Cynwyd, Pennsylvania.

The cemetery is divided, with sections representing prominent African-Americans and friends such as Benjamin Banneker, Octavius V. Catto, and white friends such as Abraham Lincoln, Thaddeus Stevens, and Senator Charles Sumner.

> Location: Pennsylvania State Historical Marker on Pa. Rte. 23, Conshohocken State Road

Montgomery County – Merion Station – The Barnes Foundation

In 1922, multimillionaire Dr. Albert C. Barnes, who made a

fortune from Argyol, established an endowment of $10 million for an institution where masterpieces of paintings and sculpture were to be displayed in connection with courses of instruction in the fine arts. Barnes' collection of paintings is considered to be one of the finest and most valuable in the world.

His collection includes the works of Cezanne, Matisse, Monet, Picasso, Renoir, Gauguin, Degas, Modigliani, and others. Influenced by his African-American friend Dr. Alain Locke, a Rhodes scholar, Barnes also developed a fine collection of African-American art. Artist Horace Pippin especially impressed him. Barnes acquired the core of his collection of African art from 1922 to 1923 through Paul Guillaume's gallery in Paris.

The main entrance walls of the Barnes Foundation are decorated with colored ceramic tiles representing the African people of the Ivory Coast and Ghana. Barnes was particular about who he would allow to see his collection. It is housed in his 18th century style French Chateau situated on 12 acres. Nine months before he died, Barnes rewrote his will to empower Lincoln University to name the foundation's future caretakers.

Location: 300 North Latches Lane

Montgomery County – Gladwyn – Woodmont: Father Divine's Estate and Shrine

Thousands filled streets, churches, and halls to see and hear words of inspiration from one of the most fascinating religious personalities of the 20th century. Known to millions as "Father Divine," along with other such heavenly titles such as "Prince of Peace," "Everlasting Father," and "Mighty God," the Rev. Major J. Divine attracted both white and black to his flock.

He was a brilliant organizer and businessman. His material kingdom has been estimated to be worth more than several million

Father Divine

dollars. Father Divine founded the Peace Mission Movement and preached love and hope. His estate and shrine are located in a scenic and hilly section of Gladwyn.

Location: 1522 Spring Mill Road

Montgomery County – Pottstown – Women and the Underground Railroad

In the area bordering Pottstown and going on into Berks County, Dunkard women sewing circles produced clothes for ragged runaway slaves who were inadequately dressed and whose southern-made garments revealed their identity as runaway slaves.

Women played an important role on Pennsylvania's Underground Railroad. In Philadelphia, Lancaster, and Pittsburgh, a secret African-American society of women known as the Sisters of the Tent Society could be called upon any time to assist the Underground Railroad network.

Bucks County – Morrisville – Pennsbury Manor

William Penn referred to Pennsbury as his "beloved manor." Of all his dwellings, it was the only one planned and built especially by and for him. To reach it from Philadelphia meant a 20-mile row in a six-oared barge.

When Penn originally occupied his estate in 1683, his plantation included a manor house, brew house, barn, out buildings, formal gardens, orchards, and a vineyard. The plantation also included seven slaves owned by Penn. In 1685, Penn wrote to his steward at Pennsbury from England that, "It would be better to have blacks to work the place, since they might be held for life." Three years later in 1688, the celebrated Germantown Protest Against Slavery was issued.

The library at Pennsbury contains archival information pertaining to Penn's slaves.

Location: 400 Pennsbury Memorial Road

Bucks County – Washington Crossing – Washington Crossing State Park

When General George Washington and his army made their famous crossing of the Delaware River to Trenton, New Jersey, on Christmas Eve night in 1776, it became a focal point of the American Revolution. With him were two African-American soldiers, Oliver Cromwell and Prince Whipple, bodyguard to General Whipple of New Hampshire, who was aide to General Washington.

There are two famous paintings that depict Washington crossing the Delaware. Thomas Sully painted the earlier of the two in 1819. It shows Washington astride a white horse on a snowy riverbank attended by four, mounted white soldiers and a young African-American soldier. The other, more familiar, painting by artist Emanuel Gottlieb Leutze, shows Washington standing in a rowboat as it passes

Washington crossing the Delaware River

through jagged cakes of ice. Prince Whipple is depicted pulling a stroke oar along with other soldiers.

Throughout his life, Washington was the master of about 300 slaves, but he had his favorites. History cites a certain slave named William Lee, commonly called "Billy," who accompanied Washington through thick and thin until the war ended and then to the Mount Vernon household with his wife, Margaret Thomas, a free woman from Philadelphia.

In his will, Washington freed Lee; "to my mulatto man William, (calling him William Lee,) I give immediate freedom." Washington's Crossing State Park includes several interesting visitor attractions, including an excellent reproduction of Leutze's "Washington Crossing the Delaware."

Location: River Road, Pa. Rte. 32

Bucks County – Quakertown – Former home of Richard Moore

The home of Quaker Richard Moore in Quakertown was a major station on Bucks County's Underground Railroad freedom network. Moore, a potter by trade, was the son-in-law of Quakertown Mayor Edward Foulke, whose Welsh Quaker relatives had arrived with William Penn and helped found Gwynedd Friends Meeting in 1699.

Moore was that uncompromising and righteous type of Quaker known and revered for his integrity. He harbored William Parker in his home and forwarded him to Canada. Parker, the subject of the Christiana Riot in 1851, was being sought for the killing of a Maryland slave owner, who had attempted to recapture his runaway slave in Lancaster County.

Both Underground Railroad chroniclers William Still and Robert Smedley gave an account of Moore and his station. He forwarded escapees to Montrose or Friendsville in Susquehanna County and to stations in New York State. Runaway slaves were hidden in Moore's barn during the day and were transported in his large pottery wagon covered with hay.

Some escapees were also hidden in his home built in 1834. Now an apartment building, Moore's former home is located between 10th and Edgemont Avenue in Quakertown.

Location: 10th and Edgemont Avenue

Bucks County – New Hope – Underground Railroad Escape Route by Land and Water

The Rev. Henry Highland Garnet

In an historic and scenic area of Bucks County, the Delaware River separates New Hope from the New Jersey town of Lambertville. During the era of the Underground Railroad, members of Mount Gilead A.M.E. Church and their white sympathizers assisted runaway slaves to their destination.

One of the runaways, Henry Highland Garnet, who later became a noted Underground Railroad agent, minister, editor, diplomat, and the first African-American to deliver a sermon before the U.S. House of Representatives, wrote about the assistance he and his family received from New Hope friends of the Underground Railroad. Sometimes, escapees were sent by trusted friends to agents and conductors on the New Hope to Easton line, and then to Stroudsburg.

For some runaway slaves, the canal and river

121

Dr. Selma Burke, renowned sculptor, was commissioned to design the bust and profile of President Franklin D. Roosevelt in 1943. Her former home and studio still stands in New Hope.

became their Underground escape route to freedom. The Delaware-Lehigh Canal was well traveled by barges carrying coal, lumber, and hay, and sometimes slaves were concealed among the cargo mules who pulled the barges from town to town along the Delaware River.

The water route led from Bristol, Fallsington, Yardley, and New Hope up the river to Easton. Aaron La Rue, a Quaker and Underground Railroad sympathizer, operator of Canal House #10 in Yardley, loaded his passengers at night on barges and covered them with cornstalks and leaves as they lay flat on the decks of the barges until they reached the next station 10 to 20 miles away.

Location: River Road, Pa Rte. 32, adjacent to Delaware River

Bucks County – Buckingham – Mt. Gilead African Methodist Episcopal Church

Up a curving path, up a hill or two, and around a few bends in a grove of trees, Mt. Gilead A.M.E. Church stands on top of Buckingham Mountain. It was the last main stop of Bucks County's Underground Railroad before escaping slaves were smuggled into New Jersey to continue their journey towards freedom. Rebuilt in 1852, the small, one-room stone church was originally built of logs in 1832.

A former Maryland runaway slave called "Big Ben" served as the church's first minister at the religious services, sometimes known at that time as "camp meetings." He is buried in the small cemetery in front of the church. "Big Ben" stood 6' 10" tall and weighed nearly 300 pounds. When slave-hunters tried to return him to slavery, he fought them off with a club. Today the congregation meets approximately three times a year.

Location: Holicong Road, at the top of the hill

CHESTER AND DELAWARE COUNTIES

HOSANNA
African
Meeting House

CHESTER
Ethel Waters Park

Chester County – Lower Oxford – Lincoln University

Ashmun Institute, today named Lincoln University, was originally established to provide education for male African-American youth. It was founded in 1854 by John M. Dickey who, after serving as a missionary preaching to slaves in Georgia, became pastor of Oxford Presbyterian Church in 1832.

During the days of the Underground Railroad, a number of runaway slaves were given assistance here as they passed through the tree-lined campus.

In 1859, the school's first three graduates all left for missionary work in Liberia, Africa, starting a link that Lincoln kept throughout the 20th century.

The institute was renamed for Abraham Lincoln in 1866, and is the oldest African-American university in the nation.

Many famous African-Americans and Africans are associated with Lincoln, including United States Supreme Court Justice Thurgood Marshall; poet and writer Langston Hughes, whose private collection of books is housed in a library that bears his name; Nnamdi Azikiwe, first president of Nigeria; Kwame Nkrumah, first president of Ghana; Dr. Horace Mann Bond, the first African-American president of Lincoln University, and Paul Robeson, who coached football for several years during the early 1920s. Robeson's father, William Drew Robeson, who escaped as a slave from North Carolina during the Civil War, was graduated from Lincoln University.

Location: Pennsylvania State Historical Marker at Old U.S. Rte. 1, Baltimore Pike

Chester County – Cheyney – Cheyney University

Established in the pre-Civil War years, Cheyney University originally opened in Philadelphia in 1837 as the Institute for Colored Youth with a mission to train African-American teachers. Charles L. Reason, a nationally known African-American educator and lecturer, served as principal of the institute from 1852 to 1856. Ebenezer D. Bassett followed him in that position, and remained with the institution for 15 years.

The campus building known as Glen Burnie was a station on the Underground Railroad. The building is still standing today.

The school prospered under the leadership of Fanny M. Jackson (Coppin), who promoted academic and industrial education. She served as the institute's principal into the 20th century. Later, Dr. Leslie Hill, a noted educator, author, and poet who had been graduated from Harvard University with high distinction during the 1920s, transformed the college into a respected liberal arts institution.

During this period, Cheyney entered the Pennsylvania educational system upon a promise that its graduates would be permitted to teach in white schools, a promise that was not honored for three decades. In 1902 the Institute for Colored Youth changed its name to Cheyney State College. Its name was changed to Cheyney University in 1963.

Location: Pennsylvania State Historical Marker at Cheyney and Creed Roads

Chester County – Cheyney – Fanny M. Jackson Coppin's Marker

Educator, writer, humanist, missionary Fanny M. Jackson Coppin, a former slave, was graduated from Oberlin College in 1865, one of the first African-American women to be graduated from college.

She began teaching at the Institute for Colored Youth shortly after graduation, and was its principal from 1869 to 1902.

Fanny Coppin also was active in a variety of educational activities in the Philadelphia community and stressed the importance of industrial as well as academic training. Booker T. Washington, the famous African-American educator, adapted a number of her ideas pertaining to industrial education and incorporated them into a curriculum at Tuskegee Institute that he founded in Alabama.

Location: Pennsylvania State Historical Marker at Cheyney University Campus, off Dilworthtown and Cheyney Roads

Chester County – Kennett Square – John and Hannah Cox Home: A Major Station on the Underground Railroad

There were no more staunch abolitionists than Quakers John and Hannah Cox. This husband and wife knew intimately most of the leading anti-slavery champions of their day.

Poet John Greenleaf Whittier commemorated the Cox's 50th anniversary of marriage with his poem, "Golden Wedding at Longwood," in which he wrote, "Blessing upon you, what you did for each sad, suffering one. Some homeless, faint and naked, unto our Lord was done."

Their former tract of 500 acres and home, Edgewood Farm, is now called DuPont Pierce Park Estate. As recorded in *Recollection and Experiences of an Abolitionist* by Dr. Alexander Ross, the house of Hannah Cox, had for many years been one of the principal stations on the

Fanny Coppin

127

Underground Railroad for fugitive slaves escaping from Maryland and Delaware, where many poor fugitive slaves came with bleeding and tattered garments, relying upon the humanity of this noble woman, who shielded the outcasts from their pursuers.

It is now a private estate; visitors must ask permission to tour the property.

Location: One half-mile west of the Anvil on Nottingham Road, now U.S. Rte. 1

Chester County – Kennett Square – Longwood Progressive Friends Meetinghouse and Cemetery

Not all Quakers in Chester County took an active part in the anti-slavery movement and Underground Railroad. However, those who did not take an active part did not talk about the involvement of those who did. Quakers who had been cast out by their co-religionists because of their anti-slavery sentiments formed Longwood Meeting in 1854.

Many prominent leaders in the anti-slavery movement spoke here, including Thomas Garrett, John Greenleaf Whittier, Lucretia Mott, Sojourner Truth, Susan B. Anthony, and William Lloyd Garrison.

In the graveyard of Longwood Meetinghouse sleep great conductors of the Underground Railroad. Cox, Darlington, Mendenhall, and Taylor, were families whose members were dedicated to the mysterious freedom network and who represented the morality of antebellum America.

Today, the meetinghouse is the site of the Brandywine Tourist Information Center. A permanent exhibit tells the story of the Underground Railroad in Chester County and elsewhere.

Location: At the entrance of Longwood Gardens, U.S. Rte. 1 and Kennett Square

Chester County – Lower Oxford – Hosanna African Union Methodist Protestant Church

Founded by free people of African descent who had settled in Upper and Lower Oxford Township in 1829, this small church was first known as the "African Meetinghouse," and was a station on the Underground Railroad.

It was formally organized in 1843 as an African Union Methodist Protestant church. From 1855 to 1862, a very large number of runaway slaves received shelter, food, and clothing from trusted members of this church. Its many visitors included Frederick Douglass and Sojourner Truth. According to oral tradition, Harriet Tubman occasionally stopped there also. She was known to have used this route, broken here and there by clumps of woodland, on her way to Kennett Square, West Grove, Avondale, and Philadelphia.

In the church's cemetery are tombstones bearing the original African names of the church's earlier members. Also buried in the

Hosanna Meetinghouse

cemetery are the remains of 17 veterans of the famous United States Colored Troops of the 54th Massachusetts Infantry Regiment who fought in the Civil War.

The church is known today as Hosanna AUMP Zion Church. It shares its border with Lincoln University's property. A Pennsylvania State Historical Marker stands in front of its present site.

Location: **Old U.S. Rte 1 (Baltimore Pike)**

Chester County – West Chester – Artist Horace Pippin

Horace Pippin, an African-American artist noted for his "primitive" paintings, was born in West Chester in 1888. He started his career late, and was entirely self-taught. His work has been acclaimed throughout the world.

Pippin's first experiments with wood-burnt panels came after he suffered a debilitating wound in World War I. The panel called "Losing the Way" was produced in 1930, and is one of the earliest examples of his work. Three of his most important paintings are "John Brown Goes To His Hanging," "Domino Players," and the "Holy Mountain" series. Other famous works include "Buffalo Hunt," "After Supper," "West Chester," "The End of the War," "Mother and Child," "Cabin in the Cotton," and "Roses with Red Chair."

Pippin's works are found in the collections of the Barnes Foundation of Merion, Philadelphia Museum of Art, the Whitney Museum of Art in New York City, and many others. A Pennsylvania State Historical Marker stands in front of the house that Pippin occupied from 1920 until his death in 1946.

Location: **Pennsylvania State Historical Marker at 327 Gay Street**

Horace Pippin

Chester County – West Chester – Bayard Rustin Home

Scholar, athlete, pacifist, civil and human rights activist, and bibliophile Bayard Rustin, who died in 1987, was born in West Chester in 1910. For more than half a century before his death, Rustin planned and implemented national and international activism on behalf of humanity.

Rustin excelled in high school academics and athletics, winning varsity letters in football, basketball, track, and tennis. He also participated in extra-curricular club activities including French, drama, and glee clubs, and later excelled in academics as a college student. He held various jobs during his early career, including serving as part-time director of Harlem Youth Center in New York.

In 1941, he helped A. Phillip Randolph, head of the Brotherhood of Sleeping Car Porters, and became director of that organization from 1966 to 1979. In 1963, he offered Martin Luther King, Jr., his services and became the principal organizer of the March on Washington D.C. After his death, Rustin was elected to the Henderson High School Hall of Fame, located in West Chester. A Pennsylvania State Historical Marker is located at the school.

Location: Lincoln and Montgomery Avenues

Chester County – West Chester – Star of the West (Tent #6) Marker

A Pennsylvania State Historical Marker recognizes an African-American women's community services organization known as Star of the West (Tent #6).

This organization, chartered in 1865, was a part of the United Order of Tent, J.R. Giddings and Jollifee Union, a secret organization founded in 1847 and named for an abolitionist congressman and his law partner.

Joshua R. Giddings, a giant, broad shouldered, deep-chested attorney of Jefferson, Ohio, went to Congress in 1838. He had a sincere abhorrence of slavery and immediately threw himself into the struggle for freedom of the slaves held in bondage in the south. His law office served as a stop on the Underground Railroad. He counted abolitionist John Brown and President Abraham Lincoln as two of his friends. As a young congressman in Washington, he lived in the same boarding house as Lincoln and lived in the same Ohio County where John Brown's family resided.

Location: 113 S. Adam Street

Chester County – West Uwchlan Township – Thomas Bonsall Home and Farm

An important Underground Railroad station was the home and farm of Thomas Bonsall, who operated this farm as a station for some 30 years. Escapees were hidden in the granary. Bonsall and his Underground Railroad co-workers Lindley Coates, Thomas Whitson, and Amos Gilbert met and signed a document to abolish the use of a jail in Washington, DC, as a slave pen and sent it to John Quincy Adams, then a member of Congress, asking him to present it.

Delaware County – Drexel Hill- Thornfield – Home of Thomas Garrett

A Quaker, Thomas Garrett wore no pistol and carried no knife. He was born in Upper Darby, Pennsylvania, on August 21, 1789. Garrett lived at Thornfield before 1822, when he moved to Wilmington, Delaware.

He refused to budge an inch for his abolition principles while living and working in a slave state. According to tradition, by the 1860s Garrett, with the assistance of Wilmington's African-American community, had helped 2,700 slaves to escape to freedom on the Underground Railroad.

His large home at 227 Shipley Street in Wilmington welcomed his friend Harriet Tubman, who led many of her "passengers" there for assistance as she made her way north to Canada. "Among the manliest of men, and the gentlest of spirits," wrote his friend William Lloyd Garrison.

William Still, indefatigable worker in the Philadelphia Underground Railroad, wrote about Garrett's daring exploits on the freedom network. Once the Maryland State Legislature offered $10,000 for Garrett as a "slave stealer," and he wrote to the parties saying it was not enough. "If they would send $20,000," he said, "I'll show up in person."

His father (also named Thomas) had built Thornfield in 1800; his great-great-grandfather William had arrived in Darby in 1684. A Pennsylvania State Historical Marker stands at this site.

Location: Garrett Road and Maple Avenue

Delaware County – Chester – Upland

Two Pennsylvania State Historical Markers honor Dr. Martin Luther King, Jr. A few years before King became one of the most important leaders of the 20th century and a spokesman for a non-violent revolution during the Civil Rights era of the 1950s and 1960s, he lived for a short period in Chester.

The first Pennsylvania State Historical Marker, reads: *Martin Luther King lived three years in this community and ministered under the mentorship of J. Pious Barbour. He graduated from Crozer Theological Seminary 1951. A leader of the 1963 March on Washington. King won a Nobel Peace Prize, 1964.*

The second marker is located in nearby Upland at Crozer-Chester Medical Center. The inscription reads: *Minister and Civil Rights Leader. Here at Crozer Theological Seminary, he earned his Bachelor of Divinity degree, 1951. King's three years here were a key period in shaping his philosophy of non-violent social change.*

Location: Pennsylvania State Historical Markers
at 1616 W. Second Street, Chester, and
One Medical Center Drive, Upland.

Delaware County – Upper Darby – Hoodland, the Former Residence of Abraham L. Pennock

A Pennsylvania State Historical Marker now standing on this site is dedicated to Abraham L. Pennock and his home Hoodland. The wording on the marker reads: *This prominent abolitionist and patron of the arts resided here at Hoodland until his death in 1868. The home had been built in 1832 by his father-in-law, John Sellers. A leader in the Pennsylvania Anti-Slavery Society, slaves escaping on the Underground Railroad, sent by Pennock's friends, Thomas Garrett and his brother Edward were duly cared for by the Pennock family."*

Pennock once met President John Quincy Adams and discussed the abolition of slavery in the nation's capital. He also founded the *Non-Slaveholder*, an anti-slavery newspaper, and he provided an illustration of Paul Cuffee's vessel, *The Traveler*. Cuffee was a famous New England African-American ship builder and sea captain who transported freed persons from America back to their motherland, Africa.

Notable visitors to Hoodland included John Greenleaf Whittier and James Russell Lowell. The Pennock, Garrett, and Seller families were instrumental in building Pennsylvania Hall in 1838. This majestic structure located in Philadelphia was burned to the ground by an anti-abolitionist mob.

Location: 76 South State Road

Delaware County – Chester – Ethel Waters Park

Renowned actress, dancer, singer, and film star Ethel Waters was born in Chester. Before breaking into show business, she moved to Philadelphia and worked as a maid in a

Ethel Waters

135

Philadelphia hotel and at Swarthmore College. During that period, she sang in Philadelphia nightclubs and beer gardens to earn additional money to support her family.

Later, when she substituted for the famous Florence Mills in a New York stage production, she was nicknamed "Sweet Mama Stringbean" for the way she danced the Charleston. Her stage roles were in *Blackbirds, Rhapsody in Black, As Thousands Cheer,* and *Home Abroad.* Film roles included *Cabin in the Sky* and *Pinky.*

She is remembered for the Broadway production of *The Member of the Wedding,* in 1950. Television performances rounded out her theater career until her death. A park is named in her honor on Second Street in Chester.

Location: Second Street

Delaware County – Sharon Hill – Bessie Smith's Gravesite

North of Chester, Mt. Lawn Cemetery in Sharon Hill holds the grave of Bessie Smith, queen of the blues singers and perhaps the most famous of all blues singers. Her discovery was owed to Ma Rainey, another legendary blues singer, who persuaded her to join the Rabbit Foot Minstrel Group after hearing her sing in Chattanooga, Tennessee.

Bessie Smith's best-known songs are "Nobody Knows You When You're Down and Out," and "St. Louis Blues." She was married to a Philadelphia policeman.

Due to the combined efforts of Bessie Smith's former maid and popular singer Janis Joplin, a white woman, Smith's grave that had suffered for years from neglect was restored to its present condition.

Location: Mt. Lawn Cemetery, 84th Street and Hook Road

Civil War recruitment poster

CAPITAL AREA

HARRISBURG
Thomas Morris
Chester Marker

ALLENTOWN
Harriet A. Baker House

CARLISLE
Dickinson College
and the Carlisle Riot

PINE FORGE
Manor House

YORK
William C. Goodridge
former home

LANCASTER
Bethel AME Church

CAPITAL AREA – BERKS, LANCASTER, LEBANON, DAUPHIN, CUMBERLAND, PERRY, YORK, NORTHAMPTON AND LEHIGH

THIS REGION CONTAINS HARRISBURG, THE STATE CAPITAL AND POLITICAL FOCUS OF MORE THAN 11 MILLION PENNSYLVANIANS. THE MAGNIFICENT CAPITOL IS THE DOMINANT BUILDING IN HARRISBURG'S CAPITOL COMPLEX.

The Susquehanna River travels through these counties and cuts across the state capital, providing one component of industries that dot the river valley towns. South of the area and west of the Susquehanna is York in the county of the same name—a town that was at one time the capital of the United States.

African-Americans were slaves of various ethnic owners, but Lancaster County's Amish and Mennonite families did not favor the use of slaves. Consequently, the anti-slavery sentiment in this region's atmosphere led to a sense of confidence and security among those African-Americans who called this area home.

The town of Steelton, outside of Harrisburg, has had a large African-American population since after the Civil War. Prior to the Civil War, the African-American community in Carlisle, Cumberland County, produced a number of abolitionists and harbored many run-away slaves passing through their community. A small African-American community has always represented Lebanon and Perry counties.

Berks County – Elverson – Hopewell Village and Furnace

Among historic Berks County landmarks, located in a green valley by French Creek, Hopewell Village and Furnace today stands tribute to people of African descent, both enslaved and free, who have been associated with Hopewell Furnace since its erection in 1770. The builder and owner of the village and furnace, Mark Bird, who originally built a brownstone structure in 1744 as his manor house, was a slave owner. The 1790 census listed Bird as being the largest holder of slaves in Berks County, having 10 adult males, three boys, and one girl.

There was bustling during the American Revolutionary War era when cannons were made with a labor force of slaves and other workers. Although slavery declined rapidly after the Pennsylvania Assembly passed an emancipation bill in 1780, people of African descent continued to work at Hopewell; some highly skilled laborers were wage earners.

Some of Hopewell's black workers lived in the "Forest." Beginning in 1835, this remote wooded area served as a safe haven for slaves seeking freedom on the Underground Railroad, along Six Penny Creek. By 1856, the community of African people established Mount Frisby A.M.E. Church. This church also was connected with the Underground Railroad. There is a cemetery south of the church site with tombstones for Isaac Cole and James Jackson, African-American veterans of the Civil War.

Hopewell Village and Furnace has been meticulously restored to its 1820-1840 appearance.

Location: Pa. Rte. 345, north of Elverson

Berks County – Bally – The Grave of an African-American Revolutionary War Soldier

Laid out in 1742 on land owned by the Society of Jesus, Bally later was named for the Rev. Augustin Bally, who ministered to Roman Catholics in the surrounding area. Here, in 1743, the chapel of St. Paul was built and later changed to the Church of the Most Blessed Sacrament, erected in 1827. Buried in the cemetery of this picturesque tree-lined hamlet is Isaac Jones, a former slave who was born in Africa and served under General George Washington during the War for Independence.

Berks County – Reading – Bethel A.M.E. Church

Only Bethel African Methodist Episcopal Church survives of the three African-American Churches that served the city of Reading in 1840. "Old Bethel," as the church is commonly called, is the oldest African-American church in Berks County. Erected in 1837 by free African-Americans, it became an Underground Railroad station for escaping slaves passing through the city.

Some runaway slaves were forwarded to designated points along the Pennsylvania Railroad and placed on trains traveling to Philadelphia and northward into New York State. Slaves were in a crawl space below a room in the church. In this church today is the Central Pennsylvania African-American Museum, founded by Frank Gilyard, a local historian.

The artful stained glass windows set in the once elegant Romanesque Revival façade of this church can still be seen. The church is listed on the National Register of Historic Places.

Berks County – Douglass Township – Pine Forge

Thomas Rutter, an English Quaker blacksmith, came to America with William Penn. Rutter built the first iron forge in the province in 1716 on Manataway Creek near what is now Pottstown.

During the course of his life, Rutter built an iron industry that provided George Washington's army with cannons during the Revolutionary War. An ardent opponent of slavery, he employed African-Americans as domestics, field workers, and laborers in his iron industry.

After Rutter's death, members of his family harbored escaping slaves in his large manor house. Pine Forge was remote from the cities where slave hunters usually prowled, and those runaway slaves just passing through the area could hide in the manor house tunnels and elude the slave hunters who pursued them. African-Americans owned the manor house and the property surrounding it. Today, it is a Seventh Day Adventist secondary boarding school. A Pennsylvania State Historical Marker stands in front of the manor house.

Location: Pine Forge Road

Berks County – Ontelaunee Township– Parvin House

Recently, a series of tunnels were discovered on the property of a stone house built in 1758 by Quaker Francis Parvin in Ontelaunee Township. In 1856, a two-room addition was built above a tunnel that is believed to have been part of the Underground Railroad. The Parvin family was ardent abolitionists; Francis Parvin had once signed a document that called for the abolition of slavery.

Members of an excavation project have found supportive evidence that these tunnels were connected to the Underground Railroad network in Berks County. A tunnel appeared to link a cellar to a barn along Maiden Creek. One tunnel runs under the road that is only .1 mile long and connects Rte. 61 to Beverly Road.

It is believed that the tunnel starts in the barn, which would have been a strategic location to conceal runaway slaves.

Location: Berkley Road

Lancaster County – Lancaster City – Bethel African Methodist Episcopal Church

Founded in 1817, Bethel A.M.E. Church is the oldest African-American church in Lancaster County. Like other African-American churches located in towns such as Marietta, Columbia, Mt. Joy, Little Britton, Casrastogen, Wrightsville, Little York, and Russellville, Bethel A.M.E. Church was the center of anti-slavery activities during the era of the Underground Railroad.

Members of this church sometimes concealed escaped slaves until the word was given to travel to the next Underground station. Members of the church also provided funds when it was necessary. Several of Bethel's preachers who were circuit riders carried secret messages pertaining to the Underground Railroad from community to community. The church still stands today.

Thaddeus Stevens

Location: Pennsylvania State Historical Marker at 450 East Strawberry Street

Lancaster County – Lancaster City – Thaddeus Stevens' Grave

Lancaster was the home of United States Rep. Thaddeus Stevens, one of the most ardent supporters of the abolition of slavery and a champion of African-American equality. Stevens, a native of Vermont, was a lawyer and lived first in Gettysburg, where he met Lydia Hamilton Smith, his attractive part African-American housekeeper, who later presided over Stevens' Lancaster residence on South Queen Street.

During the congressman's tenure in Washington, his southern enemies and political opponents in the north assumed that Lydia Hamilton Smith was his mistress, for Stevens was a bachelor. Stevens

Lydia Hamilton Smith

neither confirmed nor denied rumors of their relationship. She was constantly spoken of as Mrs. Stevens. In his will, he directed that she could receive either $500 per year for life or $500 in one lump sum.

Known as the "Old Commoner," the "Great Leveler," the "Father of the Free School Act in Pennsylvania," and the "Father of the Reconstruction Act in Congress," Stevens once said, "Give the Negro 40 acres and a mule." Stevens insisted on being buried in an African-American cemetery. He ordered that his gravestone read: "I repose in this quiet and secluded spot, not from any natural preference for solitude, but, finding other cemeteries limited as to race by Charter Rules. I have chosen this that I might illustrate in my death the principle, which I advocated through a long life: Equality of man before his creator."

He also stated that five of his pallbearers were to be drawn from the 54th Massachusetts Regiment. His request was denied, however, and he was not permitted a burial in Lancaster's only African-American cemetery. Instead he was buried in Schreiner Cemetery, a white burial ground. Lydia Smith was buried in another cemetery.

Location: Chestnut and Mulberry Streets

Lancaster County – Columbia – Wright's Ferry Mansion

Escaping slaves were cared for by abolitionist William Wright, who began assisting them as early as 1804. From Columbia in Lancaster County, Wright forwarded his passengers to the home of his sister, Hannah Gibbons, and her husband Daniel. The Gibbons, who had kept an accurate record of their long Underground Railroad experience, destroyed their documentation with the passage of the Fugitive Slave Law of 1850.

William Wright also worked with his well-known African-American neighbors, stationmasters Stephen Smith and William

Whipper. Some years ago, when Wright's home was restored, an 1829 anti-slavery pamphlet was found in a wall, and slave manacles were discovered in the attic dating from 1738. The mansion is still standing.

Location: Second and Cherry Streets

Lancaster County – Christiana – the Christiana Riot

In 1850, the federal Fugitive Slave Law strengthened the position of slaveholders seeking to capture runaway slaves. In 1851 in Christiana, the first blood was shed in resistance to this law, when a Maryland planter, Edward Gorsuch, with his son and a deputy United States marshal, tried to serve warrants for the return of some runaway slaves.

Threats were exchanged at the home of William Parker, an African-American who sheltered runaway slaves. While Parker's wife

The home of William Parker where Maryland planter Edward Gorsuch was killed.

Eliza sounded a horn over and over again to summon help, a force of free African-Americans accompanied by Quaker sympathizer Castner Hanway arrived. In the ensuing melee, afterward known as the "Christiana Riot," the runaways escaped and Gorsuch was killed.

Parker was charged with treason and became the object of a celebrated manhunt, but he escaped to Canada. More than 30 people were arrested and jailed in Philadelphia. Friend Hanway, charged not with violation of the Fugitive Slave Law, but with "wickedly and traitorously [intending to levy war against the United States]" went on trial in a federal courtroom in Independence Hall.

Thaddeus Stevens led the defense. A federal judge, who otherwise was no friend of abolitionists, was forced to say the charges against Hanway were absurd, and a verdict of "a charge not guilty" was returned in 20 minutes.

A Pennsylvania State Historical Marker honors the site today.

Location: Lower Valley Road, Sadsbury Township

Lancaster County – Lancaster City – Wheatland, The Home of President James Buchanan

From 1849 until his death, Wheatland was the home of James Buchanan, 15th President of the United States and the only Pennsylvanian so honored. Although Buchanan and Thaddeus Stevens' homes were both located in Lancaster and the two men died in 1868, their political views on slavery and equality for African-Americans were miles apart.

The aristocratic and cautious Buchanan sympathized with slaveholding southerners. He supported the infamous U.S. Supreme Court Dred Scott decision that was announced by 75-year-old Chief Justice of the United States Roger Taney on March 6, 1857, two days after Buchanan's inauguration. Taney had declared that, "Negroes had no rights which the white man was bound to respect."

Dred Scott, a former Virginia slave, had been carried by his owner, an Army doctor, from Missouri into the free state of Illinois, and then to the free territory of Minnesota. On grounds that he had become a free man by virtue of residence on free soil, Scott had sued for his liberty in St. Louis, Missouri, in 1846. Taney's decision denied Scott his freedom.

Location: 1120 Marietta Avenue

Lebanon County – Cornwall – Cornwall Iron Furnace

Built by English settler Peter Grubb in 1742, Cornwall Furnace is the oldest fully preserved example of an early iron furnace in Pennsylvania. As a self-contained "iron plantation," Cornwall Furnace manufactured its own raw material. For the most part, the labor force consisted of free African-Americans, slaves, and indentured servants.

During the Revolutionary War, Cornwall Furnace produced 42 cannon, as well as other munitions and equipment. The wives and daughters of the workers were employed as domestics or put to work spinning thread and weaving clothes for the iron master and his family.

Although large numbers of slaves were brought to America to work in the plantation, significant numbers also were used in manufacturing operations in the north. At the time of the War for Independence, approximately 6,000 slaves lived in Pennsylvania. In 1780, as emancipation took hold, the slave labor force at Cornwall Furnace began to decline and by 1792 only one African-American was listed as still working at the furnace. A hill in nearby Mt. Gretna is named "Governor Dick" after a slave who ran away from Cornwall Furnace on April 17, 1796.

Location: Rexmont Road at Boyd Street

Dauphin County – Harrisburg – John Harris Mansion

Built by John Harris, Jr., founder of Harrisburg, construction of the house was begun in 1740 by John Harris Sr. (1691 – 1748), the first settler in the region. Prior to the purchase, the region had been owned and controlled by Native Americans. According to local tradition, a group of drunken Native Americans stopped at the home of John Harris demanding an additional supply of "Lum" (meaning a container of rum.) They dragged Harris to a nearby mulberry tree with the intention of burning him to death.

"Hercules," his black slave, heard the cries of his owner and came to his aid with a group of friendly Native Americans, saving Harris. Immediately after the heroic rescue mission, Harris freed Hercules. A number of Hercules' descendents remained in the area for years.

Location: 219 South Front Street

Dauphin County – Harrisburg – The Pennsylvania Anti-Slavery Society

The Pennsylvania Anti-Slavery Society was organized at Harrisburg in 1837, at a convention that was held between January 31 and February 3, and called for immediate emancipation of slaves held in bondage. By 1838, women were welcomed as active members, and later several served as officers.

Shown here are members of its executive committee in 1851. Left to right, front row: Oliver Johnson, Mrs. Margaret Jones Burleigh, Benjamin C. Bacon, Robert Purvis, Lucretia Mott, James Mott. Back row: Mary Grew, Edward M. Davis, Haworth Wetherald, Abby Kimber, J. Miller McKim, and Sarah Pugh.

Dauphin County – Harrisburg – Thomas Morris Chester

The Pennsylvania Anti-Slavery Society Executive Committee

Born in Harrisburg on May 11, 1834, Thomas Morris Chester was a tall, illustrious African-American who distinguished himself as a journalist, educator, lecturer, and lawyer. His parents operated a restaurant in Harrisburg and were connected with the Underground Railroad.

Chester was one of a few African-American correspondents during the Civil War. He recruited African-American soldiers during the conflict. At the surrender in Richmond, sitting in the hall at the desk of the Speaker of the Virginia House of Representatives, Chester wrote his dispatch for the *Philadelphia Press*, describing the Union army victory.

After the war, he taught in Liberia, West Africa, and traveled to Europe for the Freedman's Society. He was admitted to the English

Thomas Morris Chester

bar in 1870. He also held a major post in Louisiana during the Reconstruction Era, 1873-83. In 1881, Chester became the first African-American admitted to practice before the Pennsylvania Supreme Court. He probably would be proud that African-Americans are represented in the National Civil War Museum that opened in 2000 in Harrisburg's Reservoir Park.

Chester died in 1892 and is buried in the Lincoln Cemetery in Penbrook, outside of Harrisburg. A Pennsylvania State Historical Marker honors his life and career.

> Location: Market Square near Third Street on the Capitol side of Market Street

Dauphin County – Harrisburg – State Convention of Colored Citizens

An informal meeting was held at the Wesleyan Church December 13 and 14, 1848. The Rev. George Galbraith was appointed chairman. Martin R. Delany, formerly of Pittsburgh and now living in Rochester, New York, and Charles Lennox Redmond, the nationally-known anti-slavery orator from Massachusetts, were received as honorary members of this convention. Redmond made a short but spell-binding address on the subject for which the convention had assembled.

Those present:

Allegheny County	John B. Vashon
Berks County	Joseph E. Gardiner, Joseph Murray, George C. Anderson
Columbia County	William Thompson
Cumberland County	William Webb, Edward Hawkins, Richard Johnson, Joseph Johnson, Jacob Stratton
Centre County	Joseph St. Clair

Chester County	Abraham D. Shadd, John N. Bond, Charles E. Clayton, William Lewis
Dauphin County	John F. Williams, John Wolf, Henry Price, Thomas Earley, Aquilla Amos, John Gray, Andrew Gorden, William Spence, Joseph Popel, Charles Dorris, Edward Thompson, George Adley, Henry Johnson, Richard Brown, James Popel, James Reese, William H. Davis, Charles Robertson, Daniel Jackson, Valentine Brown
Franklin County	Nelson Turpin, Jesse Bolden
Huntington County	Isaac Dickson
Juniata County	Samuel Molston, John Griffith
Lycoming County	Philip Roderic
Lancaster County	William Whipper, Leonard A. Williams, William H. Wilson, Washington Webster, Robert Boston
Mifflin County	David Roach
Philadelphia County	Isaiah C. Weir, Stephen Smith, George Galbraith, Robert Purvis, James G. Bias, David Bustill Bowser, John C. Bowers, James Knight, Mifflin W. Gibbs, Francis A. Duterte, James McCrummel, Isaiah Ware, Samuel Van Brakle, Dr. David J. Peck, Henry Cooper, Joshua Eddy, Benjamin Moore, Robert Brown, William Marten, William Jackson, Perry Miller
Schuylkill County	John Lee
York County	William Stanford, William Cupit

Many of these delegates were connected with the Underground Railroad in Pennsylvania.

Dauphin County – Penbrook – Lincoln Cemetery

A Pennsylvania State Historical Marker emblazoned with bright gold letters on a background of blue and topped by the Coat of Arms of the Commonwealth reads: *A landmark of Central Pennsylvania's African-American history. Established in 1827 by Wesley Union A.M.E. Zion Church. Among those buried here are T. Morris Chester, William Howard Day, Catherine McClintock, and at least twenty veterans of the Civil War.*

Location: 30th Street and Booser Avenue

Dauphin County – Steelton – William Howard Day

William Howard Day

Abolitionist, editor, printer, educator, orator and clergyman William Howard Day was born in 1825 of well-to-do parents, John and Eliza Day, who sent their son to private school. After passing a difficult examination in Latin and Greek, he was sent to Oberlin College in Ohio. His ability as an exceptional printer made it possible for him to pay his own way through college.

Day was graduated in 1847, the only African-American in a class of 50. He later became active in the Underground Railroad movement and traveled to Canada, where nearly 40,000 former slaves had settled, including some that he had previously assisted to freedom from the United States.

A Pennsylvania State Historical Marker describes Day's other activities: *Born in New York City, traveled in the United States, Canada, and Britain on behalf of anti-slavery and free blacks, General Secretary, A.M.E. Zion Church. He lived after 1870 in Harrisburg, where he edited the newspaper* Our National Progress. *The first African-American elected to the Harrisburg School Board in 1878; its president 1891 – 1893. Buried in Lincoln Cemetery.*

Location: Lincoln and Carlisle Streets

Dauphin County – Harrisburg – Tanner's Alley

The entire story of the Underground Railroad in Harrisburg will never be known because of the very nature of the movement. However, we do know through documentation that the flow of freedom-seeking slaves through Tanner's Alley was constant and always increasing.

A Pennsylvania State Historical Marker records the involvement of Tanner's Alley residents. It was a predominantly African-American section of Harrisburg during the era of the Underground Railroad. Joseph C. Bustill, a member of a prominent Philadelphia family whose lineage stretches back more than 200 years into American history, was the leading conductor for Harrisburg's Underground Railroad while teaching school there. His two brothers, James and Charles (maternal grandfather of Paul Robeson) were active in Underground Railroad activities in Philadelphia.

Joseph Bustill frequently sent coded letters (right) to his friend and fellow agent William Still in Philadelphia. A number of his letters were published in Still's book on the Underground Railroad. This correspondence reveals some of Bustill's activities and the working of the Railroad.

Location: Market Street between Aberdeen and 4th Streets

Cumberland County – Carlisle – Bethel African Methodist Episcopal Church

Located 18 miles west of the Susquehanna River, Carlisle today retains some of its colonial atmosphere, with shady streets camouflaging its sprawling industrial center. African-Americans have been living in Carlisle since the late 18th century. Nowhere did the Underground Railroad function more effortlessly than in Carlisle. The African-American community supported the anti-slavery cause with pride and vigor. They relished the opportunity to flaunt its defiance of slave law.

Harrisburg, May 26, 1856:
*"Friend Still: I embrace the opportunity presented by the visit of our friends, John Williams, to drop you a few lines in relation to our future operations. The Lightening Train was put on the Road last Monday, and as traveling season has commenced and this, the Southern route for Niagara Falls, I have concluded not to send by way of Auburn, except in cases of great danger; but here after we will use the Lightening Train (code word for Underground Railroad) which leaves here at 1 – and arrives in your City at 5 – o'clock in the morning, and I will telegraph about 5 – o'clock in the afternoon, so it may reach you before you close. These four are the only ones that have come to me since my last. The woman has been here some time waiting for her child and her beau, which she expects here about the first of June. If possible, please keep knowledge of her whereabouts to enable me to inform him if he comes. Yours as ever,
Jos. C. Bustill."*

J. Miller McKim accompanied Mary Brown to Harper's Ferry to retrieve John Brown's body.

At the center of this activity was Bethel A.M.E. Church. Built during the 1820s, this church welcomed escapees with open arms. When the American Anti-Slavery Society was formed in Philadelphia in 1833, the Carlisle African-American community sent their white friend J. Miller McKim to represent them. In later years, he worked with William Still in Philadelphia coordinating Underground Railroad operations throughout the East Coast.

In 1838, a juvenile anti-slavery society was formed with the assistance of several members of Bethel A.M.E. Church. The society's function was to promote the abolition cause and to disclose the evil of slavery to children. The Carlisle African-American community also organized the Toussaint L'Ouverture Club, named for the great Haitian hero. The club participated in social and political events and also in Underground Railroad activities.

Probably the two most important men in the community were John B. Vashon and John Peck, who were prominent businessmen and anti-slavery activists. The pair later moved to Pittsburgh, where they continued their campaign against slavery. Four important white Underground Railroad conductors in the county were Daniel Kaufman, Stephen Weakley, Richard Woods, and Mode Griffith.

Location: 131 East Pomfret Street

Cumberland County – Carlisle – Dickinson College and the Carlisle Riot

Founded in 1783 by Dr. Benjamin Rush of Philadelphia, who was dedicated to the abolition of slavery, Dickinson College grew out of a grammar school established through the deed of Thomas Penn in 1733. It was named for John Dickinson, who was president of the Supreme Executive Council of Pennsylvania.

Early in June 1847, an incident occurred in Carlisle that created national attention. Two Maryland slaveholders came in pursuit of three escapees. In the confrontation that followed, one of the slave-holders was severely beaten and died three weeks later.

Dr. John McClintock, a professor at Dickinson College, assisted the escapees and attempted to prevent their recapture. McClintock was arrested and later tried along with a number of free African-Americans who also had participated in the attack. McClintock and some of the African-Americans were acquitted, while others were fined. Newspapers referred to the incident as the Carlisle Riot.

Location: West High Street

Perry County – New Bloomfield – The County Courthouse Square

Perry County was formed March 22, 1820, from Cumberland County, and named for Oliver Hazard Perry, hero of the War of 1812. African-Americans were part of the area since its founding.

As early as 1776, a slave named Bob and his wife were baptized as members of St. Michael's Lutheran Church. Due to the strong anti-abolition feelings in the county, citizens held a well-attended emotional meeting at the Perry County Courthouse in New Bloomfield in 1834 to oppose the organization of an anti-slavery society.

Some Quakers and others were active here transporting runaway slaves through the county's communities of New Bloomfield, Newport, and Ickesburg. Felty Powell of Newport operated a business capturing escapees and free African-Americans and selling them to southern slave hunters. Eventually the citizens made it necessary for him to "disappear" from the county.

On at least one occasion, an unfortunate slave was drowned attempting to flee from his owner. On July 18, 1841, Coroner David Tressler held an inquest into the death of an unnamed man who drowned in the Juniata River above Newport.

Location: On the square

Northampton County – Nazereth – The Whitefield House

Originally called Ephrata, and now known as Whitefield House, this three-story, colonial limestone building with slate-covered gambrel roof and hand-hewn timbers was completed in 1743. As early as 1740, the Rev. George Whitefield, a Methodist preacher from England, purchased 5,000 acres at the bank of the Delaware River, where he proposed to establish a school for Negroes, a revivalist headquarters, and a communal church home for 32 newly-married German couples brought over in 1744. This house honors Whitefield's name.

> Location: Off Pa. Rte. 191 (East Center Street) at South New Street

Northampton County – Bethlehem – Moravian Cemetery

Used as a burial place from 1742 to 1910, this site was selected and consecrated by Count von Zinzendrof. Only flat gravestones were permitted. People of African descent are buried side-by-side with whites and Native Americans. Early African people, freedmen and women who were Moravian converts took part in the regular religious and secular life of the community.

The Moravians, a German Protestant group known formally as the *Unitas Fratrum*, founded Bethlehem in 1741 as a missionary center for the conversion of North American Indians and others who had no formal church affiliation. Among the first Moravian settlers at Bethlehem was Andrea der Moor, or Andrew the Black. Andrew often participated in an activity assigned the "single men"—to partake in Saturday evening serenades by singing hymns outside of the religious sect building complex.

The Moravians also brought Africans out of slavery and employed them as wage-earning servants. The very first Moravian foreign mission was established among the African slaves of St. Thomas in the Virgin Islands in 1832. Several African-Americans living in Lehigh and Northampton counties can trace their genealogy to slaves freed by the Moravians.

Location: West Market Street

Northampton County – Easton – Lafayette College

Lafayette College, named for the French marquis who aided the American cause during the War of Independence, was chartered in 1826. The college is situated on a hill in the oldest section of Easton.

After the Revolutionary War, Lafayette, who had the highest regard for George Washington, sent a letter from France on February 5, 1783, stating: "Now, my dear General, that you are going to enjoy some ease and quiet, permit me to propose a plan to you which might become greatly beneficial to the black part of mankind. Let us unite in purchasing a small estate, where we may try the experiment to free Negroes and use them as tenants. Such an example as yours might render it a general practice; and if we succeed in America, I will cheerfully devote a part of my time to render the method fashionable in the West Indies."

Washington replied on April 5, 1783, "The scheme, my dear Marquis, which you proposed as a precedent to encourage the emancipation of the black people in this country from that state of bondage in which they are held is striking evidence of the benevolence of your heart. I shall be happy to join you in so laudable a work but will defer gong into a detail of the business till I have the pleasure of seeing you."

Although the plan never became a reality, it is the first call for reparations for African-Americans in the U.S. During the next century, Thaddeus Stevens was the next person to call for reparations when he said, "Give the Negroes 40 acres and a mule." It is ironic that two white men were the first to call for reparations.

Location: 3rd Street

Lehigh County – Allentown – Harriet A. Baker's Mission House

Eminent scholar Dr. W.E.B. Dubois wrote in 1918, "Black women are the pillars of those social settlements which we called churches and they have with small doubt raised three-fourths of our church property." This statement aptly applies to women such as Harriet A. Baker.

A Pennsylvania State Historical Marker pays tribute to her dedication and work with the following inscription: *This African-American evangelist opened a mission about 1900 at 738 North Penn Street, where she preached until her death. In 1914 her mission became the first home of St. James A.M.E. Zion Church, which was built at this location in 1936.*

Location: 410 Union Street

York County – Shrewsbury – Amanda Berry Smith

Evangelist Amanda Berry Smith

Born a slave January 23, 1837, in Long Green, Maryland, an elder daughter in a family of 11, Amanda Berry Smith was denied an education because of local prejudice. She learned to read and write at home. Later in her life, she was called "the singing pilgrim," and "God's image carved in ebony," by newspapers of her time. She participated in Underground Railroad activities while living in Shrewsbury.

During her 45 years as an evangelist, Smith won international acclaim after traveling in Europe, India, and Africa.

Location: 108 South Main Street

York County

Its traditional bonds with Lancaster County made York County an important center for the Underground Railroad. Due to its location close to the Mason-Dixon Line, many southern escapees passed through York City and other towns in the county. Local residents such as William C. Goodridge, an African-American businessman and Underground Railroad stationmaster, Thomas Bessick, Robert Loney, Cato Jordan, and Amos Griest were the principal operators of the freedom network in the section of York City called "Crotie Row."

*York businessman
William Goodridge*

York County – York City – William C. Goodridge House

The freed African-American community of York offered constant assistance to enslaved Africans. The most important and energetic Underground Railroad agent was William C. Goodridge ,an African-American businessman. Goodridge included among his friends Underground Railroad agents and conductors William Whipper of Lancaster, William Still of Philadelphia, Frederick Douglass, and the ardent abolitionist John Brown.

As early as 1851, Goodridge used special freight cars to transport several of the freed African-Americans who were involved in the infamous Christiana Riot in Lancaster County to Canada. At his home on East Philadelphia Street, Goodridge hid runaway slaves in a movable trap door in the kitchen floor covered by a carpet. He also built Centre Hall; the five—story building was York's tallest building during this time and was used as a meeting place for abolitionist and other community events.

Goodridge secreted Osborne Perry Anderson, one of John Brown's African-American compatriots, on the third floor of Centre Hall. In 1863, Goodridge fled Pennsylvania when the Confederate troops during the Civil War threatened York and were bent on

Osborne Perry Anderson

159

catching him. He never returned to his York home, and died in Minnesota in 1873.

Right: The 1803 burning of York, Pennsylvania. Photo Courtesy of York Country Historial Society.

York County – York City – The Burning of York City

Located in the York County Heritage Trust building is a water-color painting by Lewis Mill of women of African descent being arrested and convicted of attempting to poison two white women and sent to prison in Philadelphia. An outraged African-American community took to the streets in 1803 and set fire to several buildings in the town of York.

Another African-American woman was caught who had brought a pan of hot coals into a white man's barn and spread them over the hay. Governor Thomas McKean took action by initiating militia patrols and proclaiming a large reward for the captors of the arsonist. Twenty-one local African-Americans were tried, and several of them were sent to prison for the arson.

A statement issued by government officials at the time gives an idea of the climate in which the burning of the city took place.

To the Inhabitants of the borough of York and its vicinity to the distance of 10 miles. You are hereby notified, that such of you as have Negroes or people of colour, to keep them at home under strict discipline and watch; so as they may be under your eye at all times. You are not to let them come into the borough of York on any pretense whatever without a written pass,...Given under the hands of the Justices and Burgesses of said borough, this 21st day of March 1803....

York has had a long history of tense relations between whites and African-Americans,and the tension continues today. In 2001, arrests were made in the death of an African-American woman, Lillie Belle Allen, who had been visiting relatives when race riots erupted in 1969. Authorities say she was killed by members of a white gang who opened fire on the car in which she was riding after it stalled in their neighborhood.

Location: 250 East Market Street

Large Fire in York Borough 1803.
Set on fire by the negro's

George Spangler taking his Black
boy Abe prisoner, at the Shop of
Peter Reisenger, Black Smith in
South duke Street. he was one of the
Burners, caused the fire,

CENTRAL REGION

BELLEFONTE
The Mills Brothers
Family Marker

HOLLISDAYSBURG
Dr. Daniel Hale Williams

MT DAVIS
Negro Mountain

CHAMBERSBURG
John Brown's
Headquarters

GETTYSBURG
The Dobbin House
Gettysburg National Park
St Paul's AME Church

CENTRAL REGION – JEFFERSON, CLARION, ARMSTRONG, INDIANA, CLEARFIELD, CAMBRIA, BLAIR, CAMERON, HUNTINGDON, MIFFLIN, JUNIATA, CENTRE, SNYDER, UNION, MONTOUR, COLUMBIA, FULTON, NORTHUMBERLAND, SOMERSET, BEDFORD, FRANKLIN, ADAMS

A terrain of great diversity with heavy forests, cleared pastures, and mountain ranges running southwest to northeast characterizes the central region of Pennsylvania. A number of cities of varying sizes have attracted African-Americans to their industries, which include tanning and allied trades, light manufacturing and, during the early part of the 20th century, coal mining.

The river bisecting this area is the Susquehanna. During the antebellum period, a small number of runaway slaves escaping from below the Mason-Dixon Line settled in various towns and cities in this stretch of counties. Many of their descendants have long since been attracted to the opportunities in the larger cities east and west.

Blair County – Hollidaysburg – Dr. Daniel Hale Williams

Blair County is called the "Gateway to the Alleghenies," and is located in a region known for its beautiful caverns. The county's African-American population has always been fairly well dispersed, with Hollidaysburg and Altoona being the most populated centers.

Hollidaysburg was the home of the Williams family, proud and independent descendants of African-Americans, Native Americans, and white ancestry. The family participated in anti-slavery, Underground Railroad, and equal rights activities.

Daniel Hale Williams became one of the great heroes of African-American history. In 1893, "Dr. Dan," as he was affectionately called, performed the world's first successful open-heart operation in Chicago at Provident Hospital, the nation's first hospital and training ground for African-American nurses and interns.

Williams established a nursing school for African-Americans at Freedman's Hospital in Washington, D.C., and a surgery practice at Meharry Medical College in Nashville, Tennessee. He died August 4,

"Dr. Dan" Williams

1931, in Idlewild, Michigan. A Pennsylvania State Historical Marker stands at the location of his boyhood home.

Location: U.S. Rte. 22 Eastbound (Blair Street, 300 Block)

Blair and Huntingdon Counties – Underground Railroad Network

During the era of the Underground Railroad, an influx of runaway slaves caused temporary increases in the African-American population when some runaways risked staying in this region. George A. Wolf wrote in *Blair County's First Hundred Years*: "Hollidaysburg was on the network of the Underground Railroad. Residents told many stories about fleeing slaves. A concerned slave owner pursed one of his slaves to Hollidaysburg and attempted to take him, but was prevented by a householder who protected him. The fleeing slave was spirited to Chimney Rock and resumed his journey under cover of night."

Perhaps the most often noted Underground Railroad agent in Blair County is William Nesbit. For a short period, Nesbit resided in Altoona before moving to Chimney Rock, an African-American community in Hollidaysburg and the county's best-known rendezvous for runaway slaves. Long before, Native Americans had used Chimney Rock as a lookout area and hiding place.

Sidney Carr and the Reverend James Graham of Hollidaysburg A.M.E. Zion Church were also agents of the Underground Railroad. Huntingdon County received escapees in a small-secluded settlement known as Black Log Valley. The small community of Mt. Union was also connected with the freedom network; some escapees made their homes here instead of following the Underground to distant stations north.

John Chaplin, a resident of Huntington County, an African-American barber and painter, was connected with the Underground Railroad before he studied in Europe and won fame as an artist while living in Philadelphia.

Cambria County – Johnstown – First Cambria A.M.E. Zion Church

Right: Famed singing legends The Mills Brothers

First Cambria A.M.E. Zion Church was formed in 1873 in the loft of the Woodvale Tannery, which was owned and operated by William H. Rosenstell, an African-American who relocated to Woodvale from Adams County, where he was connected with the Underground Railroad. According to his obituary, Rosenstell set up tanneries in a number of towns.

He moved to the Woodvale section of Johnstown in 1873 and recruited African-American workers from Maryland to work in his tannery. The church was organized as Cambria Chapel A.M.E. Church in 1874, at Napoleon and Dibert Streets. About 1877, it moved to its present location. In 1889 during the Johnstown flood, one of the greatest disasters in Pennsylvania history washed the church from its foundation, but it later was restored. Located also in Cambria County is the town of Wilmore founded and settled by an African-American named Godfrey Wilmore.

Location: 409 Haynes Street

Centre County – Bellefonte – A Tribute to the Mills Brothers Family

Standing at 213 West High Street in Bellefonte is a Pennsylvania State Historical Marker commemorating the internationally-known singers The Mills Brothers and their grandfather. William H. Mills, a venerable African-American citizen in Bellefonte, operated the town's oldest barbershop until his death on July 17, 1931.

He was born in Bellefonte in 1847, and was the foremost member of St. Paul's A.M.E. Church, where he was an ordained minister. In 1909, Mills published a history of the church from the time of its founding. In his younger days, Mills was recognized as a singer and

together with other local musicians formed a concert company that played engagements in many parts of Centre and adjoining counties from 1871 until 1931.

His son John went to Ohio, where his famous sons were born and carried the family tradition of music around the world. The Mills Brothers were the first African-American vocal group with sponsored national radio hookups and top billing. They appeared on numerous radio, film, and television programs, performing from 1925 to 1983.

Centre County – University Park – Paul Robeson Cultural Center – Penn State University

Located on the campus of Penn State University is an elegant, spectacular center honoring the great African-American scholar, athlete, singer, actor, lawyer, and human rights activist Paul Robeson. The Paul Robeson Cultural Center is located in the Hetzel Union Building.

Robeson brought to his audiences not only a melodious baritone voice and a great presence, but also magnificent performances on stage and screen. He eagerly immersed himself in the study of world cultures and mastered more than a dozen languages. He was more committed to the oppressed people of the world and particularly people of African descent than to any honors and accolades he received as a performer. At the height of his career in the 1930s and 1940s, Robeson was one of the most recognized persons in the world.

On permanent display at the Paul Robeson Cultural Center is African-American sculptor Oliver LaGrone's bronze bust of Robeson. The center is a popular meeting place for students, alumni, and visitors from other areas. Also on display are photographs of Robeson and distinguished African-Americans. Penn State alumni, lecturers, meetings and exhibits pertaining to African-American culture also are held at the center.

Legendary singer
Paul Robeson

Location: Penn State University

Centre County – Milroy –
Milroy Presbyterian Church

Previously called Perryville, the little village of Milroy is the site of the Presbyterian Church where the Rev. James Nourse served as pastor from 1834 to 1849. A strong and able man, Nourse denounced the pro-slavery forces in the country.

Under his leadership, an anti-slavery society was organized. Dr. Samuel Maclay, John Thompson, and Samuel Thompson assisted the Reverend Nourse in transporting runaway slaves seeking freedom through the Underground Railroad over the Seven Mountains from Milroy to other stations in surrounding counties. Nourse also worked with African-American Samuel Henderson of Half Moon, who was considered the most prominent Underground Railroad conductor in Centre County. This former church that still stands today was a station on the Underground Railroad.

Location: Lower Main Street

Centre County – Bellefonte – African-American
Heroes of Bellefonte and The Marker Honoring
Governor Andrew G. Curtin

Due to the strong Quaker anti-slavery influence in Bellefonte, many fugitive slaves from southern states who reached Centre County settled in Bellefonte prior to the Civil War. St. Paul's Church, organized in 1859, served a black population of several hundred shortly after emancipation.

African-Americans representing Bellefonte as well as several other sections of Centre County gave evidence of their loyalty to the Union by serving in the Civil War. The first known abolitionist was William H. Robinson, who said, "May the swarthy sons of Africa be free as the white population in the United States and slavery no longer stain the annals of our history."

The history of Centre County, Pennsylvania, lists the following names of blacks who were members of the Sixth Regiment, United States Colored Soldiers in Companies F and G.

August 26, 1863 to September 20, 1865:

Delige, Harsock, Patton; died at Wilmington, N.C., August 3, 1865
Derry, William, Bellefonte; killed at Petersburg, July 8, 1864
Green, William, Bellefonte; disch. September 20, 1865
Johnston, Washington, Bellefonte; disch. July 12, 1865
Johnston, Moses Bellefonte; drowned in James River, August 29, 1864
Lee, Benjamin, Bellefonte
Lee, Charles, SnowShoe; Corp; disch. September 20, 1865
Miles, Lewis, Bellefonte; disch. September 20, 1865
Whitten, John W. Bellefonte
Whitten, John, Patton
Worley, Aaron C. Bellefonte

John W. Whitten was a private in Company K, 8th Pennsylvania Regiment, United States Colored Troops. Captured in early 1865 by the Confederate Army, he was later sold by the Confederates into slavery in Cuba. Whitten escaped in 1889 and returned home to Bellefonte. He was a prisoner of war for 24 years, a record unequalled by any other American soldier. Sarah Whitten Stoner, his mother, is buried in the small Methodist Cemetery at the Centre County town of Pleasant Gap.

Bellefonte also is the home of Pennsylvania Governor Andrew G. Curtin who was governor during the Civil War. When African-Americans volunteered their services to defend Pennsylvania during the Battle of Gettysburg, Curtin refused to accept them to fight against the enemy. While visiting the Gettysburg battlefield shortly after the troops departed, Curtin was shocked to find that shallow, scattered graves revealed portions of uniformed corpses above ground. He took measure to collect the bodies and inter them decently.

Location: Pennsylvania State Historical Marker at Allegheny Street and Cherry Lane

Centre County – Philipsburg

Runaway slaves who stayed in Pennsylvania and other northern states did so at their own risk and generally against the advice of friends on the Underground Railroad. Although their liberty was still in danger, a small number of runaway slaves settled in Philipsburg.

In1860, Samuel Green, a Virginia slave, was found hiding in the woods near Moshannon Creek. A group of Philipsburg residents offered him food and shelter and later helped Green and his wife to build a house in Stumptown.

Riley Jackson was another runaway slave who made Philipsburg his home. Jackson lived at Halehurst Estates, which was rumored to be a station on the Underground Railroad. Green and Jackson were two of many former slaves and their descendants who made up a population of 91 African-American citizens in Philipsburg during the 1930s.

Somerset County – West Salisbury

A short distance from the small town of Casselman are two mountains, Mt. Davis, the highest point in Pennsylvania, and Negro Mountain, named, according to tradition, in honor of a slave. The slave was with Captain Andrew Friend's party that came to Somerset County from Maryland in 1775 to explore the mountain region's rich preserve of deer, elk, wild turkey, panthers, bear, and other game. The Native Americans who inhabited the area served notice to the white men not to enter the game territory, and they mortally wounded the slave, said to have been of gigantic stature, very strong, and armed.

Captain Friend and his party fought their way back to him and though he pleaded for their hasty retreat without him, they stayed until his death and buried him among the roots of a fallen tree. Friend and his party returned safely to Fort Cumberland.

Location: Pa. Rte. 669

Fulton County – McConnellsburg – Last Confederate Bivouac

Formed April 19, 1850, out of Bedford County, Fulton County was named for steamboat inventor Robert Fulton. Even during the early years of its founding, the African-American presence was sparse in this once rugged south central part of the state. A few African-Americans established farms in certain areas of the county.

At the same time, Fulton County became a thoroughfare for runaway slaves fleeing from Maryland and Virginia. During the Civil War, General Albert Jenkins' Confederate Cavalry, after the burning of Chambersburg, occupied McConnellsburg for a short time, the same as the Confederate soldiers who fought under General Bradley T. Johnson, who camped there July 30, 1864.

Attached to these regiments were African-American cooks, teamsters, and laundresses. Wherever the regiment went, there were men and women of African descent. In the Union Army, each company was allowed four launderers. Their quarters were set apart from those of the soldiers. The bivouac at McConnellsburg was the last Confederate encampment on Pennsylvania soil during the war.

Location: U.S. Rte. 522, six miles south of McConnellsburg

Bedford County – Chaneysville – The Chaneysville Incident

Located about four miles north of the Pennsylvania-Maryland border, on the outskirts of Bedford County, is the small town of Chaneysville. Here, according to local tradition, there are 13 graves marked only by gray, rough-cut fieldstones. No one knows the names of the people or how the bodies got there. What we do know is that they were runaway slaves who were buried on the Imes Farm, just beyond the family cemetery according to several Bedford County historical sources.

Lester Imes and his neighbors attempted to protect a group of runaway slaves who had escaped over the Cumberland Mountains with slave catchers closely pursuing them. The slaves, filled with rage, anxiety, frustration, and fear reportedly told Imes that they would rather die in freedom than to return to slavery.

Although the natural protection afforded by the mountain terrain and heavy foliage were excellent camouflage for the Underground Railroad, those 13 graves can still be seen at the remote burial grounds. Did they commit the ultimate act of suicide or did the Maryland slave hunters kill them? The answer is not known. In 1981, David Bradley Jr., an African-American native of Bedford, wrote a prize-winning novel, *The Chaneysville Incident*, about the mysterious event.

Location: Pa. Rte. 326 at the junction of Rte. 26

Bedford County – Bedford Springs – George Washington Williams

A large monument located in Bedford's public square provides a listing of locals who fought in the Civil War for the Union Army. However, there is no public recognition or historical marker honoring the name of George Washington Williams, who was born in Bedford Springs in 1849.

Wealthy southerners, often accompanied by their slaves, traveled to the famous mineral baths that were located in Bedford Springs in spite of the state law that had abolished slavery in 1780. However, local officials tolerated the free-spending southern slave-holding visitors.

At 14, Williams ran away from home to enlist in the Sixth Massachusetts Regiment in 1862 and served throughout the war.

George Washington Williams

Later, Williams distinguished himself as a lawyer, minister, gifted orator, and politician. He was appointed to the Internal Revenue Service by President Rutherford Hayes, and was elected to the Ohio legislature in 1879. He served as United States minister to Haiti in 1885-86, and near the end of his life conducted an investigation into the state of the Congo in Africa for the Belgian government.

Williams' greatest contribution to American and African-American history is his massive two-volume classic *A History of the Negro Race in America*, published in 1882. Williams died in 1891 at the age of 42.

Location: Juliana Street

Franklin County – Waynesboro – The Underground Railroad Narrative of Hiram E. Wertz

Hiram E. Wertz' narrative first appeared in the *Waynesboro Record* newspaper in 1911, 46 years after slavery was abolished. Wertz was a resident of Quincy, three miles north of Waynesboro. His former farmhouse represents one of the best-documented accounts of local Underground Railroad history.

Wertz stated in 1911, "I am the sole survivor of the captains of the Underground Railroad and it is also a fact that all who engaged in the nefarious work of capturing fugitive slaves also passed to the Great Beyond." Wertz estimated that from the time he first became a conductor on the Underground Railroad around 1845, "I piloted at least forty-five to fifty Negroes, none of them to my knowledge were captured or returned to slavery." He continued, "Runaways usually came from the south in the morning to this place or Anthony Highway."

Wertz said that he would hide them in his barn or cellar before leading them north eight miles to a settlement called Africa, near Thaddeus Stevens' furnace at Caledonia. Wertz recalled that, "I was familiar with every station along the South Mountain and Antietam

Creek, led from the Potomac River to the Pennsylvania border. The first station in Pennsylvania was known as Shockey's. It was near the present village of Rouzerville, at the foot of the mountain."

Although Wertz protected runaway slaves, one of his neighbors, Dan Logan, often captured runaways and held them by securing them to rings in his attic floor. Slave catching was a lucrative business in this area of south central Pennsylvania. Many escaped slaves found sanctuary in Needy Cave, reputed to be the first station north of the Mason-Dixon Line.

Franklin County – Mercersburg – "Little Africa"—A Historic African-American Community

Mercersburg's proximity to the Mason-Dixon Line made it an ideal theater for Underground Railroad activities in the middle 1800s. Here and there through Blair Valley to Mount Parnell was the secret freedom network. Fleeing to safety from a distance as far as Maryland, escapees were oriented by the light on top of Mount Parnell.

Here too, the agents of the slaveholders operated. Though many of the runaway slaves made Canada their destination, 25 families established a community called "Africa," now Cove Gap, at the foot of the mountain.

Included in the vibrant community were farmers, carpenters, laborers, blacksmiths, quarrymen, and teachers. Today, several African-American families such as the Cautions, Rileys, and Trinnwells can trace their heritage in Mercersburg to the late 18th century.

Mercersburg had other homes and buildings that were connected with the Underground Railroad. According to tradition, the present Hamilton Memorial Free Library located on East Main Street has a room with a crawl space under the stairwell that leads to a cave under the building.

Location: Junction of Pa. Rte. 75 and U.S. Rte. 30

Franklin County – Caledonia Furnace – Thaddeus Stevens Ironworks

Erected in 1837 by Thaddeus Stevens and James D. Paxton, the furnace was destroyed during the Civil War because of Stevens' anti-slavery and Underground Railroad activities. Franklin County counted both cold-blooded slave hunters and armed anti-slavery abolitionists among its citizens.

One of the most prominent of the latter was United States Congressman Thaddeus Stevens. Included among the labor force at Caledonia Furnace were African-Americans, both freed and those who had fled from slavery through the Underground Railroad. Other slaves fled to the African-American community of Yellow Hill that had been established earlier.

Confederate General Jubal A. Early's cavalry raiders sacked Stevens' ironworks. Early remarked that he was sorry he had not found Stevens there. "I would hang him on the spot and divide his bones and send them to several states as curiosities." The day after the raid, General Robert E. Lee issued a reproof, "We cannot take vengeance…without…offending against Him to who vengeance belongeth."

Runaway slaves at Steven's furnace were warned to avoid the nearby town of Shippensburg because of its pro-slavery views.

Location: Junction of U.S. Rte. 30 and Pa. Rte 233 in Caledonia State Park

Franklin County – Mont Alto

Located a few miles from Chambersburg is the scenic and hilly village of Mont Alto. A few years before the Civil War, this little village became the subject of national attention when one of John Brown's men was captured there. A Pennsylvania State Historical Marker recalls the event. The marker reads: *John Brown Raid, Captain*

John Cooke, one of Brown's followers, was captured here on October 25, 1859, nine days after the raid on Harper's Ferry. He was hanged on December 16th, two weeks later, after John Brown.

According to newspapers at the time, Cooke was apprehended by two of the regions' most notorious slave catchers, Dan Logan and Clagett Fitzhugh, who collected a $1,000 reward. Also located at Mont Alto is Emmanuel Chapel, a small church where John Brown attended services and taught Sunday school under the name of Isaac Smith. The small 149-year-old chapel still stands.

In recent years, the Episcopal Diocese of Central Pennsylvania gave the building to Penn State University for the Civil War era price of $1. The university now has a campus located at Mont Alto. The chapel today offers non-denominational spiritual services, speakers, art exhibits, plays, and weddings.

Location: Pa. Rte. 233, one mile east of Mont Alto

Historical Marker
Captain John Cooke

Franklin County – Chambersburg – Old Franklin County Jail

A Pennsylvania State Historical Marker standing on East King Street reads: *Of Georgian design, this jail was built in 1818, and was continuously used for 152 years. The third oldest building in the borough, it survived the burning of Chambersburg by Confederate forces during the Civil War.*

Local tradition holds that the old jail and tunnels connected with it were used to hide runaway slaves on the Underground Railroad. Historians speculate that an almost forgotten cavern now under a downtown parking lot may have been used as a secret passageway. The old jail was connected with an underground corridor leading to the courthouse a block away.

In February 2000, a past chairman of Kittochtinny Historical Society of Franklin County stated, "The whole jail was the Underground Railroad."

Location: Pennsylvania State Historical Marker on East King Street

Franklin County – Chambersburg – Brown/Douglass Meeting

Standing at the site of an old stone quarry in Chambersburg is a Pennsylvania State Historical Marker documenting the place where John Brown met his friend, the noted abolitionist Frederick Douglass. Also attending the secret meeting were John Kagi, a white associate of Brown's, and two African-Americans, Shield Green, a runaway slave who would be killed during Brown's infamous attack on Harper's Ferry, and Henry Watson, a local Underground Railroad conductor at Chambersburg, who arranged the meeting during the summer in 1859.

Brown attempted to persuade Douglass to join the expedition, but Douglass would not go with him, even after Brown told him, "I will defend you with my life. I want you for a special purpose." The quarry where the secret meeting was held was located near the property of Joseph Winters, one of Chambersburg's illustrious African-American citizens.

Frederick Douglass

Some historians believe that Winters also had arranged the meeting with Brown. He was living in Chambersburg during the Civil War when the Confederate Army burned the town. Winters later wrote an 11-stanza song, "Ten Days After the Battle of Gettysburg," to be sung to the tune of "Bobtail Horse." He is credited with inventing the hook and ladder used during fires to reach extended heights.

Location: Pennsylvania State Historical Marker on West Washington Street

Joseph Winters

Franklin County – Chambersburg – John Brown's Headquarters

John Brown was known by many names—Captain Brown, the Old Man, Osawatomie Brown, Brown of Kansas. He came to Chambersburg in the summer of 1850, describing himself as a prospector and calling himself Isaac Smith, and told local residents that he was in the area to develop iron mines.

A bold stroke for freedom— escaped slaves defending themselves against armed slave hunters.

John Brown

At the house he rented, Brown quietly purchased tools and weapons for his planned 1859 raid on the United States Arsenal at Harper's Ferry, West Virginia. Brown and his men stored the tools and weapons in a warehouse in Chambersburg and a small farm in Maryland where he assembled 21 followers. Brown also preached at the Falling Spring Presbyterian Church in Chambersburg.

Location: 255 East King Street

Franklin County – Greencastle – a Profile of Courage by African-American Women

Laid out in 1782, Greencastle prior to the Civil War was a quiet, little town of red brick houses. The Old Central Church was a station stop on the Underground Railroad, as was the home of abolitionist Joseph White.

During the Battle of Gettysburg, the local residents displayed acts of defiance and bravery when Confederate forces under General Albert Jenkins invaded Greencastle on June 16, 1863. Jenkins had been instructed by the military high command to capture all freed African-Americans living in the Chambersburg, Mercersburg, and Greencastle area, and send them south to be sold on the auction block.

Unfortunately, a great number had been captured. Between 30 and 40 African-American women and children were captured in Chambersburg and taken to Greencastle. As the captured free African-Americans under a Confederate chaplain and four soldiers came through the town, the local residents disarmed the Confederates and locked them in the town's jail.

When General Jenkins received words of this bold act, he demanded $50,000 in compensation for his lost property and threatened to return in two hours to burn the town. Upon hearing of Jenkins' threat to the town, about 14 courageous African-American women offered to give themselves up to save Greencastle, but the town officials refused their heroic offer. Jenkins failed to carry out his threat, and Greencastle was spared.

Location: US Rte. 11 or Interstate 81

Franklin County – Mercersburg – Bethel African Methodist Episcopal Church and Zion Union Cemetery

Mercersburg has a proud tradition with Bethel A.M.E. Church and the Civil War. Many of the male members of this church enlisted in the Army. Nearly half served with the famous 54th Massachusetts Volunteer Infantry Regiment.

At the close of the war, there were 149 African-American regiments, of which 120 were infantry, 12 were heavy artillery, 10 were light artillery, and seven were cavalry, for a total of 123,156 men.

Included among the 54th Massachusetts volunteers were two sets of four brothers from Mercersburg, the Christys and the Krunkletons. Seven of the brothers were killed, and 30 others from this regiment also were casualties of the war.

Many of the Civil War veterans are buried in Zion Union

cemetery. Others were buried on Park Street at the former site of the African-American Community First School and Church.

Location: 24 West California Street

Adams County – Gettysburg – Gettysburg National Park

The Battle of Gettysburg was the biggest and bloodiest encounter of the Civil War. During the afternoon of July 3, 1863, this small Adams County community trembled under the heaviest artillery duel ever fought on the American continent.

Until recent years, most historians have failed to record the vital role played by African-Americans, both men and women. Although they did not serve with any military unit, African-Americans were present on the battlefield serving as cooks, laundry workers, teamsters, nurses, and aides-in-camp with both Union and Confederate armies.

As the Battle of Gettysburg was fought, the Philadelphia Supervisory Committee for Recruiting Negro Regiments issued a call for volunteers. Smarting from an earlier insult at Harrisburg, they avoided the recruitment center.

In June 1863, a company of volunteers of about 100 men had traveled to Harrisburg to defend Gettysburg as an emergency militia; however, they were sent home. At that time about 75,000 Confederate soldiers were advancing toward Harrisburg threatening to destroy the Capital. A group of untrained African-American men from Columbia, Lancaster County, and three white companies saved Harrisburg, destroying the bridge linking Columbia and Wrightsville over the Susquehanna River.

There were other unknown acts of bravery by the African-Americans in Gettysburg. Nelson Royer, a local resident, was hired as a servant with Union Army surgeon T.T. Tate and assisted him in the field hospital. Basil Biggs helped to gather the bodies of dead soldiers, numbering over 3,000. Also, there was the gallant deed of Lydia Smith, not to be confused with Lydia Hamilton Smith, the house-keeper of Thaddeus Stevens also of Gettysburg. This brave woman with a horse and wagon gathered food and clothing and distributed the items to the battlefield and hospital to both Union and Confederate soldiers.

Location: U.S. Rte. 30, east and west of junction with Pa. Rte. 94

Adams County – Gettysburg – Daniel Alexander Payne

Clergyman, educator, church historian, civil leader, and a bishop of the A.M.E. church, Daniel Alexander Payne was born in 1811 in Charleston, South Carolina, of free parents. Payne studied at Lutheran Theological Seminary in Gettysburg, from 1835 to 1837, when poor eyesight caused him to discontinue.

He supported himself by blacking boots, working at tables, and doing other menial jobs. While living in Gettysburg, Payne was authorized by the trustees of Lutheran Theological Seminary to conduct Bible classes and later served as Pastor of St. Paul A.M.E. Church.

After leaving Gettysburg, he served briefly as pastor of a Presbyterian Church in East Troy, New York. In Philadelphia in 1840, he founded a school that grew rapidly. The following year, he joined the African Methodist Episcopal Church in Philadelphia and was connected with the Underground Railroad.

Upon moving to Ohio, he founded Wilberforce University and became its first president. In 1888, Payne published his autobiography, *Recollection of Seventy Years*, and in 1891, he published *History of the African Methodist Episcopal Church*. A Pennsylvania State Historical

Daniel Alexander Payne

Marker was erected on the former site of the Lutheran Theological Seminary (now Gettysburg College).

Location: 239 N. Washington Street

Adams County – Gettysburg – Thaddeus Stevens' former home

Born in Vermont in 1792, Thaddeus Stevens attended Dartmouth College and then studied law in York, Pennsylvania. In 1816, Stevens opened his practice in Gettysburg, where he befriended several members of the African-American community, who respected his strong opposition to slavery.

While living in Gettysburg, Stevens met Lydia Hamilton Smith, an attractive fair-skinned African-American woman who was born free in Gettysburg in the early 1800s. Smith was the daughter of a white father and African-American mother who was a good friend of Stevens' servants.

When Lydia was about 20, she married an African-American barber and had two sons. Several years after her husband's death, Lydia moved with her two children into Stevens' Gettysburg home. She was 35 and he was 56. When he moved to Lancaster, she once again lived in his home as his housekeeper, always referred to as "Mrs. Stevens."

A Pennsylvania State Historical Marker stands on the site of his Gettysburg home.

Location: 51 Chambersburg Street

Adams County – Gettysburg – The Dobbin House

Built in 1776 by the Reverend Alexander Dobbin, a slave owner, the 2-1/2-story Dobbin House is the oldest house in Gettysburg. The Dobbin family lived in the house until 1825.

The Georgian-design house changed owners several times. During the era of the Underground Railroad, the Dobbin House was used as a safe house for unknown numbers of exhausted and frightened runaway slaves. Now a restaurant, the home has sliding shelves in the wall of an addition to conceal a crawl space large enough to hide several adults.

During the Civil War, the Dobbin House sustained minor damage from gunfire. The restaurant's furnishings today correspond with the Dobbin's 1809 inventory. It is ironic that the Reverend Alexander Dobbin, the original owner of the house, used his two slaves to build his home and that the house in later years served as a station on the Underground Railroad.

Location: 89 Steinwehr Avenue

Adams County – Gettysburg – Abraham Brien Family Farm

Abraham Brien was a successful 63-year-old farmer in 1863 during the Civil War battle at Gettysburg. Brien had originally purchased 12 acres in 1857, and grew wheat, barley, and hay, along with a small apple orchard.

Before the Civil War, Brien was connected with the Underground Railroad, and an unknown number of escapees found a safe haven on his property. He worked with Basil Biggs, Edward Matthews, John Hopkins, Michael Buck, and James A. Griest, five of the most prominent African-American conductors in Adams and Franklin counties. He also worked closely with James McAlister, a white mill owner whose station was an important stop in the Adams County network.

During the war, Brien and his family fled their home and farm during Confederate General George Pickett's gallant charge at the Battle of Gettysburg. Brien's 12-acre farm, located on the Union defensive line, received heavy destruction prior to the charge by Pickett's troops.

Included among Brien's losses were his furniture, 4-1/2 tons of hay, two acres of barley, his house and apple orchard, and valuable farm animals. When Brien filed his claims to the federal government, he was heartbroken when he received $15 for the destruction of his property that he claimed was worth $570. The $15 was payment for the amount of hay Brien could prove was consumed by Union Army horses when they stayed on his farm after the Confederate Army fled the battleground. After the war, Brien was so successful that he was able to sell his farm for a profit in 1869 and move into town.

Location: Gettysburg National Park

Adams County – Gettysburg – John Hopkins and Eden Devan

John Hopkins, an African-American custodian at Gettysburg College, alerted runaway slaves passing through Gettysburg to be on the lookout for Eden Devan, a large, fair-skinned African-American slave catcher who lived there. Devan was described as the "most efficient ally of slave catchers in the town of Gettysburg."

Devan was not the only slave hunter in Pennsylvania. As early as 1826, Patty Cannon, a white woman, ran an underground railroad in reverse from a base on the eastern shore of Maryland, a short distance from Seaford, Sussex County, Delaware, where my great-grandfather and other relatives lived in slavery. A notorious kidnapper, Cannon employed both white and African-American renegades to carry out foul, foul deeds.

Historians estimate that in one year as many as 20 African-American children and adults were kidnapped from Philadelphia and the surrounding suburbs in New Jersey and forced into slavery. Sometimes Cannon's gang tortured and murdered her victims after they were placed upon her slave boat that was docked at various rivers.

She finally was apprehended and committed suicide in jail. Numerous books have been written about her and her terrible deeds connected with the Underground Railroad.

Adams County – Gettysburg – St. Paul's A.M.E. Church and The Story of Margaret Palm

Right: Margaret "Maggie Bluecoat" Palm

Five members of Gettysburg's African-American community who were members of the Slave's Refuge Society founded the church in 1841. St. Paul's African Methodist Episcopal Church's early congregation played a prominent role during the era of the Underground Railroad and the Civil War.

Margaret Palm was a formidable enemy of slavocracy. According to local tradition, Margaret was a runaway slave from Maryland. She settled in Gettysburg as a young woman with her husband Isaac. Some time later, she became active in the Underground Railroad movement, assisting and protecting other slaves.

She wore a sky-blue broadcloth uniform coat of an officer of the War of 1812 and protected herself with a musket. A woman of enormous proportions, she was fondly remembered as "Maggie Bluecoat." She was also one of a group of local residents who warned African-Americans of approaching slave hunters.

During the Battle of Gettysburg, she rendered valuable service on the battlefield and at Gettysburg Hospital, helping the sick and wounded. In later years, she successfully assisted a local druggist, despite her lack of education.

Location: 269 S. Washington Street

Northern Tier

Brooklyn
The Perkins-Dennis
Farm and Cemetery

The Medbury House

Wilkes Barre
The powder horn o
Gershom Prince

Williamsport
Freedom Road Cemetery
and Underground
Railroad Marker

Pottsville
Marker and Cemetery
honoring Nicholas Biddle

NORTHERN TIER – LYCOMING, LUZERNE, SCHUYLKILL, SUSQUEHANNA, MONROE, WAYNE, LACKAWANNA, WYOMING, PIKE, BRADFORD, POTTER, FOREST, ELK, CLINTON, CAMERON, VENANGO

Lycoming County – Pennsdale – The House of Many Stairs

Probably no house in the Quaker village of Pennsdale has been the subject of more fantastic tales than the House of Many Stairs. Built of limestone and fossil, with a red tin roof, the house was known for years as Bull's Head Tavern. Although it is only two stories high, it is an imposing place that once served as a stagecoach stop.

Edward Morris, the owner of Bull's Head Tavern, offered many sleeping rooms, food, and drink to his customers. Because people were always coming and going to and from the tavern, it helped Morris, who was a stationmaster on the Underground Railroad, to shield escapees. If any customers were slave hunters, the escapees could be found resting and eating. When danger was present, they could exit into various stairways until it was safe for them to be smuggled to the next Underground Station.

There are a total of seven staircases in the home, with five steps leading into and out of each room. Passage to a secret hideaway is through a small attic door at the top of a stairway. There is also a window that could serve as a lookout. The ceilings in each room are seven feet high; the house's complexity often caused confusion for pursuing slave hunters. A stone's throw beyond the House of Many Stairs is a small 200-year-old Quaker cemetery, where Native Americans and African-Americans are buried among the dead in unmarked graves.

The House of Many Stairs is now a private residence.

Location: Pa. Rte. 220, near junction with Pa. Rte. 147

The House of Many Stairs

Lycoming County – Williamsport – Freedom Road Cemetery

Williamsport was one of the prominent stops on Pennsylvania's Underground Railroad. The major station was the home and property owned by Daniel Hughes on Freedom Road. Hughes, a large, full-blooded Native American from the Mohawk people and his African-American wife, Annie Rotch Hughes, along with their children, hid runaway slaves and provided for their needs.

A river raftsman, Hughes transported escapees concealed in his boat to stations in nearby towns. One of Hughes' Williamsport friends, Robert Faries, an ardent abolitionist and the first president of the Williamsport-Elmira railroad, also participated in the secret operation. Faries and his employees often stowed escapees in the baggage cars of trains bound for Canada.

For almost a century, Freedom Road, located on Williamsport's northern outskirts, bore the name "Nigger Hollow." In 1936, however, at the request of an enraged African-American community, the name was changed to "Freedom Road." Although Hughes' large home no longer stands, a State Historical Marker was erected at the former site. Hughes gave part of his land for a cemetery, and among those buried here are nine known African-American veterans of the Civil War.

Location: Pennsylvania State Historical Marker at Highland Terrace and Grampian Boulevard

Lycoming County – Muncy – Henry Harris, Former Slave Inventor

Henry Harris, known as "Black Henry," was an ex-slave, who was born in 1800 and died in 1887. He had been owned by the aristocratic Baynard family of Maryland and Delaware, and was a butler at Bohemia Manor on the Eastern Shore. He bought his freedom and moved to Muncy long before the Civil War.

Harris later bought the freedom of his wife. Together they became famous caterers in Muncy using Bohemia Manor's recipes. Six feet, six inches tall, he was also a body servant to Captain John Bowman and successfully nursed many of the soldiers in Bowman's company through typhoid fever.

Harris was a highly respected citizen throughout Lycoming County. Many imitators copied his original walnut butcher's tray. Another Muncy African-American was Harris' friend John Warner, who operated an Underground Railroad station there. Warner's distinguished group of friends included the well-known African-American anti-slavery writer and lecturer Frances Ellen Watkins Harper. She once approached President Abraham Lincoln and gave him a photograph with the words, "I give you my portrait with a white back, I should like to have yours with a greenback."

Lycoming County – Thomas Lightfoote Inn

Thomas Updegraff was a Quaker who originally settled on the stretch of the Susquehanna River known as the "Long Reach" at the invitation of prominent surveyor Thomas Lightfoote. Two of Updegraff's ancestors were among the 14 members who signed the first recorded declaration against slavery on the North American continent that was written by Francis Daniel Pastorius in 1688 in Germantown (now Philadelphia).

Updegraff and his son Abraham sheltered slaves in a barn and gave directions to them, most of whom arrived on packet boats at the port by the old Exchange Hotel. Already old when Thomas Updegraff ran his Underground Railroad Station from it, the inn was built more than 200 years ago, and was a stop on the Pennsylvania Canal as well as a refuge for runaway slaves. The old Updegraff house is now the Lightfoote Inn.

Location: South Reach Road

Lycoming County – Muncy – McCarty Wertman House

Constructed of logs in 1779, the McCarty-Wertman house was at one time used as a station on the Underground Railroad. In this two-story clapboard building, runaway slaves were concealed in a large stone cellar. Today the McCarty-Wertman house is a charming inn, and there is little evidence to show that the house once served as a way-station on the clandestine network known as the Underground Railroad.

Other Lycoming County communities such as Williamsport, Montoursville, and Pennsdale often transported runaway slaves from Trout Run to Horseheads in New York State. Quaker Thomas Mendenhall, who moved with his family to Pennsdale in 1852, while living in Columbia County received escapees seeking freedom from his relatives, the Mendenhalls of Chester County.

The residents of Columbia County were no friends of runaway slaves or those who protected them. Many citizens of Columbia County sympathized with southern slave hunters who sought and kidnapped freed African-Americans in the county. On one occasion, Mendenhall's life was threatened when a bullet whistled past his head while he was living in Berwick, Columbia County. He died in Pennsdale in 1883.

Location: 858 W. Fourth Street

Luzerne County – Wilkes-Barre – Kings College Chapel

During their lifetime, coal sculpture has been practiced and perfected in the Patience family for more than 80 years. Harry Patience, the son of a former slave, originally started the coal sculpture business in Pittston. Harry's fourth son, Edgar, transferred it to Wilkes-Barre.

The hardness of anthracite and the craftsmanship employed in its carving won an international reputation for a range of Edgar Patience's products. His jewelry was worn by such heads of state as the Prime Minister of Barbados, Queen Juliana of the Netherlands, wives of United States presidents and legislators, and Hollywood celebrities.

The Chapel of Kings College in Wilkes-Barre has a 4,000-pound coal altar sculpted by Edgar Patience that is one of the largest

This Edgar Patience coal bust of an African-American woman is called "Amalrice," which means "meek one" in one of the many African dialects.

works of art created by an African-American in the U.S. It is unique in its style. There also is a coal replica of the Hoover vacuum cleaner in Canton, Ohio, sculpted by Patience.

Location: Jackson and North Franklin Streets

Luzerne County – Wilkes-Barre

Luzerne County was formed September 25, 1786, from Northumberland County and named for Chevalier de la Luzerne, the French ambassador to the United States at the time. Wilkes-Barre, the county seat, was settled in 1769. One of the most significant events that occurred in this area was the Wyoming Massacre that led to the Sullivan Expedition.

The expedition was named after General John Sullivan, who was sent by General George Washington to destroy a small group of Native Americans that supplied the British with men and ammunition. One of the participants in the Battle of Wyoming that preceded the massacre was Gershom Prince, an African-American soldier, who was a slave of Captain Robert Durkee of the Connecticut militia. He fought with Durkee in the British victory at Quebec during the French and Indian War, and died on July 3, 1778, during the Battle of Wyoming, a skirmish in the border dispute with Connecticut that took place in northcentral Pennsylvania.

The Wyoming Historical and Genealogical Society has on display a crown point powder horn that was decorated with pictures of houses and ships by Gershom Prince. Wilkes-Barre was also connected with the Underground Railroad. The recently demolished Bethel A.M.E. Church was a major site of activity.

Location: Plaque on River Commons, River Street near West South Street

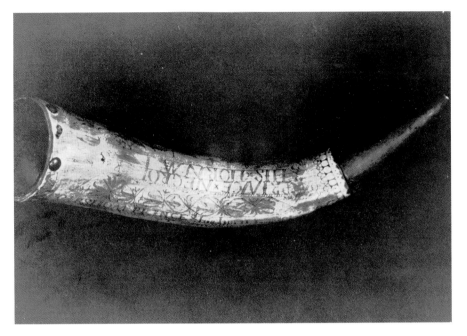

The crown point powder horn was decorated by Gershom Prince. Photo courtesy of Wyoming Historical and Genealogical Society.

Schuylkill County – Pottsville – Nicholas Biddle

Nicholas Biddle, an African-American native of Pottsville, is reported to be the first man in the union to spill blood for his flag as the Civil War commenced. A brick that was thrown as his regiment traveled through Baltimore, a city with Southern loyalties, injured Biddle, a servant for a Pottsville officer, on April 17, 1861.

Inscribed on his tombstone behind Bethel A.M.E. Church are the following words: *In the memory of Nicholas Biddle, died August 2, 1876, age 80 years. His was the Proud Distinction of Shedding the First Blood in the later war for the Union being wounded while marching through Baltimore April 17, 1861. Erected by his friends in Pottsville."*

Biddle worked with James Gillingham (see page 203) on the Underground Railroad. Bethel A.M.E. Church is located at Ninth and Laurel Streets. A bronze plaque also commemorating Biddle was placed in Garfield Square in Pottsville. However, on the 100th

Nicholas Biddle

anniversary of the day he shed the first blood marching to save the Union, his tombstone was broken in half by vandals.

Location: 5th and Market Streets

Schuylkill County – Pottsville – The Gillinghams' House

James Gillingham, one of the first Quakers in Schuylkill County, was an active stationkeeper on the freedom network. Runaway slaves were seen doing chores around Gillingham's red brick home located on Mahantango Street. On one occasion, his daughter Phoebe begged a neighbor not to tell anyone about a runaway slave in the Gillingham yard. The house is now a private residence.

Location: 622 Mahantango Street

Susquehanna County – Brooklyn Township – The Perkins-Dennis Farm and Cemetery

Located on a desolate hilltop in Brooklyn and Hartford Townships of Susquehanna County, roughly midway between Scranton, Pennsylvania, and Binghamton, New York, is the Perkins-Dennis 153-acre farm and cemetery. The cemetery has been in the ownership of the Perkins-Dennis family from before 1800 to the present, and is probably the oldest African-American cemetery in Pennsylvania. It contains the grave of Bristol Budd, who joined the Connecticut Line in March 1777, and in 1779 was chosen by General George Washington to be a member of the elite "Light Infantry Corps" commanded by General "Mad" Anthony Wayne.

Budd was one of the few who served in the Revolutionary Army for the entire war. In 1810, he moved to Brooklyn Township and lived there for 38 years. The cemetery also contains the resting-place of a number of Civil War veterans and a number of slaves who escaped on the Underground Railroad, and then decided to remain in Susquehanna County.

Substantial evidence suggests that Montrose and Brooklyn Township played a significant role in the network for slave freedom.

This striking illustration by C.G. Lewis for the cover of Henry Wadsworth Longfellow's poem The Slave in the Dismal Swamp *is from a painting entitled* The Hunted Slave *by British artist Richard Ansdell. Unlike much abolitionist art, which portrayed slaves as prayerful victims, Ansdell and Lewis show the tension and defiance of escaped slaves cornered by bloodhounds.*

African-American inhabitants in these communities played an important role in the development of the county since the Revolutionary War era. The Perkins-Dennis Cemetery is one of the oldest African-American burial grounds in continuous use in this country.

Before the Civil War, the two communities were connected with the Underground Railroad. During the war, 20 African-American men from Montrose joined the Union Army, a substantial representation from a small community. One tombstone of a former slave reads, "Born in slavery—Died in Freedom."

Location: Pa. Rte. 167

Susquehanna County – Montrose – First African-American Admitted to the Bar

Jonathan Jasper Wright

Jonathan Jasper Wright (1840–1887) was born in Wilkes-Barre, Luzerne County, but spent most of his childhood in the Springville section of Montrose, where his family moved shortly after his birth. After attending Lancastrian University in Ithaca, New York, he had law offices in Montrose and Wilkes-Barre and taught school during the same period. He represented Luzerne County as a delegate at the State Equal Rights Convention for Colored People of Pennsylvania, held in Harrisburg in 1865. That same year, Wright went to Charleston, South Carolina, where he attended a colored people's convention that protested an attempt of the state legislature to keep former slaves in their servile status.

Wright also served as an organizer of schools for freedmen under the auspices of the American Missionary Association. He returned to Pennsylvania where, in 1866, he became the first African-American in Pennsylvania admitted to the bar. Wright returned to South Carolina and continued his public life; he died in his rooming house in 1887.

Location: Wright's former family home in Springville is now a private residence

Susquehanna County – Montrose – Galusha Grow: Father of the Homestead Act

A Pennsylvania State Historical Marker dedicated July 5, 1982, at Hartford Cemetery reads: *Susquehanna County was the home of Galusha Grow, sponsor of the 1862 Homestead Act. Montrose County Seat was an early abolitionist center and stop on the Underground Railroad. Grow died in 1907 and is buried in the Hartford Cemetery.*

Location: Pa. Rte. 547

Monroe County – Stroudsburg – Major Underground Railroad Station

In Monroe County, where Quaker influence was strong, Stroudsburg was one of the chief stations on the Underground Railroad freedom route to Canada. Dr. Sydenham Walter was a well-known stationmaster, and at the same time he was a strong supporter of the Republican Party.

The African-American male citizens of Monroe County participated actively in the Civil War. They served as both volunteers and draftees in the 22nd, 24th and 25th U.S. Colored Regiments and in Company Nine in the Eighth Colored Regiment. Military records report this regiment to have suffered heavy losses: 51 killed and 252 wounded in the battle of Oluster Swamp, Florida, on February 20, 1864.

Right: Celebration of Emancipation Proclamation by African-Americans

Wayne County – Bethany – David Wilmot

Wayne County was formed on March 21, 1798, from Northampton County. It is named for Revolutionary War General Anthony Wayne. David Wilmot, a county politician born in Bethany, Pennsylvania, is chiefly known as the author of the Wilmot Proviso (see below).

As a young man, he practiced law in Towanda. In 1845, he entered politics and served as representative in Congress until 1851. In 1854, Wilmot helped found the Republican Party, and was its first candidate for governor. He was elected to the United States Senate in 1861.

The Wilmot Proviso

On August 8, 1846, an important bill was offered for approval of the United States House of Representatives. The bill provided an appropriation of $20 million for the negotiation of peace with Mexico, which was then at war with the United States. The money was to be used for the purchase from Mexico of new territory for the United States.

David Wilmot, a Democratic member of the House, offered an amendment to the bill. The amendment, called the Wilmont Proviso, declared that slavery should be forbidden in any territory obtained by the United States. The House of Representatives approved the amendment but the Senate refused to pass it.

WESTERN REGION

ERIE
Harry T. Burleigh's
Pennsylvania State
Historical Marker

MEADVILLE
John Brown's Tannery

PITTSBURGH
Pittsburgh Courier
State Historical Marker

Dr. Frances
LeMoyne House

WESTERN REGION – BEAVER, ALLEGHENY, CRAWFORD, MERCER, LAWRENCE, FAYETTE, WASHINGTON, WESTMORELAND, GREENE

Beaver County – Beaver Falls – Geneva College

Geneva College was deeply involved with the Underground Railroad and took a strong stance against human slavery. Founded in 1848 by the Reformed United Presbyterian Church in Northwood, Ohio, it was moved to Beaver County in 1880.

While it was known that many Quakers and other religious groups received credit for their involvement with the anti-slavery movement, the Covenanters, as the college founders were called, did their work as silent sentinels. They made significant contributions to the Underground Railroad and the immediate emancipation of African-Americans held in bondage.

Wilbur H. Siebert, an Ohio Underground Railroad historian who wrote *The Underground Railroad: From Slavery to Freedom*, published in 1898, notes: "Family ties, Church fellowship, journalistic and political, were the leavening influences of institutions like Oberlin College, Western Reserve College and Geneva College. All contributed to propagate a sentiment that was ready to support the fleeing slave." The college library houses a major collection of archival documents related to Geneva's involvement with the Underground Railroad.

Location: Campus on a wooded bluff overlooking Beaver Falls

Beaver County – Darlington – Markers Dedicated to Underground Railroad Sites

In 1979, the Little Beaver Historical Society dedicated two markers commemorating the Underground Railroad. The first dedication was held at the Reform Presbyterian Church, and the second was at the former home of the Reverend Arthur B. Bradford.

The Reform Presbyterian Church was formed in 1847 and was led by Bradford. After the infamous Fugitive Slave Law of 1850 was passed, the congregation declared that the law was un-Christian and vowed that they would not respect it. About this time, the members of this church became involved with the Underground Railroad.

The point where these supporters most often rallied seems to have been the home of Evan Townsend, with an ingenious trapdoor to the cellar where slaves were hidden. His relatives Benjamin, David, and Milo Townsend were also active. Stationkeepers included James Irvin, Timothy White, and Elwood Thomas.

Among the noted anti-slavery lecturers who spoke at the Presbyterian Church and "Shuster's Abolition Hall" were Frederick Douglass, Abby Kelley, and Steven Foster. Buttonwood, the Bradfords' home, also welcomed abolitionists and served as a station on the Underground.

Location: Pa. Rte. 551 between Darlington and Enon

Allegheny County – Pittsburgh – The Cathedral of Learning's African Heritage Classroom.

The University of Pittsburgh was founded in 1787. Located on its campus is a 42-story skyscraper known as the Cathedral of Learning. This building, constructed of Bedford stone with Gothic ornament, dominates a 14-acre quadrangle. The Cathedral of Learning's immense Commons Room on the first floor goes up four stories to a vaulted ceiling.

A number of Nationality Rooms in the Cathedral of Learning commemorate various ethnic groups in Pittsburgh's population. The African Heritage classroom interprets the history and culture of the African continent. It is organized around the concept of courtyards of various types and the focus of family activities in Africa.

The classroom is modeled on a central courtyard of an Ashanti royal residence, though the style is found among the African cultures in present-day Nigeria, Ghana, Benin, Togo, and the Ivory Coast. Today, this model has added symbols and artifacts from other African peoples.

Location: Fifth Avenue at Bigelow Boulevard

Allegheny County – Pittsburgh – Josh Gibson of The Homestead Grays

Born December 21, 1911, in Buena Vista, Georgia, Josh Gibson, the eldest of three children, moved to Pittsburgh with his family, where he enrolled at Allegheny Prevocational School to study to be an electrician. However, he left school to become an apprentice in an air-brake factory.

In 1927, he began his baseball career in Pittsburgh playing with a sandlot team called the Pleasant Valley Red Sox, before joining the Pittsburgh Crawfords. Because of his exceptional skill as a baseball player, Gibson attracted the attention of the Homestead Grays of the Negro Professional Baseball League and began to win fame as a catcher and home run slugger.

In one season, Gibson is credited with 75 home runs. In 1932, he left the Homestead Grays to play with the Pittsburgh Crawfords and recorded batting averages of .464, .384, .440, and .457, and hit 69 home runs.

Gibson is credited with 962 home runs in his 17-year career, many against non-league teams. Due to racial prejudice in white

professional baseball leagues, Gibson was denied the opportunity to exhibit his great talent before all American baseball fans. He suffered a fatal stroke a month before his 35th birthday and just a few months before Jackie Robinson became the first African-American to play in professional baseball's major league.

A Pennsylvania State Historical Marker reads: *Hailed as Negro Leagues' greatest slugger, he hit some eight hundred home runs in a baseball career that began here at Ammon's Field in 1929. Played for Homestead Grays and Pittsburgh Crawfords, 1930 – 1946. Elected to Baseball Hall of Fame, 1972.*

Left: Josh Gibson

Location: 2217 Bedford Avenue

Allegheny County – Pittsburgh – Jazz Composer Mary Lou Williams

Mary Lou Williams, a celebrated jazz pianist, arranger, and composer was born in Atlanta, Georgia, May 8, 1910. She moved to Pittsburgh with her mother and sister at the age of four. A child prodigy, Williams began playing the piano from an early age. She studied at Lincoln Elementary School and then toured on a circuit accompanying a group headed by two local Pittsburgh musicians before resuming her studies at Westinghouse Junior High School in Pittsburgh.

She returned to the tour circuit during the mid-1920s until the early 1930s, when she performed at the Pearl Theater in Philadelphia. Later, she performed with several nationally known bandleaders such as Benny Goodman, Louis Armstrong, Earl Hines, Tommy Dorsey, and Duke Ellington from the mid-1930s until the mid-1940s.

During the decade of the 1950s, she established residency in New York City and did extensive composing and then moved to Europe, performing in England and France. Returning to America in 1957, Williams performed at major jazz festivals until 1969, when she again went to Europe and also performed in South America.

In 1978, she appeared before President Jimmy Carter at a White House jazz party. Williams' major compositions include "Zodiac Suite" and "Mary Lou's Mass."

> Location: Pennsylvania State Historical Marker at Lincoln Elementary School, 328 Lincoln Avenue

Allegheny County – Pittsburgh – National Negro Opera Company

The Pennsylvania State Historical Marker honoring this organization reads: *Here at Caldwell School of Music, this first national Black opera company was founded in 1941 by Mary Caldwell Dawson. Noted for its musical genius, the Black Opera Company performed for twenty-one years in Pittsburgh, Washington, New York and other cities.*

> Location: 7101 Apple Street

Allegheny County – Pittsburgh – Bethel African Methodist Episcopal Church

The Pennsylvania State Historical Marker for this historic church reads: *Founded 1808 and known as the African Church. Chartered in 1818. Located nearby in early years, church was site of area's first school for colored children, 1831 and statewide Civil Rights conventions, 1841. Congregation moved to Wylie Avenue, 1872; Webster Avenue, 1959.*

Determined to see their children educated, members of the African-American community, led by businessmen Benjamin Richards, the Reverend Lewis Woodson, and John B. Vashon, opened the first school for African-Americans in 1831 in the basement of Bethel A.M.E. Church located on Front Street at that time. The school's most prominent student was Martin R. Delany. John Vashon's son, George, was graduated from Bethel's school and went on to become one of the first African-Americans to earn a law degree from Oberlin College in Ohio.

David J. Peck, the son of Underground Railroad agent and businessman John C. Peck, also was graduated from Bethel's church school. In 1847, he became the first African-American to earn a medical degree when he was graduated from Rush Medical College in Chicago.

> **Location: First Avenue at Smithfield Street**

Allegheny County – Pittsburgh – Robert L. Vann

Lawyer, politician, entrepreneur, and publisher Robert L. Vann, the son of a tenant farmer from North Carolina, rose to a position of prominence among African-Americans of Allegheny County. One of the first African-Americans to be graduated from the University of Pittsburgh, Vann set up a law practice in the city in 1910. Shortly thereafter, he helped to found the influential *Pittsburgh Courier*, a widely circulated African-American newspaper that presented African-American views to a national audience, and he also became its editor.

From its first edition, March 10, 1910, the *Pittsburgh Courier* grew over the years and hundreds of people found employment in various branch offices. Most importantly, many of today's well-known African-American authors were able to learn journalism when doors of white newspapers and magazines were closed to African-American interest.

President Franklin D. Roosevelt appointed Vann Assistant U.S. Attorney General. The battleship USS Robert L. Vann was named in his honor during World War II. He died in 1940.

Robert Vann

> **Location: Pennsylvania State Historical Marker at Center Avenue and Frances Street**

Allegheny County – Pittsburgh – Jazz Composer and Arranger William "Billy " Strayhorn

A graduate of Westinghouse High School, in the city's Homewood section, William "Billy" Strayhorn had his musical talents nurtured there. In 1939, he joined the famous Duke Ellington Orchestra as a pianist, composer, and arranger. The two musicians worked so intimately and with such rapport that, according to some jazz critics, their styles became indistinguishable.

Location: Pennsylvania State Historical Marker at Westinghouse High School, 1101 N. Murtland Street

Allegheny County – Pittsburgh – Singer Billy Eckstein

Known as "Mr. B" among his jazz fans throughout the world, Billy Eckstein was in the true sense of the word a "pioneer" in the world of jazz. His career started in 1939 when he joined the Earl Hines Band as a vocalist. Following four years with Hines, Eckstein formed his own orchestra, and employed young jazz personalities such as Dizzy Gillespie, Charlie Parker, Miles Davis, Dexter Gordon, Gene Ammons, Sonny Stitt, and Art Blakey, along with a very talented singer named Sarah Vaughn, who later became a jazz legend.

In 1947, he recorded, "Everything I Have Is Yours," a record that gained international acclaim. One of the nation's most popular vocalists, Eckstein had 11 gold records. A Pennsylvania State Historical Marker is erected at the site where he lived.

Location: 5913 Bryant Street, Highland Park

Allegheny County – Pittsburgh – K. Leroy Irvis

A native of Albany, New York, K. Leroy Irvis has had a life-long career in public service. He has been a public man, teacher, lawyer, civic leader, politician, poet, sculptor, and the first African-

K. Leroy Irvis

American Speaker of the House of Representatives in the General Assembly of the Commonwealth of Pennsylvania.

In 1969, he organized the Pennsylvania Legislative Black Caucus to monitor legislation that advanced the interest of minorities in the commonwealth. He also sponsored a resolution for the establishment of a community college system within the state during the 1960s.

He was a mentor to both African-American and white legislators during his tenure in office. At the suggestion of his many admirers, a bronze bust of Irvis was placed on display in the rotunda in the state capitol in Harrisburg. The Hillman Library at the University of Pittsburgh houses his private papers and other archival materials.

Allegheny County – Pittsburgh – Daisy E. Lampkin

Daisy E. Lampkin was born in Washington D.C., and grew up in Reading, Pennsylvania. She moved to Pittsburgh in 1909 and married William Lampkin of Rome, Georgia, in 1912. In Pittsburgh, she became a tireless fundraiser and fighter for African-American and American civil rights organizations as well as a longtime vice president of the *Pittsburgh Courier* newspaper.

Lampkin was best known for her work as national field secretary for the National Association for the Advancement of Colored People. On August 9, 1983, a Pennsylvania State Historical Marker was dedicated in her honor with the following inscription: *Outstanding as an NAACP organizer, Mrs. Lampkin was its National Field Secretary 1935-1947. President of the Lucy Stone Civic League, 1915-1965. A charter member of the National Council of Negro Women, and Vice President of the Pittsburgh Courier. She lived here until her death in 1965.*

Location: 2519 Webster Avenue

Allegheny County – Pittsburgh –
The Hannibal Guards

At the outbreak of the Civil War, the following letter was sent to General James S. Negley by a group of black Pittsburgh citizens known as the Hannibal Guards:

As we sympathized with our white fellow citizens at the present crisis, and to show that we can and do feel interested in the present state of affairs, and as we consider ourselves American citizens and interested in the Commonwealth of all our white fellow citizens, although deprived of all political rights, we yet wish the government of the United States to be maintained against the tyranny of slavery, and we are willing to assist in any honorable way or manner to sustain the present administration. We therefore tender to the state the services of the Hannibal Guards.

Yours, Capt. Samuel Saunders.

The Civil War raged for three years before Governor Andrew G. Curtin accepted the services of the Hannibal Guards and the Fort Pitt Cadets, another African-American volunteer unit. The guards and cadets were based in Allegheny County and had offered their services shortly after the outbreak of the war. Curtin accepted the offer only after it was rumored that Confederate forces led by General Robert E. Lee were about to march upon Pennsylvania. It is estimated that during the course of the war, 500 African-Americans from the Pittsburgh area served under the Union flag.

Allegheny County – Pittsburgh –
Stephen C. Foster Memorial

Stephen Collin Foster was born of Scotch-Irish descent on July 4, 1826. Known as the "American Troubadour," he was the greatest of white minstrel composers. His first known composition was "Tioga Waltz" (1840); he published his first song at age 16.

As a child, Foster early came into contact with the music of African-Americans. A family servant, Olivia Pise, took him to African-

American church services. In 1845, Foster decided to become "the best Ethiopian songwriter," when he composed "Ethiopian Songs." He consciously based some of his songs on tunes that he had heard sung by African-American stevedores on the wharves in Pittsburgh and the songs sung by black boatmen on the steamboat *James Miligan*.

When he visited New Orleans, his only journey into the south resulted in the song "My Old Kentucky Home." He also composed popular songs such as "Oh Susanna," "Old Black Joe," "Camptown Races" and others. Foster drank to excess and had an unhappy marriage. He died in New York City on January 13, 1864, from a fall in a Bowery lodging house. The memorial depicts Foster seated with a young African-American man looking at him.

> Location: Forbes Avenue just east of Bigelow Boulevard

Allegheny County – Pittsburgh – Avery College

Charles Avery, Methodist preacher, abolitionist, and philanthropist, is honored by a Pennsylvania State Historical Marker standing 10 feet high, shining blue and gold, bearing the state insignia at the former site of Avery College and Avery Memorial Church. The buildings derived their names from Avery, whose wealth came from the production of pharmaceuticals and a cotton mill.

A member of the Pennsylvania Abolition Society, Avery gave large sums of money to African-Americans, whom he proclaimed were intellectually equal to whites. In 1849, he founded a college for African-Americans known as the Allegheny Institute and Mission Church.

Avery died on January 17, 1858, and was buried in the God's Acre section of Pittsburgh's Allegheny Cemetery. There is a marble statue of Avery on his grave; on one side there is a figure of charity and the other side a figure of justice. Avery also provided for Oberlin College in Ohio, and for the Avery Institute in Charleston, South Carolina.

Charles Avery

Location: 619 Ohio Street

Allegheny County – Pittsburgh – Martin R. Delany

Martin R. Delany (1812-1885) was an editor, author, physician, abolitionist, colonizationist, Underground Railroad agent, and

Martin R. Delany

army officer. The dynamic father of black nationalism was born of free parents in Charles Town, West Virginia, on May 6, 1812. He grew up in Chambersburg, Pennsylvania, and settled in Pittsburgh with his family in 1831.

He did his undergraduate work in Pittsburgh and then applied to Harvard Medical School, where he was accepted after a year. Delany and two other African-Americans were dismissed from the school because of a petition signed by bigoted fellow students. Returning to Pittsburgh, where he had earlier edited an African-American newspaper, *The Mystery*, he completed his medical studies and began his practice.

Early in his professional life, he defended his views of African-American colonization to Africa, and later served as editor of Frederick Douglass' famous newspaper *North Star*, from 1847 to 1849. Delany presided over the National Emigration of Colored Men, an organization that prescribed that African-Americans were to explore the possibility of immigrating to other places such as Canada, Central America, and South America.

A man of many facets, during the Civil War he was the first African-American to be appointed to the rank of major in the United States Army. He proposed to President Abraham Lincoln that there should be "an Army of Negroes commanded by Negroes," but he was not successful in winning Lincoln to this proposal. Delany died in 1885. A Pennsylvania State Historical Marker is located at the former office of his newspaper *The Mystery*.

Location: Third Avenue and Market Street

Allegheny County – Pittsburgh – Jane Grey Swisshelm

Pittsburgh was a town of fewer than 5,000 inhabitants when abolitionist, editor, Underground Railroad agent, and Civil War nurse

Jane Grey Swisshelm was born on December 6, 1815. A renowned editor, her sharp, witty writing style carried her to Washington as a correspondent for Horace Greeley's *Tribune*. A white, anti-slavery newspaper publisher, Swisshelm is best known for her colorful autobiography, *Half Century*, published in 1880. It was a popular and significant document.

The frequently-erected banner of "no women need apply" did not stop her foray into journalism and criticism. With tongue and pen, she lashed out at public officials and politicians. Mrs. Swisshelm was an early advocate of women's rights and temperance. She died in 1884 at the homestead on Braddock and Greendale Avenues in Pittsburgh.

Swisshelm wrote in her autobiography that she assisted runaway slaves and her home was a station on the Underground Railroad. In her abolitionist newspaper *The Saturday Visitor*, she vigorously opposed the Fugitive Slave Law of 1850, calling for total resistance to its implementation.

Jane Grey Swisshelm

Allegheny County – Pittsburgh – Martin R. Delany's Speech on the Infamous Fugitive Slave Law of 1850.

On September 30, 1850, the *Pittsburgh Gazette* reported that Martin Delany had delivered a speech on the topic of the Fugitive Slave Law before a group of prominent white citizens in Allegheny City (now Pittsburgh.)

Delany stated:

Honorable Mayor, whatever ideas of liberty I have, have been received from reading the lives of your revolutionary fathers. I have therein learned that a man has a right to defend his castle with his life, even unto the taking of life. Sir, my home is my castle, in that castle are none but my wife, and my children, as free as the angels of heaven, and whose liberty is as sacred as the pillars of God. If any man approaches that house in search of a slave – I care not who he may be, whether constable, or sheriff, magistrate or even judge of the Supreme Court – nay, let it be he who sanctioned this act to become law, surrounded by his bodyguard, with the Declaration of Independence waving above his head as his banner, and the Constitution of this country upon his breast, as a shield – if he crosses the threshold of my door, and I do not lay him a lifeless corpse at my feet, I hope the grave may refuse my body as a resting place and righteous Haven, my spirit a home. No! He cannot enter that house and we both live.

Allegheny County – Pittsburgh – Crawford Grill No. 2

Crawford Grill No. 2 opened in 1943 as a companion to the first Crawford Grill. It also became a major center for social and cultural life in Pittsburgh's Hill District, an African-American community.

Notable musicians such as Mary Lou Williams, John Coltrane, Dizzy Gillespie, and Art Blakely played there to racially mixed international audiences. The grill was owned by William A. (Gus) Greenlee, who also owned the Pittsburgh Crawfords Negro League baseball team, and later by Jackie Robinson.

This was and continues as the second of three Crawford Grills that enriched the cultural scene for decades.

Location: Pennsylvania State Historical Marker at 2141 Wylie Avenue

Warren County – Sugar Grove – Families Aid the Underground Railroad

Warren County was formed March 12, 1800, from Allegheny and Lycoming counties. It was named for General Joseph Warren, who was killed at Bunker Hill during the Revolutionary War era. The village of Sugar Grove was a station on the Underground Railroad with several families involved in its operation.

The William Storum family, originally from Hartford, Connecticut, migrated to Pennsylvania in 1816 and frequently played host to leading Sugar Grove citizens who were interested in the anti-slavery movement. It was said that the family was part African-American, but the records are not clear.

The Underground Railroad routes in Warren County led into Chautauqua County in New York State. Located outside of Garland, in Spring Creek Township, Warren County, there is a natural slope called African Hill. At one time a small mill and several homes were built on the hill. Today, an abandoned cemetery with more than a dozen fieldstone markers is all that can be seen.

Erie County – Erie – Harry T. Burleigh

Eminent African-American baritone, composer, and arranger of "Nobody Knows The Trouble I've Seen," Harry Burleigh has visited the lips of millions of African-Americans and white Americans. He was famous for that song and many others such as: "Deep River," "Were You There?" and "Balm In Gilead."

He was born in 1866 in Erie, and at a young age revealed a musical talent. His father died when he was young and, like many other African-Americans, he had no resources for formal training. So even as a boy, Burleigh worked in Erie hotels when not attending school.

He earned a scholarship to the National Conservatory of Music, from which he was graduated, and he soon established himself as a soloist in a white Episcopal Church and on the concert stage, where he appeared before presidents and royalty. He composed more than 250 songs, many in the tradition of spirituals. His ballads and songs were performed by many well-known singers of his day.

Among the many awards and honors Burleigh received was the Spingarn Medal of the National Association for the Advancement of Colored People. Burleigh was a charter member and the first of his

Harry Burleigh

race to serve on the board of directors of the American Society of Composers, Authors, and Publishers.

Location: Pennsylvania State Historical Marker at Burleigh's former home on East Sixth Street, Alternate Pa. Rte. 5

Erie County – North East

During the era of the Underground Railroad, North East, then a town of only a few hundred people, was a jumping off place for escaping slaves seeking passage to Canada by crossing Lake Erie. Many escapees feared the larger neighboring town of Erie because of federal agents who were stationed around the waterfront to watch for escapees.

The former home of Underground Railroad worker Theodore Sprague was an important station. He hid slaves in the basement of the house, located a short distance from the lakefront. According to local tradition, the harbor at North East was called Freeport because it was where escaping slaves found freedom as they were transported on fishing boats to Long Point, Canada.

Erie County – Erie – St. James A.M.E. Church

A Pennsylvania State Historical Marker honors St. James African Methodist Episcopal Church. The marker's inscription reads: *Founded in 1874, this was Erie's oldest African-American congregation. Five of its first six members were women. Originally, at 3rd and German Streets, this church has ministered to the spiritual and social needs of the Erie community.*

Location: 236 East 11th Street

Erie County – Erie – African-Americans in Battle of Erie Maritime Museum

One of the major battles of the War of 1812 against England was fought at Lake Erie. African-American seamen under Commodore Oliver Hazard Perry played vital and heroic roles in the bloody victory. Initially, Commodore Perry objected to the many black sailors. He questioned their qualifications as seamen and as fighting men, even though he had great difficulty getting men.

Perry wrote a letter to a fellow naval officer saying, "The men that came are a motley set of blacks, soldiers and boys. I cannot think you saw them after they were selected. I am, however, pleased to see anything in the shape of a man."

However, he later paid high tribute to their bravery and courage for their participation was critical to victory, and secured a place for African-Americans in the region's history. One of Perry's closest friends was Hannibal Collins, an African-American who commanded Perry's barge on Lake Erie.

Location: Pennsylvania State Historical Marker in front of the Erie Maritime Museum at 150 E. Front Street

Erie County – Erie – Sailing Point for Underground Railroad Escapees

The Stanton House was a station on the Underground Railroad. The foundation walls of the building were built with double thickness and hidden passages for secret tunnels to the water's edge, where restless slaves were quickly placed in boats and transported to Canada. For many of them, Erie was their last view of the United States.

Location: Second and French Streets

McKean County – Smethport – The Medbury House

Formed in 1804 out of Lycoming County and named for Governor Thomas McKean, this county was a stopping place on the ancient Native American trail that crossed the Big Level when traveling south. The trail was once on the main route from Onondaga, the Iroquois capital, to the Ohio River and the Carolinas. Smethport, the county seat, was incorporated in 1853.

Documented evidence points to the Medbury House as an important station on the Underground Railroad. A hiding place for runaway slaves can still be seen in the cellar of this house, which is now a private residence.

Location: 604 East Main Street

Crawford County – New Richmond – John Brown's Tannery

Leading the aggressive abolitionist and Underground Railroad supporters in Crawford County was the legendary John Brown. Although he was born in Torrington, Connecticut, in 1800, everywhere he traveled and lived he was connected with the Underground Railroad. Brown, a deeply religious man and the father of 20 children, did not hesitate to say that slavery was wrong and should be eliminated by any means necessary.

In 1825, Brown and his family moved to Randolph, later called Richmond, in Crawford County, not far from Lake Erie. Located on a side road, a short distance, stands a Pennsylvania State Historical Marker with the following inscribed, *John Brown of Ossawatomie and Harper's Ferry worked here as a tanner 1825-1835, employing as many as fifteen men in producing leather.*

According to oral tradition, the tannery and barn had a trapdoor leading into a partial cellar, where runaway slaves were hidden. His children had memories of his interest in runaway slaves. John Brown, Jr., said that a fugitive and his wife came to the door, sent by a neighbor. His father took them to the woods to hide.

The tannery has been rebuilt on its original location and is operated by the John Brown Heritage Association. The remains of Brown's former home can be seen at this site. His first wife, Dianthe, and son, Frederick, are buried in a cemetery a short distance away from the tannery. The Historic John Brown Museum has opened on an adjoining property.

This last painting of John Brown was by David Bustill Bowser, noted Philadelphia African-American artist.

Location: Township Road (former LR 20118) south of Pa. Rte. 77

Crawford County – Meadville – Richard Henderson Home

Richard Henderson, a friend of John Brown, was probably the most active Underground Railroad agent and conductor in northwestern Pennsylvania. He was born in 1801, in Hagerstown, Maryland, of slave parents. At the age of 15, he and his brothers Edward and Robert and a sister, whose name is not known, ran away from their Maryland slave owner. They followed a branch of the Underground Railroad known as Jefferson's Route.

This route began near the Mason-Dixon Line and extended through Bellefonte, the Grampian Hills, Punxsutawney, Brookville, and points west. Due to difficulties crossing a stream of water, the sister died of pneumonia. Although saddened by the death of their sister, the brothers continued on to safety.

Upon settling in Meadville, Henderson became a barber. His Arch Street house, since torn down, is estimated to have harbored some 500 hundred runaway slaves prior to the Civil War. The Pennsylvania Historical and Museum Commission erected a marker to commemorate Richard Henderson's Underground Railroad activities on June 1, 1980.

> **Location: Pennsylvania State Historical Marker at Liberty and Arch Streets**

Mercer County – Sandy Lake – Freedom Road Cemetery

In Sandy Lake, there stands a Pennsylvania State Historical Marker inscribed: *Freedom Road. In search of freedom, men, women, brought from the south by the Underground Railroad settled near here about 1850 and later, after 1850, most of them went to Canada. The cemetery, still in use, lies a short distance above the road.* The members of the community once called "Liberia" fled in masses due to the enactment of the Fugitive Slave Law of 1850.

Few laws of Congress have ever produced more bitterness and widespread disobedience than this one. No other was held by the people to be so flagrantly unconstitutional. The law of 1850 gave slave hunters or those hunting their escapees the power to organize a posse at any point in the United States to aid them in running down slaves.

It provided for the delivery of fugitive slaves without allowing them a trial by jury. African-Americans in northern cities organized groups armed with weapons to protect their families and friends. Columbia, Lancaster County, lost 487 of its 943 African-Americans. In Philadelphia, the well-respected and normally mild mannered Underground Railroad agent and stationkeeper Robert Purvis declared, "Should any wretched enter my dwelling, any pale faced spectre among ye, to execute this law on me or mine, I'll seek his life, I'll shed his blood."

Hundreds of lawfully free African-Americans were unlawfully shackled and dragged away in slave cuffs to be sold into slavery. Many vowed that they would die before being taken back into slavery.

Location: Pa. Rte. 62, southwest of Sandy Lake

Mercer County – Dr. Charles Everett

Until 1781, Westmoreland County embraced the whole western section of the state. Mercer was one of the counties formed from it, and produced the second-earliest instance of slaveholding, when John Calvin of Salem Township bequeathed a mulatto to his wife in 1804.

Virtually nothing remains of the ill-fated settlement of 61 freed slaves called Pendenarium. Dr. Charles Everett, a wealthy land and slave owner, formerly of Charlottesville, Va., liberated his slaves and arranged for 50 acres of land in Indian Run to be used as a settlement for his former slaves. The land was located in southern Mercer County near East Lackawannock, Springfield, and Wilmington townships. He commissioned the building of a road, homes, wells, and a church on his property in 1854.

This settlement also welcomed runaway slaves. Despite their attempts to maintain Everett's original settlement, by the turn of the 20th century, most of the descendants of this free African-American community had fled to more prosperous communities like Sharon, Farrell, and New Castle. Virtually nothing remains of the settlement today but a few foundation rocks of its former buildings.

Lawrence County – New Castle – The White Homestead and Other Underground Railroad Stationkeepers

Built in 1840 by ardent abolitionist Joseph White, this two-story, brick house was one of the most important stops on the road to freedom. A large Dutch oven and fireplace were constructed to conceal and provide food for exhausted and hungry escaping slaves. St. Paul's Lutheran Church now owns the old home, that is still standing.

J. C. Furnas recounted an interesting incident of aid given to a runaway slave in his book *Goodbye to Uncle Tom*: "When a slave catcher seized on a girl fugitive working in a tavern in New Castle, the landlord's daughter working upstairs heard the girl cry out, rushed down and screamed and beat the intruder with her broom until the wagon maker next door could come and knock him cold. Before the lowly slave catcher regained his consciousness, the girl fugitive was led to safety on the Underground Railroad."

The minister and the congregation of Old Central Presbyterian Church were a station on the Underground Railroad in New Castle. The minister was jailed at one time for harboring slaves. In 1949, the church building was destroyed by fire. In 1950, the property was purchased and the church was renamed Northminster United Presbyterian Church. In New Wilmington, Lawrence County,

Underground Railroad conductor Robert Ramsey, an undertaker and cabinetmaker, transported his passengers concealed in a box.

Other Lawrence County conductors included Judge Mather McKeever, Benjamin Sharpless, Dr. A. G. Hart, Joseph Minch, Alexander Wright, and the Young Family—Donald, John, and William.

Location: 305 N. Jefferson Street

Fayette County – Brownsville – Nemacolin Castle

Fayette County was formed September 26, 1783, from Westmoreland County and named for the Marquis de Lafayette. Among the French and Indian War sites here is Fort Necessity. Uniontown, the county seat, was incorporated in 1796. Located in Fayette County, Brownsville is a small community situated on the slope above the Monongahela River. An anti-slavery society was formed here on August 19, 1826, and an account of the meeting was recorded in the Washington County *Examiner*.

Members of the Bowman family were known abolitionists. Their large, stone house was built in 1786 by Jacob Bowman as a residence and trading post. In 1847, it was renovated and enlarged. Its present location is on the same site as Old Fort Burd. The Bowmans' home was a haven for escaping slaves who stopped in Brownsville. A secret room in the rear of the mansion that is sometime called "Nemacolin Castle" was used as a lookout for approaching slave hunters.

The African-American conductor Howard Wallace wrote in his pamphlet *Historical Sketch*, of the Underground Railroad from Uniontown to Pittsburgh: "The main route from William Wallace was Maple Creek, but sometimes we went by the way of Ginger Hill. When fugitive slaves were taken to Maple Creek, they were kept by George Norris, also the Bowmans from their house to the river someplace near Belle Vernon, where a small settlement of Colored People lived."

Location: Second Avenue and Front Streets

Washington County – Washington – The LeMoyne House

Wealthy Dr. Francis J. LeMoyne, professor at Washington College, led the radical anti-slavery movement in Washington County. LeMoyne was known as "The Fighting Advocate for the Right," and was a founder of the Washington County Anti-Slavery Society. He was a three-time candidate in the 1840s for governor of Pennsylvania on the Liberty (abolitionist) Party ticket.

With the help of his family, he operated a successful Underground Railroad station in the town of Little Washington. His two-story, gray stone structure of Greek Revival design housed numerous runaway slaves. At one time, the family concealed 25 slaves in a secret room on the third floor.

LeMoyne was well acquainted with the Underground Railroad stationmasters in the Washington County towns of Centerville and West Middletown and at Brownsville and Bridgeport, Fayette County. Today, the LeMoyne House is maintained by the Washington County Historical Society, which operates it as a museum that documents the LeMoyne family and information pertaining to the Underground Railroad.

Location: Pennsylvania State Historical Marker at 49 E. Maiden Street

Dr. Francis J. LeMoyne

THE UNDERGROUND RAILROAD

THE UNDERGROUND RAILROAD SEEMS TO EXCITE PEOPLE OF ALL AGES. OVER THE PAST TWO DECADES OR MORE, AMERICANS HAVE WITNESSED A HEALTHY RENEWAL OF INTEREST IN IT. BUT NOTHING GENERATES MORE MISUNDERSTANDING AND DEBATE THAN THE UNDERGROUND RAILROAD BECAUSE OF ITS CLANDESTINE NATURE.

This secret operation was filled with tales of crated escapees, murdered agents, soft knocks on side doors, and complicated routes, codes, passwords, spies, and informers. What we know is a mere fragment of the whole, but is it enough? Ordeals may have gone unrecorded and names may have been forgotten, but such records as have survived are the memoirs of those who risked all for freedom, brotherhood, and sisterhood. It is clear that the flight to freedom on the Underground Railroad was an epic of American heroism, in spite of misconceptions on the topic.

During my years of researching and writing on the subject, I have found that antebellum Pennsylvania was a hub of this nationwide escape network for several historical and geographical reasons. All 67 counties of the commonwealth had a connection with the Underground Railroad. Unlike any other state immediately north of the Mason-Dixon Line, Pennsylvania had an international port at Philadelphia that was a natural meeting point for boats traveling north from Virginia, Maryland, and Delaware.

At this busy port, there was constant traffic of foreigners as well as indigenous African-Americans and whites. Thus, runaway slaves could blend in this atmosphere with relative ease. In the south central region of the state, the Blue Mountains' hazardous and unfamiliar terrain and forest protected escapees from slave hunters. Furthermore, in western Pennsylvania, the Monongahela River was a main waterway from the south to the urban centers of Pittsburgh and Allegheny City. And in the northwest, Erie was a focal point for travel to Canada.

Pennsylvania had a significant number of abolitionists and an aggressive free African-American community, both of which were conducive to activity to aid runaway slaves. Although there was a relatively substantial abolitionist segment in Pennsylvania, many whites among the general state population exhibited attitudes and behavior towards free African-Americans and slaves that were identical with the most staunch antebellum segregationists and racists.

Other white Pennsylvanians were altogether apathetic towards the plight of enslaved African-Americans, who were looked down upon, especially in the southeastern counties. Many prominent businessmen dealt with southern states for goods and therefore did not want to arouse the wrath of their slaveholding clients. Gangs roamed towns and cities in many counties taunting and physically attacking abolitionists and sometimes even burning their property.

White churches on the whole did not participate in the Underground Railroad activities. Many Quakers displayed a paternalistic attitude towards African-Americans. The Quakers have long received credit for being the most active religious group in the Underground Railroad. While their involvement was significant, only a minority of this religious community raised their voices against slav-

ery and participated in the struggles to transport slaves to freedom. On the other hand, most African-American churches offered assistance.

It was also common for leading African-American spokespersons to be ostracized by Quakers when the latter held their social gatherings. The Quakers were not the only religious group or sect who discriminated against African-Americans. This was a common practice in most of the white churches throughout Pennsylvania.

One cannot make the generalization that Pennsylvania was a state that was "friendly" to African-Americans. A more realistic approach is to try to identify the small, yet effective network of individuals and groups in the state who actually aided runaway slaves.

Slaves are too often portrayed as passive victims to be led out of slavery. Recent research reveals that most enslaved escapees risked all they had to escape to freedom. Their routes were many and varied, and they often traveled in disguise through woods and farms by wagon, boat, and train, hiding in stables, caves, attics, churches, and storerooms. They had to flee through secret passages, but the destination they sought was always freedom.

The Underground Railroad is a story of suffering, bravery, secret codes, heroic deeds, treachery, and lofty ideas and ideals. Its coded spirituals became cries for help and pleas for escape, and melodies about freedom. It is a story about the best and worst of humankind. It is a story seldom told. Why did escapees risk death for freedom and how did they make their way out of bondage? The answers to these questions are indispensable to an understanding of the freedom network.

Slavery, known as the "peculiar institution," required unconditional submission. As one planter wrote, "We teach them they are slaves…that to the white face belongs control, and black obedience."

In the south, slavery took deepest root as gangs of unpaid laborers turned vast tracts of cheap land into productive plantations of indigo, rice, cotton, and sugar, destined for foreign markets. Though most southern whites were small farmers working for themselves, the plantation system soon dominated southern politics and traditions.

"For what purpose does the master hold the servant?" asked a southerner in the *Farmer's Journal* in 1853. Answering frankly, "Is it not that by his labor he, the master, may accumulate wealth?"

Slave dealers stood by in southern towns to pay cash for slaves who were standing on auction blocks. These dealers advertised openly that they had slaves of all classes constantly in hand. The subjects, often brought in chains, were washed and groomed for display like prize horses.

Slaves ran away seeking freedom from small towns and cities in the south as well as from plantations. Some ran away from cruel owners to join family members. Some ran away because of crimes committed against their owners, and others wanted to experience life as a free person.

Many enslaved African people in the Deep South fled to Florida to live among the Seminole Indians. Others fled to Mexico or the Caribbean Islands and lived as free persons. Most simply walked to freedom, guided by the North Star.

Underground Railroad chronicler William Still wrote that those who left were "penniless, braving the perils of the land and sea, eluding the keen scent of the bloodhounds as well as the more dangerous pursuit of the savage slave hunters, enduring indescribable suffering from hunger and other privations making their way to freedom."

The discontented and daring hoped that the North Star would guide them to stations on the burgeoning Underground Railroad, which by the early 1830s still didn't have a name. The word spread from plantation to plantation, city to city, town to town, first in whispers and then outright talk: there was a railroad to freedom.

It was a moment of great trepidation when runaways met up with a conductor in the dark who whispered, "Follow me," and then proceeded to guide them on an arduous journey on which they were constantly admonished to keep quiet.

They were disguised in various ways. They were nursed and nursed themselves through long and serious illnesses. They moved on to the next station at night on a moment's notice. When runaway slaves settled down in a free state such as Pennsylvania, it was along the Underground Railroad routes, so they could get away quickly if necessary.

Runaway slaves and their helpers left few traces for fear of jeopardizing other escapees. Invisible though it may have been, the Underground Railroad in Pennsylvania had many subsidiary routes and innumerable sidings and spurs. If the Underground Railroad had a charter and impetus apart from the longing for freedom and the urgings of conscience, it was the Fugitive Slave Law of 1850, which greatly strengthened an earlier law dating from 1793 and gave slaveholders the right to organize a posse at any point in the United States to aid in recapturing runaway slaves. Courts and police everywhere were obligated to assist them. Unlocking the shackles of slaves meant breaking the law—organized theft as southerners called it—yet abolitionists did so eagerly.

The magnitude of the Underground Railroad was immense; people of African descent in the United States have called it the first great American civil rights movement. Each escapee along the Underground Railroad had to find a place in a local, interpersonal ecology; some did in rugged iron forge settings in Berks, Franklin, and Lebanon counties. Others slipped into the larger cities such as Philadelphia, Lancaster, Harrisburg, Pittsburgh, and Erie. Many runaway slaves whose original destination was Canada risked being recaptured by settling in towns and cities such as Gettysburg, Carlisle, Reading, Williamsport, Mercer, Montrose, Meadville, and Waverly.

In each instance, escapees had to possess extremely keen perceptions and intuitions about the motives of those surrounding them and the racial dynamics of the community in which they settled before they became amalgamated into an anonymous mass. Along the way, some people died, and some were captured and returned to slavery. A small number of these courageous escapees went on to take leadership roles in the anti-slavery movement, but most remained anonymous.

In the cities, runaway slaves almost always trusted only African-Americans to protect them. However, on some occasions they were betrayed by informers and spies of their own race and turned over to local authorities or slave hunters for a reward. As a scholar attempting to research the Underground Railroad for many years, I have found with a mixture of admiration and chagrin that the atmosphere of secrecy endures.

So much is uncertain; even the term "Underground Railroad" is obscure. No one knows how many fled from slavery along its invisible tracks in Pennsylvania or elsewhere in the country, because secrecy was crucial. Few records of the railroad's activities survive. In some areas where escaping slaves often traveled and settled, stories or legends of Underground Railroad stations and routes still persist. It is absurd to speculate, to dwell on which house, nook, or cranny might have sheltered runaways slaves on their way towards Canada, the "Promised Land," as they passed through Pennsylvania, often guided by the "Freedom Star," as Harriet Tubman called it.

Most of the agents, conductors, and stationmasters who participated in the clandestine operation destroyed their personal records to protect themselves and the escaping slaves. Of course, there were a few exceptions, such as William Still, the indefatigable worker in the Philadelphia Underground. Still kept rare day-to-day records. One extraordinary aspect of those records is Still's careful listing of escapees' names together with the new name given to them to avoid discovery.

Still turned his record-keeping experience into a book published in 1872 as *Underground Railroad*. Long before freed African-Americans and their white allies officially organized the Underground Railroad during the 1830s and 1840s, many runaway slaves had created their own methods to achieve freedom as early as the 1700s.

Another fact emerged when researching the Underground Railroad in Pennsylvania. African-American churches spread throughout Pennsylvania formed a vital portion of the network of stations for the protection of escaping slaves. Circuit riders, who were traveling preachers, often communicated information about secret underground activities.

Indeed, the most vociferous organizers of the networks to freedom were churchmen and some women. This was because many African-American ministers felt that organized assistance to runaways challenged the prevailing religious dogma of many white churches that a truly religious person was one who was patient.

Philadelphia Underground Railroad Personalities

Philadelphia was a vital junction on the Underground Railroad. Men and women, young and old, from all races, religions, and walks of life kept the "Freedom Train" rolling. Included here are some of Philadelphia's brave and courageous Underground Railroad personalities who gave of themselves for others:

William Still   – agent, major record keeper
Lucretia Mott – Quaker abolitionist, stationkeeper
The Reverend Richard Allen – stationmaster
Jacob Blockson – passenger
Henry "Box" Brown – passenger
Charles and Joseph Bustill – stationmaster, conductor
William and Ellen Craft – passengers
Lear Green – passenger
Isaac Hopper – agent, conductor
Samuel Johnson and family – stationmasters
J. Miller McKim – agent and stationmaster
Robert Purvis – agent and stationmaster
Passmore Williamson – agent

18 - year - old Lear Green was sent from Philadelphia to Elmira, NY, and freedom.

On January 15, 1990, United States Representative Peter H. Kostmayer and Charles L. Blockson held a news conference at Mother Bethel A.M.E. Church in Philadelphia and discussed proposed federal legislation to formally identify and preserve these historic sites and to designate them as part of an Underground Railroad Historic Trail.

Charles L. Blockson

During the same year, Congress passed Public Law 101-628, which recognized the significance of the Underground Railroad to American history. The legislation directed the Secretary of Interior and the National Park Service to conduct a study of the Underground

Railroad. The effort was made largely because of Charles L. Blockson's 30 years of research on the subject and the publication of his article "Escape from Slavery: The Underground Railroad," in the July 1984 *National Geographic*. He was selected as the Chairperson of an Advisory

Committee to examine the historical significance of various sites covering 23 states and territories, including linkage to Canada, Mexico, and the Caribbean Islands. The Advisory Committee's first meeting was held in Independence Hall in Philadelphia.

On July 21, 1998, President William Jefferson Clinton signed the National Underground Railroad Network to Freedom Act into law. Pennsylvania was instrumental in the start of the process for the original proposal.

Philadelphia

Anti-slavery roots were planted and nurtured in Philadelphia many years before the 1800s when the Underground Railroad is believed to have been organized. The flight to freedom in Philadelphia actually began long before the Underground Railroad was known by that name.

George Washington wrote in 1786 about runaway slaves in Philadelphia "which a Society of Quakers in the City (formed for such purposes) have attempted to liberate." Washington, a slave holder himself, was probably referring to the Pennsylvania Abolition Society, which also included among its members at various times such non-Quakers as Benjamin Franklin, Thomas Paine, Dr. Benjamin Rush, and the Marquis de Lafayette. These early white friends of freedom for enslaved African people were all dead when a new breed of fiery abolitionists laid the trackless train known as the Underground Railroad. Yet, it was they who first popularized and lobbied for total abolition in the white community.

Philadelphia's African-American community opened their churches and homes to runaway slaves seeking a place to hide. By the 1830s, many of the African-American clergy in Philadelphia permitted abolitionist and fugitive aid meetings and activities in their buildings, and even joined in these efforts themselves.

The Reverend Walter Proctor, an agent on the Underground

Railroad and pastor of Mother Bethel Church, belonged to the Philadelphia Vigilant Committee. The Reverend Stephen H. Gloucester of the Central Presbyterian Church of Color, Daniel Scott of Union Baptist Church, William Douglass, and Charles L. Gardiner, all had an Underground connection in the City.

Campbell African Methodist Church also established a reputation for helping escaping slaves. The Reverend John T. Moore, pastor of Wesley African Methodist Episcopal Church, offered his church as a temporary headquarters for escaping slaves. Ministers also were instrumental in helping to organize the Free Produce Movement, by which concerned citizens throughout the north were urged to refrain from using the products of slave labor.

John C. Bowers

Even on the Underground Railroad bigotry existed. William Wells Brown, a former slave and celebrated orator and author, said of Philadelphia in 1854; "Color-phobia is more rampant there than in the pro-slavery...city of New York."

Runaway slaves were sometimes banned from entering a conductor's home; some conductors were known to shackle runaways for "control."

It was not until the enactment of the Fugitive Slave Law of 1850 that most white anti-slavery societies began to realize the practical value of helping runaway slaves from the South.

But before that, in August 1837, more militant African-Americans and white abolitionists had created the Philadelphia Vigilant Committee to fund aid to "colored persons in distress." The association elected three African-American officers at its initial meetings: James McCrummell, President; Jacob C. White, Secretary; and James Needham, Treasurer. Also a member was John C. Bowers. On

James Needham was a major agent on the Underground Railroad.

April 16, 1838, the Zoar A.M.E. Church in Northern Liberties held a public meeting to solicit contributions and increase membership for the Vigilant (Fugitive Aid) Association and Committee.

The Vigilance Association, through its Vigilant Committee, assisted destitute slaves with board and room, clothing, medicine, and money. It also informed runaway slaves of their legal rights, gave them legal protection from kidnappers, and frequently prosecuted individuals who had attempted to abduct, sell, or violate the legal rights of free African-Americans. Moreover, it helped runaways set up a permanent home or gave them temporary employment before their departure to Canada.

At any juncture of its history, a majority of the officers in the association were African-American. In 1839, for example, nine of the 16 members of the Vigilant Committee were African-American, including James McCrummell, Jacob C. White, James Needham, James Gibbons, Daniel Colly, J.J.G. Bias, and Shepherd Shay. Others included were William Still, Robert Purvis, Charles H. Bustill, Charles Reason, and Joseph C. Ware.

Underground Railroad lore in Philadelphia provides modern readers with a vast amount of information on William Still and Robert Purvis who, along with his brother Joseph, assisted hundreds of runaway slaves after his young brother's death. Purvis destroyed many of his records of the Vigilant Committee because he feared that its members might be prosecuted or those whom the committee assisted might be recaptured.

William Still wisely hid the committee papers in the loft of a building that stood on the ground of the Lebanon Cemetery. Jacob C. White, another prominent member, and his son, Jacob, Jr., used their home at 100 Old York Road as a station on the Underground. White's office at the Lebanon Cemetery repeatedly served also as a station stop as well as a communication center and distribution point for anti-slavery newspapers. Anti-slavery newspaper members of the Vigilant Committee occasionally sent escapees to League Island, an isolated area of the city surrounded by water, until they could be passed on to the next station.

A few members of the Vigilant Committee lived on or near a street named Pascal Alley. Written accounts state that more runaway slaves were hidden in houses on Pascal Alley than in any other area in Philadelphia. In 1933, a group of Philadelphia African-American bibliophiles and collectors presented a number of documents to the Historical Society of Pennsylvania, including a notebook entitled

Jacob C. White, a prominent entrepreneur and major Underground Railroad agent, managed an African-American cemetery where Railroad records were stored.

251

Minute Book of the Vigilant Committee of Philadelphia. Until 1887, that rare notebook had been in the possession of Jacob C. White, Jr. It was found in the basement of a church about to be demolished.

Association with a few African-American women enhanced the efforts of Philadelphia's anti-slavery and Underground Railroad movement. African-American women in the female branch of the Philadelphia Vigilant Committee included Mary Dutrieulle, Eliza Bias, Hetty Reckless, and Mary Myers.

Philadelphia was the city where several Underground Railroad conductors and passengers received national attention. Harriet Tubman found employment and saved almost every penny she earned for the real work to come. Her own freedom was not enough; she made many perilous journeys leading caravans of slaves to Canada.

Henry "Box" Brown arrived in the city alive after being shipped by train from Virginia. Husband and wife William and Ellen Craft, masquerading as master and slave, arrived from Macon, Georgia. Jane Johnson, a single slave mother, received assistance from the Underground and was delivered to freedom when her owner stopped in the city while on vacation.

Henrietta Bowers Duterte, the first African-American undertaker in Pennsylvania, on several occasions cleverly concealed runaway slaves in caskets. She also led slaves dressed in northern clothes from Philadelphia to freedom.

Hundreds of runaway slaves entered Philadelphia before 1860 and were forwarded to points along the Reading and Pennsylvania Railroads to New York and New England.

Slave hunters and informers were so diligent in guarding the waterfront along the Delaware River, separating the ports of Camden, New Jersey, and Philadelphia, that sometimes escapees and their helpers could not make a safe crossing for days. Several sea captains were involved in this branch of the Underground Railroad.

When Captain William Bayliss' boat docked March 1, 1855, his cargo of escaped slaves was delivered to the Pennsylvania Anti-Slavery Society office. The slaves had been hidden in a schooner piloted by a man identified by William Still only as "Captain B." Other sources indicate the man was William Bayliss.

Bayliss was a frequent transporter of escaped slaves and Still had to protect his friend's identity. Bayliss' schooner was fitted with a false floor under the captain's cabin; the last place a slave hunter would search. However, sometimes corrupted officials and slave hunters seeking rewards for runaway slaves battened down everything on the schooner and smoked out the hull to force escapees out.

Ships out of Charleston, Savannah, and New Orleans usually were given closer inspections when they arrived in Philadelphia because they often were suspected of carrying runaway slaves. Sea captains sailing out of Philadelphia after the Civil War admitted smuggling slaves as part of their regular business, charging them $30 to $120 each.

Montgomery, Bucks, Chester, and Delaware Counties

When runaway slaves appeared at many stations in Montgomery County, they were hidden until it could be determined whether they were being followed closely and by whom. Many of them were received sympathetically in the Quaker community in Plymouth Meeting and in Norristown's African-American community.

Although there were African-American towns, the major participation was in Norristown. Though abused, insulted, and threatened by mobs, residents there held to their convictions. So strong was the faith among the residents of Norristown's African-American community that a number of runaways remained there. Among these were John and Jane Lewis, who organized the Mt. Zion A.M.E. Church in 1844. The church became an important stop on the freedom network.

The history of the Underground Railroad in Montgomery County also cannot be told without mentioning Dan Ross, an African-American Underground Railroad agent who was connected with the

253

Quaker Corson family of Plymouth Meeting. Agent Dr. Hiram Corson stated: "When fugitives had reached Norristown, they were rested and cared for; the Abolition members notified of the fact. The next step was to send for 'Old Dan' to have his counsel. They were generally taken to his home and kept until arrangements were made to forward the fugitives to Canada."

Ross lived in a spacious two-and-a-half-story frame house at Green and Jacoby Streets. For 20 years, he and his wife used their home as a station on the Underground Railroad.

Joseph H. Smith says in his article "Some Aspects of the Underground Railroad in the Counties of Southeastern Pennsylvania" that, "a great many slaves came from Wilmington and the southwestern part of Chester County on their way north. Numbers of these later passed through Kimberton, Corner Stores, by Elijah Pennypacker, and were sent across the Schuylkill River at Phoenixville by the bridge near the short-ford into the upper end of Montgomery County. Others were switched backward from the Lewis Peart farm, after 1844, nearer Valley Forge, to Charles Adamson's at Corner Stores, or into James Wood at Moore Hall, were taken across the long-ford to Port Providence in canoes, and were passed through the hands of Abel Fitzwater. William W. Taylor of Upper Providence Township directed his passengers from a concealment under a bridge of his barn to stationmaster Thomas Hopking's place west of Arcola."

Thomas and Hanna Atkinson, ardent abolitionists formerly of Warwick Township, Bucks County, assisted fugitives on this route after they moved to Upper Dublin Township in 1849. They were regular contributors to the anti-slavery fair in Philadelphia and attended all of the anti-slavery meetings within reach. The Atkinsons often entertained speakers and distributed *Uncle Tom's Cabin* and other anti-slavery literature.

They were part of a group that consisted of Thomas and Mary Lightfoot, Charles and Agnes Paxon, and Marianne Comly, all of Upper Dublin. John and Martha Shoemaker, also of Upper Dublin, warmly favored the cause but did not take as active a part as Isaac Conrad did.

The home of Benjamin Harry in Conshohocken was a minor station en route to the Corsons' at Plymouth Meeting. From Plymouth Meeting, slaves were sent to the Norristown stations or to William Foulke's near Penllyn. The next stop was the home of Richard Moore in Quakertown, Bucks County, or the Buckingham Meetinghouse.

The Isaac Michener home near Pittsville on the Limekiln Pike was a station in the route running northwest and passing near Limekiln Pike through Jarretown. Providence Meetinghouse near Yerkes also was a gathering place for abolitionists. Another known station on this route was the home of Seth Lukens, who lived on old Forty-Foot Road near Lansdale. Seth Lukens, father of George Lukens of Towamencin Township, was a Mennonite and one of the earliest abolitionists in Montgomery County. The Lukens station dates as early as the 1820s, and slaves reportedly were hidden in a well near the house. Lukens' co-workers in the network were James Harner of Skippack and Charles T. Jenkins of Hatfield. They worked with conductors from Penllyn, Gwynedd, and Plymouth Meeting.

Abolitionist Peter Dager had a huge home at the crossroads of Spring Mill Road and Ridge Pike, Whitemarsh Township, where he often housed fugitive slaves. One day in 1829, John Lewis' owner found him in Dager's stable. Shortly thereafter, Lewis' brother Westley was captured in the same place. Both slaves were tied up and taken by wagon to a magistrate four miles away in Norristown, where they were awarded to their southern master.

Dager, however, had summoned a friend, Ezra Comfort, and the two hurried to the magistrate to buy the men from their owners. Dager bought John Lewis and his freedom for $600, and Comfort bought Westley for $300.

John P. Rutter, Henry Potts, Jesse Ives, Joseph Neide, and John Titlow operated stations in Pottstown. The Potts were all abolitionists and Pottstown offered no sympathy or protection for slave hunters. Due to the vigilance of the brave group of abolitionists there, no slave arrest occurred in this part of the county.

Located between Pottstown and Pine Forge, Berks County,

was a section known as "Knock on Any Door." The Underground Railroad grapevine told fugitives that if they reached that area, they could knock on any door to find refuge. The residents of Knock on Any Door did not reflect the sentiments of everyone in that region.

Underground Railroad stationkeepers were in constant fear that someone would inform on them if runaways were seen about the house. Runaways were warned not to go near the windows. Foreign to the customs of northern cities and towns, and only partially acquainted with free African-Americans, runaways frequently betrayed themselves by leaving their hiding places. Their inquisitiveness and general lack of familiarity with their surroundings showed unmistakably that they had but recently traveled on the Underground Railroad. For this reason, slaves were quickly forwarded to safety, and did not remain in areas where spies dotted the streets, docks, and highways.

African-American agents and conductors in Norristown were William Lewis; John Augusta, a barber; and Benjamin Johnson, who escaped from Virginia by way of Harrisburg and was directed to Norristown. Usually escapees were concealed in the basement of an old paint shop located on the south side of Church Street, between Marshall and Chestnut Streets. William Parker, the subject of a national manhunt, was sheltered in the shop for a short period as he fled in 1851 from the Christiana Riot in Lancaster County.

Montgomery County had a number of prominent Underground Railroad conductors and safehouse-keepers including Lucretia and James Mott, George and Seth Lukens, Dr. Charles Shoemaker, David Newport, Thomas and Hanna Atkinson, William Foulke, Charles Todd Jenkins, John Rutter, Peter Dager, Morris Hallowell, Croasdale Twining, and John Kenderdine. Most citizens of this county maintained a "laissez-faire" attitude about slavery and would not make any great effort to help them.

Hundreds of runaway slaves and free African-American Underground Railroad workers were familiar with a secret organization known as the African Mysteries, which was based on Masonic symbols and rituals. The following dialogue is an example of a test

Manor House at Pine Forge, an important Underground Railroad station

given by members of the Philadelphia Vigilant Committee and other agents throughout the country to identify imposters:

Agent: *Have you ever been on the railroad?*
Runaway: *I have been a short distance.*
Agent: *Where did you start from?*
Runaway: *A place called safety.*
Agent: *Have you a brother there? I think I know him.*
Runaway: *I know you now. You traveled the road.*

Enslaved Africans developed codes, riddles, passwords, hand-shakes, and rituals to help each other learn the ways of the Underground Railroad. Slaves also used coded spirituals that were completely foreign to whites. Songs became cries for help and pleas for escape. For example, "Steal Away to Jesus," used Jesus as an open invitation for slaves to steal away to freedom. These coded spirituals conveyed every hidden signal imaginable. "Follow the Drinking Gourd," was a code word for the North Star, which is found from the Big Dipper constellation, a fact that most slaves knew.

Runaway slaves were sometimes told to look for weather vanes pointed in a certain direction. Conductors and agents would sometimes use coded words for passengers such as boxes, bales of black wool, and parcels; small parcels were children and large parcels were adults.

Bucks County had three main centers of Underground Railroad activity: Quakertown, in the northern section, Buckingham, and Bensalem Township. The most active station in upper Bucks County was the home of Quaker Richard Moore.

Working with the Reverend Benjamin Jones, pastor of Mount Gilead African Methodist Church in Buckingham, African-American conductor Amos Webber, who was born in Attleborough, Bucks County, received numerous runaway slaves in his home.

Webber also worked with the Philadelphia Vigilant Committee. The home of Charles W. Pierce was an important station in Bristol. He kept a secret room above the linen closet on the second floor. Charles Kirk, a Warminster Quaker, had a home that was used in conjunction with other conductors in the county whose families included Burgess, Longshore Palmer, Swain, Schofield Linton, Beance, Janney, Simpson, Buckman, Doan, Smith (Benjamin and Jonathan), and the Hamptons.

There were several stations in Perkasie and in Doylestown, the county seat, also in Pennsville and Wrightstown. Runaway slaves were sent to Elijah Pennypacker and his neighbors from the south central Pennsylvania counties of Adams, York, and Franklin. Emnor Kimber, one of his Underground Railroad co-workers, harbored numerous runaways in a boarding school for girls he founded in 1817 known as Kimber Hall.

Graceanna Lewis

Frequently, professional slave hunters visited Sunnyside Farmhouse, the home of Graceanna Lewis and her sisters, looking for runaway slaves. Looking at Graceanna, no casual observer would have suspected her as the operator of one of the most important stations in Chester County.

The Lewis sisters shared their underground activities with their neighbor Elijah Pennypacker. In 1851, while law officers throughout the nation were looking for William Parker, who was involved in the Christiana Resistance in Lancaster County, he hid for a short time at Sunnyside.

Nearly every village and town in Chester County was connected with the Underground. It was a county with pro-slavery sympathizers and zealous abolitionists. In West Chester, African-American stationmaster Abraham Shadd and his family home were an important station. Most of the members of West Chester's African-American community were connected with the freedom network as well as the members of the Longwood Progressive Friends Meetinghouse in Kennett Square.

The road to freedom passed through the communities of Oxford, West Grove, Paoli, Downingtown, Coatesville, Malvern, and Chadds Ford.

Dr. Horace Mann Bond, the first African-American president of Lincoln University, says in his book *Education for Freedom: A History of Lincoln University*, "The big brick house painted white is still visible two miles east of Lincoln from U.S. highway 1 as one approaches the campus from Philadelphia. The house had been built by Charles Hambleton and served as a station on the Underground Railroad. The big house had sheltered Harriet Tubman, Sojourner Truth, Frederick Douglass, Lucretia Mott, William Lloyd Garrison, and other anti-slavery lecturers. Adjoining its root cellar was a 'secret place' where hundreds of runaway slaves had been concealed. The Hambletons were instrumental in establishing an anti-slavery society at nearby Homeville, in 1821."

Chester County had another important agent—Abraham Shadd of West Chester. A prominent black businessman, Shadd and three other black Pennsylvanians—John Peck, John B. Vashon, and Stephen Smith—sold subscriptions for the New York-based newspaper *The Emancipator*. Mary Ann, Shadd's attractive, outspoken daughter, probably became the first woman in North America to establish and edit a weekly newspaper, *The Provincial Freedman*. When the entire Shadd family moved to Canada after passage of the Fugitive Slave Act of 1850, the newspaper provided news of blacks who were in refugee camps in Canada.

The work of assisting runaway slaves was popular in the small cohesive black community of West Chester, where homes and churches became stations on the Underground Railroad. The most renowned West Chester citizen was conductor John Price. A short account of his life was published in a local paper on March 3, 1890. It said that John Price, a colored man, furnished a reporter with some interesting reminiscences of the Underground Railroad, in which he was an active member.

An old African-American named Davey Moore who sold

peaches, fish, and other produce in Wilmington and around the neighborhood of Kennett Square was an important link from Delaware into Chester County. He connected with Thomas Garrett and Dr. Bartholomew Fussell. Moore made daily trips between Wilmington and Kennett Square to sell his goods, and often was accompanied by other blacks who carried goods. He thus was able to conduct many

Thomas Garrett: "Among the manliest of men and the gentlest of spirits," wrote William Lloyd Garrison about Garrett, who aided hundreds of slaves to Freedom.

fugitives disguised as workers over the Pennsylvania boundary to Kennett Square.

The home of Anna Preston was an important station for the Underground Railroad in Kennett Square. She was one of the members of the first graduating class (1851) of the Women's Medical College. Dr. Preston once dressed a runaway slave in Quaker clothes and drove her in a horse-drawn buggy towards Oxford. They met a group of slave hunters who did not stop them, thinking that they were both Quakers.

Two well-known pottery-making families of Kennett Square were conductors. Both Mahlan Brosius and John Vickers are given the sobriquet "Quaker potter, abolitionist." The Vickers family hid slaves in the straw covering their pottery ware and moved them on to the next station.

In another neighborhood, Isaac and Dinah Mendenhall helped several hundred slaves escape over a 34-year period. Their neighbors, Allen and Maria Agnew, Chandler and Hannah Darlington, and Samuel Pennock also played a prominent role in operating the train of freedom.

In Kennett Square, a short distance from West Chester, stood the two-story frame house of James Walker, a freed black who operated a station on South Union Street. Walker forwarded many fugitives sent from Wilmington by Thomas Garrett. Harriet Tubman, the celebrated "Moses" of the Railroad, lived and worked in the Kennett area, staying long enough to earn money to help finance some of her trips into Maryland.

Moore Hall was one of the main stations on the Underground Railroad in Kimberton. It had 10 slave stalls, each about three feet wide. An iron chain was stapled to the floor in each one. The stationmaster here locked in his fugitives because he thought they would panic from fear.

Stationmasters Norris Maris and Emmor Hunter helped Graceanna Lewis in the Kimberton area. Graceanna Lewis and her sisters Mariann and Elizabeth operated one of the most famous stations in the county on their Kimberton farm. They, like others who helped runaways, often could trick slave hunters with their charm. Their old farmhouse that still stands was visited frequently by professionals slave hunters in search of runaways. Graceanna would permit them to search the farm and every room in her home but her bedroom, which is where she hid fugitives. When one curious slave catcher attempted to enter that room she said, "No gentleman would peer into a lady's bedroom. Surely you gentlemen agree." The slave catchers left.

At Phoenixville, the home and drugstore of Elijah Pennypacker, a fearless conductor on the Underground Railroad, were regularly used as stations. Pennypacker was interested in all moral and political subjects, and especially in slavery, on which he lectured with great fervor. William Still wrote, "His home near Phoenixville, Chester County, was an important station on the Underground Railroad, the majority of fugitives proceeding through the southern rural districts of eastern Pennsylvania, passing through his hands."

Pennypacker and his wife Hannah forwarded many slaves to his co-worker Lewis Peart in Valley Forge. Peart hid the runaways in a secret room in his house. Pennypacker sent this message to William Still in the summer of 1857; it gives evidence of the large number of fugitives stopping at his station: "Respected friend, there are three colored friends at my house now who will reach the city by the Philadelphia and Reading train this evening. Please meet them. We have within the past two months passed forty-three through our hands, transported them to Norristown in our conveyance."

Delaware County

Delaware County did not have the heavy concentration of Underground Railroad stations that was found in neighboring Chester and Montgomery counties. From the region adjacent to Wilmington, Delaware, and north through Chester and Delaware Counties, the main route in this county ran along West Chester Pike from

Philadelphia to West Chester and Phoenixville.

Some stations were operated in Upper Darby, Manor, Darby, Media, Swarthmore, Newtown Square, and the crossroads settlement known today as Broomall. The City of Chester was often the first stop for runaway slaves coming from the State of Delaware and the Chesapeake Bay area.

On March 5, 1857, Chester was the scene of a bloody battle between 12 runaway slaves and 10 slave hunters. The runaways turned on their pursuers and fought until the slave hunters retreated. The runaway slaves then escaped into Knowles Pine Forest aided by abolitionists from Philadelphia.

Some Underground Railroad conductors would often appear to be carrying out normal business affairs, but were actually transporting runaway slaves. Hannah Marsh of Chester County often took garden produce to the Philadelphia and Chester markets. She sometimes used her covered market wagon, even in the daytime, to carry escapees without detection.

James Dannaker often forwarded his passengers to Philadelphia to the Arch Street wharf, where a sea captain named Whildon would transport slaves in a small horse-driven wagon to Bordentown and Trenton, New Jersey.

Runaway slaves entering Delaware County also received assistance from Quaker families in Darby—the Buntings and Jacksons.

Members of the Honeycomb A.M.E. Church in Lima also assisted runaways who crossed their path, most of whom were using the route from Wilmington, Delaware, forwarding them into Philadelphia.

Lancaster, Dauphin, Berks, and York Counties

According to my research and the research of Charles D. Spotts, author of the pamphlet *The Pilgrim Pathway* on the Underground Railroad in Lancaster County, three main

Underground routes passed through the county. Christiana was the main center for escapees from Maryland and Virginia. Other runaway slaves came from Franklin, Adams, and York Counties, and entered Lancaster County at Columbia.

The second route ran from Baltimore and moved along the banks of the Susquehanna River at Peach Bottom, where African-American conductors met the passengers. A third route traveled along the Susquehanna River to the mouth of the Octorara Creek near the Maryland border.

William Whipper, who lived in Columbia, wrote: "My house was at the end of the bridge and as I kept the station, I was frequently called up in the night to take charge of the passengers. On their arrival, they were generally penniless and hungry. I have received hundreds in that condition, fed and sheltered from one to 17 at one time in a single night. Some went to Pittsburgh by boat, others in cars to Philadelphia. Until the passage of the Fugitive Slave Law in 1850, many remained in Columbia to work in the lumber and coal yards."

Numerous Quakers and a few Amish and Mennonites living in the Columbia area and southern Lancaster County assisted the slaves in their travels. These supporters most often rallied in the Gap and Christiana areas in eastern Lancaster County. Many fugitive slaves stayed here rather than move on. It is thought they came to that area from the western shore of Maryland and Delaware, as well as from southern Maryland and Virginia.

Wealthy abolitionist William Whipper

Anti-slavery activity in Lancaster County was such that William Lloyd Garrison's newspaper *The Liberator* had correspondents in Columbia. The town was known to confront any slave hunters who were bold enough to enter the community seeking runaway slaves. On one occasion, citizens fell upon Isaac Brooks, a slave hunter, dragged him through deep snow, stripped him, and beat him with hickory sticks.

With the passage of the Fugitive Slave Law of 1850, it is reported that nearly 500 of the 942 African-Americans who lived in the Columbia area left for other northern U.S. towns and Canada. An incident that occurred in Columbia illustrates the oppressive effects of the Fugitive Slave Law.

William Smith, a slave who had escaped long before 1850, lived in Columbia, where he was a respected and industrious member of the community. When he was at work one day, he noticed a group of men approaching and, suspecting they were slave hunters, began to run. Smith was fatally wounded by the hunters as they tried to capture him.

Most runaway slaves leaving Columbia, including Mary Epps, initially followed the Susquehanna River by foot or wagon. Later, some were able to catch a northbound train in Harrisburg, about 30 miles away. The train took them to Elmira, New York, a major Underground Railroad entry point in that state.

Mary Epps' journey began on the docks in Richmond, Virginia. Historical documents indicate that she boarded a Northern Central train in Elmira with at least two other escapees. After arriving in Niagara Falls, the train crossed a suspension bridge into Canada, eventually stopping in St. Catherine.

In a letter to William Still in Philadelphia, Epps reported that she was living in Toronto, where British law protected runaway slaves. She signed her new name, Mary Brown. Runaway slaves from Frederick, Maryland, and Winchester, Virginia, as well as from areas farther south, traveled through Franklin, Adams, and York counties in Pennsylvania to William Wright's home on south Second Street in Columbia. The house still stands with its backyard slopes through woods hugging the river.

Dauphin County

The city of Harrisburg was an important terminal on Pennsylvania's Underground Railroad. In 1847, Harrisburg's African-American community had expanded to nearly 800 citizens. In August

Frederick Douglass, as a young man

1847, abolitionists William Lloyd Garrison and Frederick Douglass spoke at the Wesley A.M.E. Church without interruption. However, Douglass was attacked by catcalls and pelted with rotten eggs and several firecrackers were exploded when he spoke before a predominantly white audience at another location.

William Jones, the African-American pastor of Wesley A.M.E. Church, was one of Harrisburg's leading agents on the Underground. For many years, Jones was one of the most efficient men connected with the Underground Railroad in the city. He acquired a thorough knowledge of the routes leading northward, and would always provide competent guides.

Jones owned two horses and a large covered wagon in which he took fugitives with a load of rags. He often worked with local stationmasters such as Dr. William Rutherford, who lived at 11 South Front Street. He was assisted by his next-door neighbor, Wilson Kelker. The McClintock family also participated in assisting and hiding escapees. Mary Ann and her sister were among a small group of women who organized the Philadelphia Female Anti-Slavery Society, on December 9, 1833.

A noted station in Harrisburg was a restaurant operated by the African-American family of George and Jane Chester. Perhaps the most active Underground agent in the city was Joseph C. Bustill, while he taught school in Harrisburg. He often forwarded escapees to his brothers Charles and James, William Still, and other prominent African-American conductors and agents.

Bustill, along with other members of Harrisburg's African-American community such as the Reverend William Jones, George Chester, and Abraham Lewis, harbored numerous weary and hungry escapees in Tanner's Alley, an important section in Harrisburg. The congregations of two other African-American churches also were active in Harrisburg's Underground Railroad.

A grandson of Dr. William Rutherford revealed in 1928 that graves of two fugitive slaves could be found near Harrisburg on the north side of the mountain north of Linglestown. One of the small gravestones was placed for an unknown slave in 1858 and reads: *"Here in the solitude of God's acres lies one whose life was filled with pathos and suffering and who had a tragic end. He took the North Star as a guide to liberty, yet in a fitful moment in fear of betrayal he took the deadly cup to save himself from bondage by his fellow man. Erected by C. H. Smith, M.D."*

Berks County

Slave ownership throughout Berks County died out in the early decades of the 19th century. The county was the scene of substantial Underground Railroad activities. About 1835, Berks County started receiving significant numbers of runaway slaves led by conductors in Chester, Lancaster, and Montgomery Counties.

Elizabeth Scarlet, a Quaker widow, and her son, Joseph, operated a well-known station in Robeson Township near Birdsboro. Their home, "The Forrest," was in a remote region safe from slave hunters. Later, while he was living in Lancaster County, Joseph Scarlet was indicted for participating in the Christiana Riot of 1851.

In Christiana, Scarlet operated under the name "Abolitionist Jim Shadbury." Along this dangerous route waited a notorious group of kidnappers known as the "Gap Gang," who terrorized the community as well as adventurous travelers. William Padgett, an itinerant repairer of clocks, visited homes and farms pretending that he was looking for work, when actually he was seeking to expose runaways.

Padgett, a light-skinned black, reported to the gangs those citizens harboring fugitive slaves. Runaways here were sometimes hunted down with clubs, chains, whips, and guns. Paid slave hunters cared little whether their victims were freed blacks or runaways. Freedom papers were taken from blacks and burned publicly, and captives were whipped and sent south without trial.

Northern Tier Counties

McKean, Potter, Tioga, Bradford, Susquehanna Wayne, Pike, Forest, Elk, Cameron, Clinton, Clarion, Lycoming, Sullivan, Luzerne, Lackawanna, Carbon, Lehigh, Northampton, Schuylkill, Monroe, and Wyoming

The natural area of northeast Pennsylvania is dominated by the Delaware River, Susquehanna River, and the Pocono Mountains, which provide resort areas that make it possible for tourism to succeed. This area of the commonwealth is the least populated. It is heavily wooded, more given over to nature than to industry or farming or cities.

Deer and bear hunting, fishing, lodging, and the like provide what prosperity there is. Scranton and Wilkes-Barre, for a time when coal mining waned, suffered some lasting ghost town effects. Bethlehem, founded by the Moravians, spewed out steel for industry all over the country for many decades.

Counties in this Northern Tier such as McKean, Potter, Tioga, Bradford, and Susquehanna share a border with New York State and are the least populated by either African-Americans or whites. During the revolution in France and Haiti, refugees who arrived in Bradford County formed the settlement of Azilum, which endured for a time.

Meanwhile, in Monroe County, Dr. Syndenham Walter, a prominent white abolitionist, supported a small community of freed African-Americans. Travelers looking for historical data and monuments of African-Americans will find little evidence in Elk County. If oral tradition is to be credited, we can learn from one account that Bill Green was the first man to be buried in a Ridgway Cemetery. Green, an African-American, was killed by a falling tree.

The *Elk County Advocate* newspaper reported August 13, 1853: "A colored lady passed through here on Wednesday last, on her way to Canada. She was on Foot, refused bread and would not say where she was from or where she was going. She was probably insane." (It was later ascertained that she was a runaway slave, who had been sent through the area by members of the Underground Railroad.)

In Clinton County, operators George R. Bliss, Thomas Curtis, and Howard Malcolm were connected with the Underground Railroad.

Central Counties

Indiana, Jefferson, Clinton, Armstrong, Clearfield, Cambria, Clarion, Cameron, Huntingdon, Mifflin, Juniata, Centre, Snyder, Union, Montour, Columbia, Northumberland, and Forest

Runaway slaves who traveled the rugged country roads received aid from several anti-slavery families in the area of Indiana, located in the county with the same name. Although other families were extremely hostile to runaways, there were enthusiastic conductors, including Dr. Robert Mitchell and his son, Robert Jr., James Hamilton, William Banks, and James Moorhead, editor of the *Clarion of Freedom*, an anti-slavery newspaper.

Escaping slaves used the Mitchell Farm, located nine miles east of Indiana. Mitchell directed his tenant, John Shields, to permit runaways to occupy a small cabin on the property and to supply them with bedding, cooking utensils, and other necessities. Mitchell also provided them with temporary employment.

In 1847, Mitchell was forced by Judge Robert C. Grier, who presided over the United States Circuit Court in Pittsburgh, to sell a large portion of his pine forest to defray the expense of a court fine for harboring a runaway slave. However, his anti-slavery convictions remained as strong as ever in securing slaves' freedom while working on the Underground Railroad.

Albert Hazlett was another active agent and conductor on the Underground Railroad in Indiana County. He later joined John Brown's group of Emancipators at Harper's Ferry in 1859. Freedom-seeking slaves who traveled the rugged and fragmented route of the Underground in Clarion, Jefferson, and Forest counties were protected by hills, forests, and valleys covered with pine, hemlock, and oak trees.

There were two routes in Clarion County. The main one was across the southwestern section of the county, with four known stations, two of which were in the Rimersburg area, one in the south and the other north. There are a number of conflicting claims as to the exact location of these stations today. The second route, which was further east, followed the old Venango-Chinklamoose Native American trail north out of the county, while runaways were led into Armstrong County at Dayton. The Reverend John Hindman, a Seceder minister near Dayton, received and forwarded his passengers to William Blair of Potter Township.

Blair in turn sent them on to the Reverend John McAuley, another Seceder clergyman in Rimersburg. A third dedicated stationmaster was a minister named Fogle at Summerville, who hid runaways in tannery vats at Welsh Run. It appears that a majority of active abolitionists in this county belonged to the Seceder denomination, a sect whose members were noted as men of strong and decided views and resolute in carrying out their principles.

James Fulton, who lived north of Rimersburg, after feeding and harboring his passengers, delivered them by wagon to Benjamin Gardner, in Locking Township, three miles north of Callensburg. Another dedicated Underground stationmaster, Elihu Chadwick in Rockland Township, concealed his passengers in a large barn designed to receive runaway slaves. When it was safe, he transported them to Franklin, 25 miles away, to a bridge, where they were met by another conductor, who guided them to permanent safety.

Clearfield County witnessed substantial Underground Railroad activity. Runaway slaves were passed through Brady Township and Grampian Hills (Penn Township). A Clearfield County historian wrote that during the late 1840s, an escaped slave who worked for Anthony Hile on the Susquehanna River near Lumber City decided to go to Canada.

He left Hile one night, taking with him one of Hile's best horses. When he reached Coal Hill, the runaway discovered that slave hunters were close at hand. He tied the horse to the fence near the edge of the woods and property of Amos Bonsall and hid in the woods. A few nights later, he stole a horse from Godfrey Zillox, traveled into Jefferson County, left the horse and made good his escape.

Another Underground stationmaster who lived on the Clearfield and Cambria County borders was George Atcheson of Burnside. He had a secret room built where he would shelter six to eight runaway slaves. Atcheson purchased land on both banks of the river where he could transport fleeing slaves.

With his brother William, he forwarded passengers to conductors in Indiana, Jefferson, and Armstrong Counties. Other known conductors in Clearfield County included Isaac Cochran, James Gallakery, William Westover, and Jason Kirk and his sons.

Lewistown, Mifflin County, was the central rendezvous point in central Pennsylvania. Written accounts reveal the dedication of African-Americans and a few white citizens in restraining slave hunters, by force when necessary, until runaway slaves could be safely hidden or moved along to other areas.

The African-American population in Lewistown began to swell with runaway slaves during the 1840s and 1850s. Even though they settled in a free state, they were still slaves in the eyes of the slave hunters and subject to recapture and return to bondage. The famous slave Charles Ball was harbored at Lewistown.

Ball was an escaped slave who was the subject of an important anti-slavery book, *A Narrative of the Life and Adventure of Charles Ball: A Black Man*, published in 1836 and reprinted in a new form with the title *Fifty Years in Chains or The Life of an American Slave*. In his narrative, Ball traces his life as a slave in South Carolina, Georgia, and Maryland, and as a runaway escaping on the Underground Railroad to Lewistown.

His slave name was Richard Barnes; he lived in Lewistown the rest of his life to be more than 100 years old. Living also in Lewistown during this period was the Reverend William Grimes, an African-

American Underground Railroad agent who was pastor of a Lewistown African-American church.

Grimes traveled as a circuit rider minister who made a regular tour around an assigned territory, often serving the congregations of two or more churches. He delivered information pertaining to the Underground while visiting various communities in Centre, Huntingdon, Juniata, and Blair Counties.

Centre County has a rich heritage of social activism and African-Americans played a leading role in that history. Due to a strong anti-slavery influence in Bellefonte among a small group of Quakers and other concerned citizens, many runaway slaves settled in Centre County.

One Centre County historian wrote: "Tradition states that The Linn House in Bellefonte was a famous stop on the Underground Railroad for runaway slaves. A secret compartment on the third floor is generally attributed to the place where they were hidden en route to Canada." The Linn House still stands today.

Centre County residents Rush Petrikin and William Robinson were known for their abolitionist views and were station-masters in Patton Township. Apparently an ill-defined route led from Centre County into Clinton County and northwest towards Erie County. A small number of slaves escaping through Centre County risked being recaptured and settled in Philipsburg, a small town located in a scenic region underlain with bituminous coal. Many runaway slaves who settled in Centre County were assisted in Half Moon, a Quaker community.

Perhaps the most often noted Underground Railroad operator in Blair County was William Nesbit. For a short period, Nesbit resided in Altoona, before moving to Chimney Rock, an African-American area in Hollidaysburg. The Reverend James Graham of the African Methodist Episcopal Zion Church of Hollidaysburg was a known agent on the Underground Railroad and assisted William Nesbit and Daniel Williams, a local barber and the father of Daniel Hale Williams, who performed the world's first successful heart operation.

A local traditional story reveals that an Underground Railroad incident occurred in the Hollidaysburg area in 1855. A slave ran away from his owner, James Parsons, in Virginia. The slave arrived in Hollidaysburg on his way to Canada, but was closely followed by Parsons who entered the same old Portage Railroad car.

Parsons caught the escapee at Gaysport. The incident provoked excitement. Concerned white citizens and the entire African-American community were aroused. They immediately came to the aid of the escapee under the leadership of Sidney Carr, an African-American barber. However, the unfortunate escapee was arrested and transported to Virginia.

Blair County neighbor Huntingdon County received numerous runaway slaves traveling on the "Freedom Train." Many remained and settled in a secluded area known as "Black Log Valley." This isolated community was renamed "Black Valley" because of the African-Americans in the area.

The small community of Mt. Union was a sub-station where runaways sometimes made their homes instead of following the Underground to distant points north.

In Cambria County, the main route of the Underground led from old Conemaugh Path through Pleasantville, Elton, and to an area now called Windber.

Another route transported passengers from Claysburg over the mountains into Beaverdale, then over the Blue Knob Mountain area, and finally into Elton and Geistown. Other runaway slaves were brought to Ebensburg, cared for, and forwarded to Harts Sleeping Place, through Cherry Tree, and north to Canada. Cambria County conductors and stationkeepers concealed their passengers by various methods. Some were hidden in wagons carrying corn shocks, others in apple carts. Runaways often received aid in Johnstown, hiding in churches and homes in the free African-American Community.

Among the known, documented conductors and stationkeepers in Cambria County are: William H. Rosensteel, Abraham Barker, John Cushon, James Heeslop, William Slick, Henry Wills, John

Myers, Wallace Fortune, Isaac Weatherington, Frederick Kaylor, Dr. George Gamble, George Atchinson, and John Manion. There is little documentation of Underground Railroad activities for Northumberland, Forest, Snyder, Union, Sullivan, and Wyoming counties. However, Underground Railroad conductors and station-keepers in the towns and cities of Emporium, Lewisburg, Selinsgrove, Kittanning, and Milton received passengers from co-workers in Schuylkill, Montour, and Luzerne Counties. The first recorded evidence of befriending a fugitive slave in Wilkes-Barre occurred in 1859. A fugitive threw himself into the river to avoid capture. One of his ears had been shot off and he was left for dead. After his former owner left, he was spirited away to safety by a group of abolitionist friends.

The case of fugitive slave William Thomas involved the rights of a free black man. Thomas became the subject of national attention when slave hunters attempted to kidnap him in 1853.

The General Vigilance Committee met in Philadelphia to consider the case. Members of the committee said that if the state government permitted the Fugitive State Law of 1850 to be enforced, the safety of every free black would be endangered. The black members of the committee raised $150 for the prosecution of the kidnappers. The courts ruled that Thomas was, indeed, a free man.

The Rev. William C. Gildersleeve, a local minister and prominent abolitionist, immersed himself in the Underground Railroad movement. He once was tarred and feathered for his clandestine activities. Another time, Gildersleeve was tried and sentenced to serve time in a Philadelphia prison for helping an escapee. His case attracted national attention. Judge William Jessup, known for his anti-slavery views, reportedly protected all fugitives presented before him.

Documented evidence points to the fact that Clinton County was involved in the Underground Railroad. Located in the interior of the western part of the county was the small community of West Keating. During the years before the Civil War, this small village surrounded by mountains was a haven for runaway slaves.

According to local tradition, there were about 20 African-

American families who offered help to fleeing runaways. Slaves who didn't feel threatened remained in the town and lived openly among the citizens. Throughout the years, several homes in Lock Haven are reported to have welcomed and sheltered runaways. One site is located at Lock Haven University.

There is little available documentation on the Underground Railroad in Wyoming and Carbon counties. However, Jonathan Drake and Nicholas Overfield were operators in Wyoming County, and stations are known to have existed in Palmerton, Carbon County

It has been assumed that the Underground Railroad operated in Lehigh, Northampton, and Monroe Counties. When runaway slaves escaping on the Underground entered Lehigh County, occasionally sympathetic Moravians assisted them. However, members of that religious sect did not want their occasional involvement generally known to the Underground Railroad network operators.

Eventually, escaping slaves were sent from Philadelphia to Quakertown before turning northwest through Allentown and Lehigh County. There is the usual traditional lore concerning the involvement of houses and buildings that were once stations on the Railroad, but little documentary evidence supports them.

Occasionally escapees were hidden by conductors in Union County at Lewisburg, near Bucknell University. A Pennsylvania State Historical Marker at 110 University Avenue reads: *The old stable was a station on the Underground Railroad. Here fugitive slaves were hidden and aided.*

The proliferation of stories about the Underground Railroad network is largely the work of latter generations. In Monroe County, Dr. Syndenham Walter, Jacob Singmaster, and the Vail Family were documented stationkeepers on the Underground. Some runaway slaves who passed through Monroe County apparently were sent by conductors from the Bucks County area through Stroudsburg, and perhaps from the Lehigh Valley area.

Lycoming County is located on the north bank of the Susquehanna River. The scenic Bald Eagle Ridge and the rugged Allegheny Mountains surround Williamsport, the major city of this county. Runaway slaves escaping to Canada often settled here.

Aid to escaping slaves in Lycoming County was extensive and organized. The citizens in this county were generally receptive to escaping slaves, hiding them from pursuers and helping them along in their flight. Robert Faries, superintendent of the Williamsport-Elmira Railroad, was an ardent supporter of the Underground. Faries and his employees transported numerous runaway slaves in the baggage cars of the train to New York State and Canada.

Robert Faries operated his Underground network with Daniel Hughes, Thomas Undegraff, Henry Harris, David and Philip Rodrick, and several other Lycoming County conductors and stationkeepers. Muncy, Jersey Shore, and Montoursville, all small towns, were on Lycoming County's railroad network.

Sullivan County was known to have Underground Railroad stations in LaPorte and Estella. King Tomkins was an operator on his farm in Estella. From Sullivan County passengers were forwarded to Bradford, Tioga, or Susquehanna Counties.

In Potter County, the Underground Railroad route led over the ridge of the Allegheny Mountain basin whose height is at least 400 feet. Here the route of the Railroad led into the heart of Pennsylvania wilderness, offering a most striking landscape.

The volume of runaway slaves who passed through Potter County is not known. However, Coudersport, a major town in the county at that time, served as a "way station" and was operated by several farmers who harbored runaways for a short period and then sent them on their own in sparsely populated regions of the state.

From Coudersport, passengers sometimes were directed to Millport. In Coudersport, stationkeeper John S. Mann maintained his home as an important station on the Underground. Mann forwarded his passengers to his brother Joseph and his brother's partner, Rodney Nichols, at their Millport station.

Stationkeepers in Potter and McKean counties were Nelson Clark, who lived in Eulalia; Ephraim Bishop, in Steer Creek; and Leroy Allen in Creres. It was John King's duty to forward his passengers to stations located in Angelica, Canandaigua, and Genesee, to Rochester and Bushnell's Cove on Lake Ontario, and across to Canada.

The town of Smethport, McKean County, was another important town on the Underground route to Canada. Runaway slaves entering the county were directed or taken along the Allegheny River at Warren through Smethport, Eldred, and Orlean and on to Buffalo, New York.

In Smethport, frightened, hungry, weary, and footsore runaway slaves who stopped at David Young's hotel were given food and money to help them on their way. Lackawanna County, where the City of Scranton is located, received and forwarded escaping slaves seeking freedom.

Waverly was the center of Underground activities in the county. The town was sparsely populated during the era of the Underground Railroad. However, a small number of runaways remained there instead of seeking freedom in Canada.

There are several homes in Waverly today that were formerly owned by local conductors of the Underground and former slaves. Another route in Lackawanna County passed through Dunmore and Carbondale, where there were a few friends of the Underground Railroad. Pike and Wayne Counties are located in the most scantily populated section of the state. These two counties offered little encouragement to escaping slaves or pursuing slave catchers.

Several families living in these two counties are reputed to have sheltered runaway slaves passing through. A family named Cuddeback is reported to have used their barn as a station, and in Milford slaves were said to have hidden in a building used as an old printing shop. Some accounts state that escaping slaves traveling to Milford followed the Owego Indian Trail through Pike County to Wayne County and north to Canada.

Bradford County with its vast forests and hills witnessed a flow of runaway slaves who followed the Old Genesee Road, a trail used by early settlers. Unknown numbers of runaway slaves from various eastern tributaries were led through Sunbury to Muncy, past the Run

House of conductor William Ellis, to agent Abraham Webster near Huntersville, across the wooded mountains at Highland Lake to Ogdonia Creek through Loyalsock, Elk Creek, Lincoln Falls, and Eldredsville. Another route led from Harrisburg, Union City, and Tidioute into Smethport and Coudersport.

One of the most effective conductors in Bradford County was Nelson Pardoe, who lived on Genesee Road near Lincoln Falls. He transported his passengers to Towanda concealed in a load of hay. The Bradford County towns of Wheelerville, Springfield, Granville, and Wellsburg were all on the Underground Railroad route to Canada.

Western Region Counties

Erie, Warren, Venango, Butler, Crawford, Mercer, Lawrence, Beaver, Allegheny, Westmoreland, Fayette, Washington, and Greene

Of the number of escaping slaves who came to or passed through Erie, Crawford, Mercer, Butler, Venango, and Warren counties over the Underground Railroad, no data are available. Yet my research, and the research of other scholars, reveals that a vital segment of the Underground Railroad ran through these counties. The town of North East in Erie County, populated by only a few hundred in the antebellum period, was a "jumping off" place for escaping slaves seeking passage to Canada by crossing Lake Erie. Runaways who lingered here and in other towns in the county did so at their own risk and in general against the advice of their helpers.

Federal agents were stationed around the waterfront to watch for escapees. Only 15 miles from Erie, North East was a logical stop for runaway slaves. Within the City of Erie itself, abolitionist and Underground activity was considerable, particularly from 1835 to 1853. Indeed, hundreds of runaways passed through Erie on their way to the "Promised Land" — Canada. At the mouth of Sixteen-

Mile Creek in Erie lived the abolitionist farmer James Crawford. His house stood in a grove of locust trees, a few yards from the beach of Lake Erie.

From here, Crawford's neighbor, a foundry owner named John Glass, forwarded passengers in small boats and transported them to Canada on the Great Lakes. The Perry Memorial House, the former home of Admiral Oliver Perry, hero of the War of 1812, on the southeastern corner of Second and French Streets, was an important station.

The operation of the Underground through this region was inspired by conductors and safehouse keepers Henry Frank, Dr. Judson Jehiel Towner, James and Job Reeder, William Gray, Stephen C. Lee, Josiah Kellog, William Himrod, and Hamlin Russell. The home of Captain Daniel Porter Dobbins was one of many "stations" on the Underground network of Northwestern Pennsylvania. It stood at Third and State Streets in Erie.

The belfry of the Old Methodist Church on Buffalo Road in Wesleyville concealed many escaping slaves until they could be safely embarked on boats to cross the lake to Canada. Other Underground routes ran north from Townsville and Cambridge Springs, Crawford County, taking their course to Albion, Branchville, Union City and Waterford, connecting with Girard in Erie County.

One route ran through Canton and Alba and then through the New York State cities of Buffalo and Niagara Falls, finally ending at St. Catherine, Canada. Meadville, located on French Creek in the western foothills of the Allegheny Mountains, played a prominent role in the Underground Railroad in Crawford County. Free African-Americans migrated to Meadville in the early 1800s, developed a small community, and won considerable prominence in the city.

Leading the aggressive abolitionists in Crawford County was none other than the legendary Underground Railroad conductor and stationmaster John Brown, who operated a tannery at New Richmond. Brown arrived in Crawford County in 1825. He frequently visited Meadville, 12 miles from New Richmond, and made his anti-slavery feelings known to the town's citizens. His cousin, Miles Barnette, operated a station at Waterford. The two men worked frequently and effectively for the Underground.

Among the whites participating in this clandestine activity in Meadville was agent Levi Barton, owner of the Barton Hotel. Barton conscientiously cared for his passengers and waited for coded messages to send then to other stations. He transported his passengers by concealing them under mattresses with straw.

Richard Henderson, John Brown's African-American friend and barber, with his brother Edward, is reported to have assisted nearly 500 runaway slaves in his home located at 371 Arch Street. Abolitionist brothers Robert and James Hanna owned and operated a livery stable next door to Henderson's home that was a station in the Meadville area.

Taylor Randolph, a most pronounced abolitionist, sheltered runaways for years in his home. John Brown converted Randolph to the anti-slavery cause. Brown also converted his friend George Dalameter and his family of New Richmond to join the Underground Railroad activities.

In 1833, Brown married his second wife, Mary Day, of Troy, Crawford County. His first wife, Dianthe, died after giving birth to several children, and she is buried on the property of Brown's New Richmond tannery. After John Brown's death at Harper's Ferry, West Virginia, in 1859, he was remembered by the county's citizens as a devout man who wanted to destroy the sordid institution of slavery by any means necessary.

Slave hunters had to face many frustrations as they pursued their human property through Crawford County because it was largely populated by people who were against slavery. The men and women in Crawford County who were connected with the Underground Railroad were activated by the highest principles. They denied the validity of the Fugitive Slave Law of 1850. They justified their illegal participation in the Underground Railroad by their belief in a higher law that gave African-Americans the same inalienable right to life, liberty, and the pursuit of happiness as they themselves enjoyed.

The Last Moments of John Brown—*Thomas Hovenden painted Brown after his hanging at Harpers Ferry.*

Several routes of the Underground passed through Crawford County. One extended from the State of Maryland, through Bellefonte, Punxsutawney, Brookville, Corry, Shippenville, and Franklin through Meadville to Lake Erie and into Canada. Another route passed through Pittsburgh to Beaver Falls, into New Castle, across Mercer, and north to Waterford via Meadville. A third route passed through Cooperstown into Townville and finally Meadville.

Some conductors led their passengers from stations in Meadville to Linesville, Conneautville, Owego, Binghamton, and Jamestown in New York. From Meadville, they also went to the Reverend Charles L. Shipman, a universalistic minister at Girard who, with his assistant Elyah Drury, harbored unknown numbers of runaway slaves.

Mercer, Butler, and Venango counties were also connected with the "road to freedom." Although a large number of runaway slaves passed through Mercer County and were assisted by Dr. Charles Everett and other sympathetic anti-slavery individuals, time has erased all indications of most of their names and the names of the runaway slaves they assisted.

However, in Stoneboro, there remains a Pennsylvania State Historical Marker inscribed *Freedom Road*, where a group of runaway slaves settled about 1825 and hastened to Canada during the enactment of the infamous Fugitive Slave Law of 1850.

Robert F. Lark stated in his article "The Underground Railroad in Mercer and Butler Counties" that, "The Fugitive could use the Philadelphia-Pittsburgh Road to reach Pittsburgh and follow the Old Plank Road to Butler, or he could use the Perry Road through Mercer County on his way to Erie." The name of the Reverend Loyal Young, pastor of the Presbyterian Church from 1833 to 1863, is frequently mentioned as a known stationkeeper in Butler County.

Other stationkeepers in Mercer County aiding runaway slaves were James Kilgore, the Reverend Edward Smalls, Elizabeth Breckinridge, John Gilbert, the Reverend George Gordon, Robert Grierson, John Houge, Jason Mathew, James Minich, John Squires,

Wilson Traves, George Wilson, John Young, the Bishop and Ward Families, and Robert Hanna, chairman of the Mercer County Anti-Slavery Society.

Mercer County's neighbor, Venango County, also had a number of stations on the Underground. Agents and conductors in Cooperstown and Franklin forwarded passengers into Mercer and Crawford Counties.

In Warren County, runaway slaves received some assistance as they traveled through that sparsely populated and wooded northwestern Pennsylvania county. The village of Sugar Grove was an important station on the Underground Railroad. Between Lottsville and Sugar Grove, James Carter harbored runaways, and in Sugar Grove ardent abolitionist Dr. James Catlin with his wife, also a physician, was a fearless defender of the Underground and harbored numerous runaway slaves who came to their home.

Other Warren County stations were the Presbyterian Church at Barnes, Sheffield Township, and the Linus Pratt and Levi Jones homes in Sugar Grove, from which passengers were led to Busti and other points in Chautauqua County in New York State.

There is much evidence to show that in the southwestern counties of Lawrence, Beaver, Allegheny, Washington, Greene, Westmoreland, and Fayette, there was some "organized" resistance to slavery in connection with the Underground Railroad. Runaways who came to New Wilmington found protection at the Underground Railroad station operated by Robert Ramsey. He was a Methodist and a staunch abolitionist, as well as an undertaker and cabinetmaker.

Ramsey sometimes transported his passengers concealed in a box from New Wilmington to other Lawrence and Mercer Counties stations. A principal Underground Railroad station in New Castle was the home of Joseph White, located on the West Side of Jefferson Street.

Ardent abolitionists, White and his wife worked tirelessly to assist the movement of the Underground Railroad in western Pennsylvania. They concealed their passengers in a Dutch oven and fireplace. Usually passengers would spend only one night in the home.

After receiving food and clothing they were taken at night to station-keepers in Mercer County.

William McAnliss of Big Beaver Township maintained a farm and transported his slaves in a wagon filled with hay to conductors in New Castle. Unfortunately, documented information on Underground Railroad operators is as difficult to substantiate in Lawrence County as in most Pennsylvania counties.

Documented correctly in the writing of Wilbur H. Siebert are the following Underground Railroad operators in Lawrence County: Alex Anderson, A. B. Bradford, Reverend Wells Bushnell, Daniel Enwer, Dr. A. G. Hart, Judge McKeever, Mathew McKeever, White McMillen, James Minich, S. W. Mitchell, Amzi C. Semple, Eli Semple, Benjamin Sharpless, E. M. Stevenson, W. W. Walker, Joseph S. White, Alexander Wright, Donald Young, John Young, and William Young.

The Underground Railroad ran directly through Beaver County, which was the center of considerable anti-slavery activity. The county was positioned along the Ohio River, which led escaping slaves from Morgantown, West Virginia, and Cumberland, Maryland, into Uniontown, Pennsylvania, and finally through Beaver County. The activities of the Quakers of New Brighton, the origin of the Free Presbyterian Movement, and the work of the Reverend Arthur B. Bradford were other forces that invited runaway slaves to stop in Beaver County.

According to Bausman's *History of Beaver County*: "The Quakers of New Brighton were always the ring leaders of the local anti-slavery movement. In some mysterious way of communication, slaves from Kentucky, Maryland, Virginia and even Huntsville, Alabama, knew that if they could reach the Quakers of New Brighton, they would be helped to freedom."

There, Edward Townsend with an ingenious trap-door to his cellar; Benjamin Townsend, with his friendly island in the Beaver River; Milo Talbot and Lewis Townsend; James Irvin; Timothy B. White; E. Ellwood and his wife; and many others were untiring in their assistance to runaways slaves.

Jonathan Morris of New Brighton was a bold and tireless worker on the Underground Railroad. Morris' home, located on the Little Beaver Creek, frequently harbored runaways. He was a friend of the noted Philadelphia Quaker Isaac Hopper. He forwarded his passengers to a famous station in Salem, Ohio.

Beaver County citizens formed two active anti-slavery societies. On January 28, 1826, a society was formed at the Greensburg Academy (until 1830 Darlington was known as Greensburg). Between 1842 and 1845 the first Abolition Society was formed in Chippewa Township under the leadership of prominent abolitionist William Scott.

The small Beaver County town of Achor near Salem, Ohio, was widely known as a key locale for Underground Railroad activities. On December 5, 1850, anti-slavery workers of New Brighton met and adopted resolutions against the Fugitive Slave Law. They declared the law was anti-Christian and vowed they would not respect it. The Covenanter Congregation of the Presbyterian Church in Beaver County was known in western Pennsylvania for its involvement in the Underground Railroad.

Also, Geneva College in Beaver Falls was a suspected station when it was located in Northwood, Ohio. Hookstown, Bridgewater, and Rochester had stations on the Underground route. The flight to freedom for many escaping slaves from the south led through the wilderness of southwestern Pennsylvania into Allegheny County.

As Pittsburgh grew, so did the controversy over slavery and abolition. During the pre-Civil War decades, The *Pittsburgh Gazette* reflected this controversy. It printed political news and articles on kidnapping, migration to Canada, Underground activities, anti-slavery meetings and other matters related to black life. Since the *Gazette* circulated far beyond the limits of Pittsburgh itself, residents in neighboring counties read its columns for information.

Heavy migration of African-Americans to the north had occurred by 1840, sweeping into Pittsburgh ever larger numbers of free and escaped African-Americans, and heating up local sentiments towards the abolition of slavery. These were heroic years for African-Americans and their white friends who participated in the anti-slavery movement.

The Fugitive Slave Law of 1850 sent shockwaves throughout the African-American and abolitionist communities in the Pittsburgh area. The *North Star* reported that on July 11, 1850, a group of African-American citizens met at Wylie A.M.E. Church and passed resolutions condemning the recently proposed fugitive slave bill. Members of this gathering called for total consolidation among their associations to ensure protection from slave catchers coming into Pittsburgh seeking fugitives.

Another anti-slavery newspaper, the *Liberator*, disclosed that by September 25, 1850, 100 fugitives had already left Pittsburgh for Canada. In one instance, the fear of recapture stimulated all of the black waiters in one hotel to leave the city for Canada. By October, an additional 200 fugitives had slipped out of this western Pennsylvania city, many severing family ties.

They left in small parties armed with rifles, revolvers, and bowie knives, all pledged to defend one another to the death. Throughout Pittsburgh, as the abolition movement gathered momentum, it drew into it all the issues of that day—women's rights; universal suffrage; freedom of speech, press and assembly; prison reform; temperance; and moral reform.

Many of these freedom-loving reformers were organizers and operators on the Underground Railroad in the city. Reports of the arrival of slave hunters caused great excitement, not only among African-Americans, but also among white anti-slavery citizens as well. So determined were these groups that no slave hunter should succeed in the city, that fugitives who arrived without proper identification were liable to be viewed with suspicion. Because of its location, the intensity of feelings, and its growing African-American population, Pittsburgh became the most active station on the Underground Railroad in western Pennsylvania.

Part of the extreme western region of Pennsylvania shares

borders with Lake Erie, Ohio, and West Virginia. Beyond the few urban areas such as Erie, very few African-Americans settled in the northwest part of the State. In 1912, Richard R. Wright, an African-American doctoral student at the University of Pennsylvania, noted that there were in Franklin (Venango County) fewer than 300 African-Americans among a population of 7,000, and in nearby Oil City, fewer than 200 African-Americans in 13,000.

In the surrounding countryside, the population was even smaller. It is a different story for African-Americans in the hills and valleys of the southwest region of the commonwealth. African-Americans arrived in this region of the Pennsylvania frontier almost as early as the English and the Scotch-Irish. They came with the first military expeditions as servants and laborers.

Moreover, African-American soldiers were with British General John Forbes when he confronted the French at Fort Duquesne, at the headwaters of the Ohio River in 1758. Others served under Colonel George Washington during the same French and Indian Wars.

By 1761, freed and enslaved African-American artisans, trappers, and wagon makers were settling around the Fort Pitt area. When the Gradual Abolition Act of 1780 passed in Pennsylvania, many runaway slaves came to Uniontown, Fayette County, from western Virginia during the last years of slavery as the courthouse records fully attest. Two routes on the Underground Railroad led to a terminal at Pittsburgh.

From this point fugitives seem to have been sent to Cleveland by rail or to have been directed to follow the Allegheny or the Ohio rivers and their tributaries north. Most of the passengers were forwarded on these two routes from Uniontown. Other slaves were forwarded northward along the Allegheny River to Erie. Pittsburgh African-American leaders such as the Reverend Lewis Woodson, John B. Vashon, John Peck, and the militant Martin R. Delany, all members of the Philanthropic Society, a secret Black underground organization.

Delany was probably the most educated and affluent of the African-Americans who lived in Allegheny City (now part of

George Washington with his slave helper on a surveying expedition in western Pennsylvania.

Pittsburgh). John B. Vashon's City Baths located between Market and Ferry Street was, by day, a business, social, and political club for the city's white leaders. By night, it became a station on the Underground. The John C. Peck Oyster House located on Market Street, operated by a friend of Vashon's, also served as a station stop. The Monongahela House and the Merchant Hotel also were important stations in the city.

Avery Memorial A.M.E. Zion Church, located at Nash and Avery Streets, has been documented as a station on the Underground Railroad. Hundreds of runaway slaves bided their time here until they could travel to the next station. It is recorded that a tunnel from the church's basement led to a former canal nearby, permitting fugitive slaves to be dropped by boat from the Allegheny River. A rowboat was used to secretly move them up the canal at night to the tunnel entrance. Information concerning the tunnel lacks full verification. Charles Avery's church was demolished to make way for the construction of a super highway.

Fugitives were secreted in private homes in the predominantly black section of Arthurville and Hayti (now the "Lower Hill"), and were aided by agents and conductors including the Reverend Lewis Woodson, Samuel Bruce, George Gardner, and Bishop Benjamin Tanner, the father of the noted black artist Henry Ossawa Tanner, who is portrayed on a United States postal stamp. The artist's mother, Elizabeth Miller, escaped from Virginia on the Underground Railroad to Carlisle shortly before she was married.

Abolitionist Charles Brewer's home was reported to have been a station, as was Thomas Bigham's home in Chatham Village. Bigham was the editor of *The Commercial Journal Anti-Slavery Newspaper*. Tradition states that Bigham's black family nurse, Lucinda, faithfully watched from the tower of the Bigham home for fugitive slaves or professional slave hunters.

One Works Progress Administration researcher wrote in 1940 that where Dalington Road runs through Murdoch Street stood the old Murdoch house, which was razed in 1920. Here too, in the barns and cornfields, slaves were said to have found refuge. Down the Ohio River near Aliquippa, the Reverend Andrew MacDonald lived in a log house where runaways on the Underground stopped for shelter.

Some Pittsburgh conductors forwarded their slaves to Venango County, a few miles north of Cooperstown on Bradleyville Road. Pittsburgh was a natural terminal on the Underground Railroad because of its location on the Ohio, Allegheny, and Monongahela rivers, and because of its wooded hills and deep ravines.

It is reported that a considerable number of fugitives were forwarded through the towns of Sewickley, Baden, Leetsdale and Rochester. Not enough is known about them to suggest their connection with certainty.

The founder and members of St. Matthew's A.M.E. Church, built in 1857 in Sewickley, served as operators on the Railroad. One frequently-used method for delivering food to fugitive slaves in the Pittsburgh area was for conductors to dress as hunters at night with a game bag filled with provisions.

Raccoon hunting was popular and used by the free blacks and their white friends. Since the masquerading party looked liked most hunters, they were seldom questioned. Wealthy Dr. Francis J. LeMoyne, a professor at Washington College, led the radical anti-slavery movement in Washington County. LeMoyne was known as "The Fighting Advocate for the Right."

With the help of his family, abolitionist LeMoyne operated the most celebrated station on the Underground Railroad in the town of Little Washington. Located today at 49 East Maiden Street, this two-story gray stone structure is of Greek Revival design. On January 26, 1824, LeMoyne was instrumental in establishing the Western Abolition Society.

Similar societies were organized in Centerville and West Middletown in Washington County, and at Brownsville and Bridgeport, Fayette County. LeMoyne won national recognition when he ran for Vice President on the Abolitionist ticket.

West Middletown, Washington County, was a major stop on the Underground Railroad where a number of routes came together nearby. Penitentiary Woods and the home of the McKeever family provided safe hiding places. John Brown made several visits to Washington County, where he was welcomed at the homes of James McElroy and the McKeever brothers.

The Underground Railroad was active in the Washington County town of Monongahela, particularly at the Taylor house on

West Main Street and at the Latta Stone house in Roscoe. Slaves were hidden in an old barn near the riverbank. As early as 1780, Westmoreland County was well acquainted with slavery.

Edward M. Burns wrote in his book *Slavery in Western Pennsylvania* that many men in the county who would not "for a fine cow have shaved their heads on Sunday" held and abused slaves. The major portion of the residents was conservative. However, by March 4, 1836, a small group of citizens formed the Westmoreland Anti-Slavery Society. They called for Congress to abolish slavery where it had jurisdiction and to allow the various state legislatures to do it for themselves.

Runaway slaves were also known to have passed through the Westmoreland County towns of New Kensington, Latrobe, Blairsville, and Jeannette. Unknown to most Underground Railroad historians is a rare, privately printed pamphlet, *Historical Sketch of the Underground Railroad from Uniontown to Pittsburgh* by Howard Wallace.

Wallace, a former conductor, lived most of his live in Centerville, Washington County. His story begins with the following words: "There was a black man by the name of Curry who cared for slaves while in Uniontown. Also another black man named John Payne. At Hopwood, a small settlement near Uniontown, the inhabitants were considered very rough, and many of them would have betrayed the escaping slaves. At night, they piloted to Brownsville by John Payne and others. There they were welcomed by other black men, Lloyd Demas, Simeon Artis and Thomas Cain, Andrew Hopkins, James Moffitt, Esq., and others contributed clothing and other means to help them along."

According to Wallace, some of the runaways would venture out at night and walk around, while others were very much afraid of the white people and would stay very close. Sometimes they were exhausted when they arrived, and welcomed the opportunity to rest. "We generally made it a point to solicit aid from the farmers and neighbors who were always willing to help."

Wallace described the main route and other helpers: "We always had plenty of help. Benjamin Wheeler, Sam Wheeler, Joseph Steward, and Henry Smith always assisted where needed. Some of our trips were made to Ginger Hill where a man by the name of Milton Maxwell lived. He would then take charge of them and forward them to Pittsburgh. The main route from William Wallace's was Maple Creek, but sometimes we went by the way of Ginger Hill. When they were taken to Maple Creek they were kept by George Norris, also the Bowmans. They were conveyed from their house to the river some place near Belle Vernon, where a small settlement of colored people lived, namely Rosses, Basiers and Minneys who were willing to help. From their homes they were taken to Robstown, now called West Newton, from there to Pittsburgh where many of the slaves found employment and remained there until the Fugitive Slave Law was enacted.

"Living in the Uniontown area during this period was the notorious slave stealer Robert Stump, with a crew of men who constantly captured and harassed runaways. Stump was encouraged to discontinue his sordid activities when the black community in Brownsville organized a protection committee. The Fugitive Slave Law created quite a lot of excitement in Pittsburgh and there was considerable trouble about the slaves. But nearly all of them went to Canada for permanent safety where they were welcomed by the subjects of Queen Victoria."

Located in Fayette County, Brownsville is a small community situated on a slope above the Monongahela River. It was a noted boatbuilding center during the early 1800s. An Anti-Slavery Society was formed here on August 19, 1826, and an account of the meeting was recorded in the *Washington County Examiner.*

The members of the Bowman family were known abolitionists. Their home was a haven for runaway slaves who stopped in Brownsville. A secret room in the rear of the mansion was used as a lookout for approaching slave stealers and catchers, so legend has it.

Runaways from Maryland and Virginia also found shelter in Uniontown. Many settled here as the courthouse records fully indicate. The town was a popular stop on the Underground Railroad, especially Baxter Ridge, a known hideaway for runaway slaves. Other places offering safety were Turkey Nest and Baker Alley, where runaways would be protected by fellow blacks. They also ventured out to the adjoining towns and some to Pittsburgh and beyond.

Among the lesser-known routes on the Underground Railroad in the tri-county areas of Fayette, Washington, and Westmoreland, were the towns of Donora, Monessen, Charleroi, Mt. Pleasant, Greensburg, Brownsville, and Fellsburg. Siebert's list of operators in Fayette County indicated one African-American operator, Joe Black. However, the great Underground Railroad historian was unaware that the following operators named by him were also African-American: John Jackson, Joseph Jackson, Potan McClure, Jacob Miller, Thomas Waller, Joe Ware, and Cato Webster.

Evidently he had no information pertaining to the activities of conductors Howard Wallace and Alexander Green with a significant population of Quakers, free African-Americans, and other anti-slavery supporters of the Underground Railroad.

Andrew J. Wayehoff, a Greene County historian declared: "Underground Railroad crossed Greene County about one half mile south of Mt. Morris on the Morgantown and Mt Morris Road, one branch led Northward through Belsontown (now Uniontown), Indiana, Punxsutawney and New York State to Canada." On the route that passed through Lenardsville and Bursville, Washington County, a community of Quakers was suspected of assisting runaway slaves. Thomas Hughes' home was an important station and the home still stands today.

The Ballad of the Underground Railroad

By Charles L. Blockson

Underground Train, strange as it seems,
carried many passengers and never was seen.

It wasn't made of wood, it wasn't made of steel;
a man-made train that ran without wheels.
The train was known by many a name.
But the greatest of all was "The Freedom Train."

The Quakers, the Indians, Gentiles and Jews,
were some of the people who made up the crews.
Free Blacks and Christians and Atheists, too,
were the rest of the people who made up the crews.

Conductors and agents led the way at night,
guiding the train by the North Star Light.

The passengers were the fugitive slaves,
running from slavery and its evil ways.
Running from the whip and the overseer,
from the slave block and the Auctioneer.

They didn't want their masters to catch them again,
so the men dressed as women and the women as men.
They hid in churches, cellars and barns,
waiting to hear the Train's alarm.

Sleeping by day, and traveling by night,
was the best way they knew to keep out of sight.
They waded in the waters to hide their scent
And fool those bloodhounds the slave masters sent.

They spoke in riddles, and sang in codes
To understand the message, you had to be told.

Those who knew the secret never did tell
The sacred message of the "Freedom Train's" bell.

Riding this train broke the laws of the land,
But the laws of God are higher than man's.

Selected Bibliography

Aldrick, Lewis. *History of Clearfield County.* Syracuse, New York.

Anspach, Marshall R. "An Account of the Muncy Abolition Riot of 1842". *Now and Then,* 7(1942): 29-37.

Auge, M. Biographies: *Men of Montgomery County.* Norristown, PA: N.P., 1879.

Ballard, Allen B. *One More Day's Journey.* New York: McGraw Hill Book Company, 1984.

Bausman, Joseph H. *History of Beaver County.* New York: Knickerbocker Press, 1904.

Bell, Whitfield J., Jr. "Washington County Pennsylvania in the Eighteenth Century Anti-Slavery Movement." *Western Pennsylvania Historical Magazine, XXV.* (September, December, 1942), 125-142.

Blackburn, Howard E. *History of Bedford and Somerset Counties with Genealogical and Personal Histories.* New York: Lewis Publishing Co., 1906.

Blackett, R.J.M. "Freedom or the Martyr's Grave: Black Pittsburgh's Aid to the Fugitive Slave." *The Western Pennsylvania Historical Magazine* 61, No.2 (April 1978.).

Blemaster, Arthur W. *The Community of Meadville on the Underground Railroad.* Meadville, PA: Allegheny College Press, 1926.

Blockson, Charles L. *Pennsylvania Black History.* Philadelphia: Portfolio Associates, Inc., 1975.

Blockson, Charles L. *The Underground Railroad In Pennsylvania.* Jacksonville, North Carolina: Flame International, Inc., 1981.

Blockson, Charles L. *Hippocrene Guide To The Underground Railroad.* New York: Hippocrene Books Inc., 1994.

Bond, Horace Mann. Education for Freedom, *A History of Lincoln University*. New Jersey: Princeton University Press, 1976.

Borome, Joseph. "The Vigilance Committee of Philadelphia." *Pennsylvania Magazine of History and Biography XCII* (July 1968): 320-352.

Brown, Ira V. "The Negro In Pennsylvania History." *The Pennsylvania History Studies 11* (1970) Harrisburg: Pennsylvania Historical Association.

Brubaker, Mariana. "The Underground Railroad." *Lancaster County Society Papers XI* (1911): 117.

Burns, Edward M. "Slavery in Western Pennsylvania." *Western Pennsylvania Historical Magazine 18* (1925): 204-214.

Carter, W.C. and A.J. Glossbrenner. *History of York County: From Erection to the Present Time, 1739 – 1834.* Reprinted by A. Monroe Aurand, Jr., The Aurand Press, Harrisburg, Pennsylvania, 1930.

Christy, Sarah R. "Fugitive Slaves in Indiana County." *Western Pennsylvania Historical Magazine 18* (1935): 278-288.

Corson, Hiram. "The Abolitionists of Montgomery County – Historical Sketches." *Montgomery County Historical Society 11* (1900): 1-76.

Davis, W.W.H., "Negro Slavery in Bucks County." *The Historical Society of Bucks County.* Doylestown, (1876): 793-803.

Delarme, Alonzo Alvin. *History of the First Baptist Church of Norristown, Pennsylvania.* Philadelphia: Lehman and Bolton Co., 1897.

Dubois, W.E.B. *The Philadelphia Negro: A Social Study.* Boston. Ginn and Co., 1899.

Duncan, John S. "John Brown in Pennsylvania." *Western Pennsylvania Historical Magazine 11* (1928): 50-54.

Griffith, Cyril E. *The African Dream: Martin R. Delany and The Emergence of Pan African Thought.* University Park: Pennsylvania State University Press, 1975.

Hill, Ruth W. "Random Ridgeway Recollections." *History of Elk County."*Pennsylvania Elk County Historical Society, 1982.

Hopkins, LeRoy. "The Negro Entry Book: A Document of Lancaster City's Antebellum Afro American Community Lancaster." *Journal of the Lancaster County Historical Society,* Volume 88, 1984. 142-180.

Katz, Jonathan. *Resistance at Christiana: The Fugitive Slave Rebellion, Christiana Pennsylvania September 11, 1851.* New York. Thomas Crowell Co., 1974.

Lane, Roger. *William Dorsey's Philadelphia and Ours.* New York. Oxford University Press, 1992.

Nash, Gary B. *Forging Freedom: The Formation of Philadelphia's Black Community 1720-1840.* Harvard University Press, Cambridge, Massachusetts, 1988.

Oblinger, Carl D. *Freedom Foundations: Black Communities in Southeastern Pennsylvania Towns 1780-1860.* Northwest Missouri State University, 1972.

Pennsylvania – A Guide to the Keystone State. Compiled by the Writers' Program of the Work Projects' Administration in the State of Pennsylvania. New York, 1940.

Philadelphia's Guide: African-American State Historical Markers. Philadelphia: Charles L. Blockson Afro American Collection/William Penn Foundation, 1992.

Salvatore, Nick. *We All Got History: The Memory Books of Amos Webber.* New York. Random House, 1996.

Siebert, Wilbur H. *The Underground Railroad: From Slavery to Freedom.* New York. Macmillan Company 1898.

Smedley, Robert C. *History of the Underground Railroad in Chester and the Neighboring Counties of Pennsylvania.* Lancaster, Pennsylvania: N.P. 1883.

Spott, Charles D. *The Pilgrims' Pathway: The Underground Railroad in Lancaster County.* Lancaster, Pennsylvania. Franklin and Marshall College Library, 1966.

Still, William. *The Underground Railroad.* Philadelphia. Potter and Coates. 1872.

Trotter, Joe William and Smith, Eric L., editors. *African Americans in Pennsylvania Shifting Historical Perspectives.* The Pennsylvania Historical and Museum Commission and The Pennsylvania State University Press, University Park, Pennsylvania, 1997.

Turner, Edward R. *The Negro In Pennsylvania: Slavery, Servitude – Freedom, 1639 – 1861.* Washington, D.C. 1911.

Walker, Joseph E. "Negro Labor in the Charcoal Iron Industry of Southeastern Pennsylvania." *Pennsylvania Magazine of History and Biography, XCII.* (October 1969): 466-486.

Wallace, Howard. *A Historical Sketch of the Underground Railroad from Uniontown to Pittsburgh.* Uniontown, Pennsylvania. Howard Wallace, 1903.

Wertz, Hiram E. "The Underground Railroad." *Paper read before the Kittochtinny Historical Society,* March 29, 1911.

Williams, George Washington. *History of the Negro Race in America from 1619 to 1880.* 2 vols. G.P. Putnam's Sons, New York. 1883.

Woodson, Carter G. "The Negro in Pennsylvania." *Negro History Bulletin, XII* (1949), 150-152-167.

Wright, Richard R. Jr. *The Negro in Pennsylvania: A Study in Economic History.* Philadelphia, 1912.

African-Americans in Pennsylvania

Book Chapters - Regions

① Philadelphia
② Montomery and Berks
③ Chester and Delaware
④ Capital
⑤ Central
⑥ Northern Tier
⑦ Western

North
↑

0   50 Kilometers

0   50 Miles

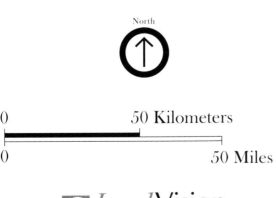
LandVision
Planning and GeoTechnologies

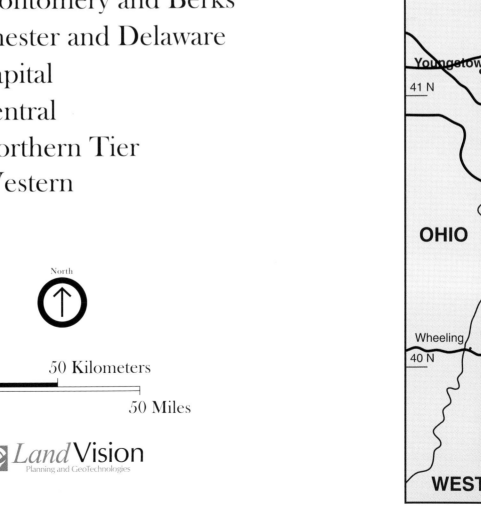

42 N

90

Youngstow

41 N

OHIO

Wheeling
40 N

WEST

THIS MAP SHOWS THE MOST SIGNIFICANT ABOVE GROUND AND UNDERGROUND COMMUNITIES FOR PENNSYLVANIA'S AFRICAN-AMERICANS.

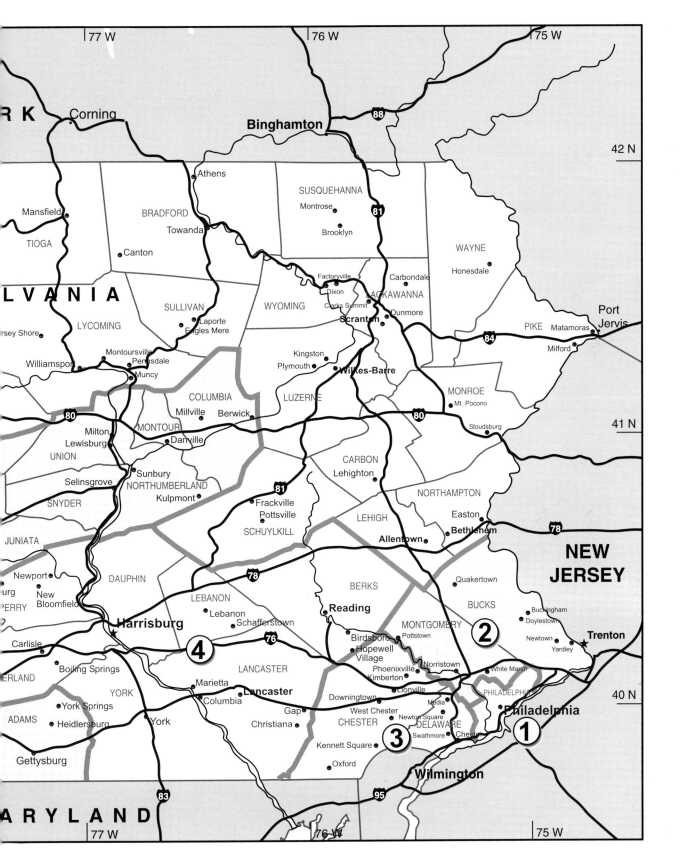

This illustration from William Still's classic book on the Underground Railroad depicts a conductor helping a group of slaves arriving at Philadelphia's League Island.

Appendix A

Underground Railroad Glossary

Abolitionist — person who demanded the emancipation of slaves

Agent — person who plotted the course of escape for runaway slaves

Baggage — slaves escaping on the Underground Railroad

Black Grapevine — method of communication in the African-American community

Bondage — the institution of slavery

Conductors — persons who directly transported escaping slaves

Drinking Gourd — a term for the constellation that points to the North Star

Emancipation Car — a name for the Underground Railroad

Flying Bondsmen — number of escaping slaves

Forwarding — taking slaves from station to station

Friends of Liberty — group of people who watched for the Underground Railroad

Freedom Network — the route of travel by runaway slaves

Fugitive Slaves — runaway slaves

Go Free — code word used by runaway slaves

Grand Central Station — city where a large number of slaves secured assistance

Gospel Train — name for the Underground Railroad

Haven — place of shelter for escaping slaves

Heaven — code word for Canada

Illegal Caravans — group of runaway slaves

John Brown's Trail — route of travel for runaway slaves

Lightning Train —name for the Underground Railroad

Load of Potatoes — wagonload of runaway slaves hidden under farm produce

Middle Passage — route of passage between slavers and freedom in the north

Mother Hubbard's Cupboard — code word for an Underground station based on a children's nursery rhyme

Operator — person who aided runaway slaves as a conductor or agent on the Underground Railroad

Overflow Stations — place of hiding of a large number of escapees

Sanctuary — a hiding place

Station — a safe place where runaway slaves could be sheltered

Stationmaster — person in charge of a hiding place

Promised Land — code word for Canada

Refugees — escaping slaves

Star Pointed North — code word for the North Star

Trackless Train — another name for the Underground Railroad

Wind Blows from the South Today — warning to Underground Railroad workers that runaway slaves were present in the area

Way Stations — hiding places for fugitive slaves

Appendix B

AFRICAN-AMERICAN POPULATION IN PENNSYLVANIA COUNTIES — 2000 UNITED STATES CENSUS

Adams County
1,105

Allegheny County
159,058

Armstrong County
592

Beaver County
10,811

Bedford County
178

Berks County
13,778

Blair County
1,535

Bradford County
251

Bucks County
19,495

Butler County
1,367

Cambria County
4,322

Cameron County
21

Carbon County
353

Centre County
3,544

Chester County
27,040

Clarion County
329

Clearfield County
1,239

Clinton County
197

Columbia County
516

Crawford County
1,437

Cumberland County
5,048

Dauphin County
42,580

Delaware County
79,981

Elk County
52

Erie County
17,202

Fayette County
5,233

Forest County
10

Franklin County
3,016

Fulton County
94

Greene County
1,585

Huntingdon County
2,342

Indiana County
1,407

Jefferson County
59

Juniata County
85

Lackawanna County
2,793

Lancaster County
12,933

Lawrence County
3,416

Lebanon County
1,548

Lehigh County
11,097

Luzerne County
5,408

Lycoming County
5,189

McKean County
860

Mercer County
6,318

Mifflin County
226

Monroe County
8,343

Montgomery County
55,969

Montour County
185

Northampton County
7,400

Northumberland County
1,439

Perry County
189

Philadelphia County
635,824

Pike County
1,513

Potter County
52

Schuylkill County
3,147

Snyder County
307

Somerset County
1,275

Sullivan County
144

Susquehanna County
128

Tioga County
250

Union County
2,878

Venango County
626

Warren County
90

Washington County
6,606

Wayne County
757

Westmoreland County
7,446

Wyoming County
149

York County
354,103

Appendix C

PENNSYLVANIA CITIES AND
TOWNS WITH UNDERGROUND
RAILROAD STATIONS 1833-
1860

Adams County
Gettysburg
York Springs
Middletown
Heidlersburg

Allegheny County
Pittsburgh
McKeesport
Sewickley

Armstrong County
Kittanning

Beaver County
Beaver Falls
New Brighton
Darlington
Rochester

Berks County
Reading
Kirbyville
Birdsboro
White Bear
Hopewell Village
Pine Forge

Blair County
Altoona
Hollidaysburg
Tyrone
Duncansville

Bradford County
Athens
Towanda
Canton

Bucks County
Buckingham
Doylestown
New Hope
Quakertown
Bristol
Newtown
Yardley

Butler County
Butler
West Liberty

Cambria County
Johnstown
Ebensburg
Geistown
Windber

Cameron County
Emporium

Carbon County
Lehighton

Centre County
Half Moon
Bellefonte
Philipsburg

Chester County
West Chester
Lionville
Phoenixville
Oxford
Kimberton
Kennett Square
Downingtown

Clarion County
Clarion
Rimersburg
Shippensville

Clearfield County
Grampian Hills
Burnside Township

Clinton County
Lock Haven
Keating
Glen Union

Columbia County
Berwick
Millville

Crawford County
Meadville
Townsville
Randolph
Cambridge Springs

Cumberland County
Carlisle
Boiling Springs

Dauphin County
Harrisburg

Delaware County
Chester
Upper Darby
Newtown Square
Lima
Media
Swarthmore

Elk County
Ridgway
Wilcox

Erie County
Erie
Girard
Union City
Corry
Waterford
Albion

Fayette County
Brownsville
Uniontown

Franklin County
Chambersburg
Caledonia
Shippensburg
Quincy
Waynesboro

Fulton County
McConnellsburg

Greene County
Waynesburg
Mt. Morris
Bobtown

Huntingdon County
Mt. Union
Huntingdon

Indiana County
Indiana
Dixonville
Homer City

Juniata County
Mifflin
Turbett Township

Lackawanna County
Clarks Summit
Dunmore
Waverly
Scranton
Carbondale

Lancaster County
Lancaster
Gap
Columbia
Salisbury
Christiana
Marietta
Wrightsville

Lawrence County
New Castle
New Wilmington

Lebanon County
Lebanon
Schaefferstown

Lehigh County
Allentown
Whitehall

Luzerne County
Wilkes-Barre
Plymouth
Kingston

Lycoming County
Williamsport
Montoursville
Muncy
Trout Run
Pennsdale
Jersey Shore

McKean County
Smethport
Uniontown

Mercer County
Mercer
Stoneboro

Mifflin County
Lewistown
Milroy

African Americans in Pennsylvania

Monroe County
Minisink
Mt. Pocono
Stroudsburg

Montgomery County
Norristown
Whitemarsh
La Mott
Horsham
Plymouth Meeting
Penllyn
Upper Dublin
Willow Grove
Pottstown

Montour County
Danville

Northampton County
Easton
Bethlehem

Northumberland County
Kulpmont
Sunbury
Watsontown

Perry County
New Bloomfield
Newport
Ickesburg

Philadelphia County
Philadelphia
Germantown
Frankford
Byberry

Pike County
Milford
Matamoras

Potter County
Coudersport
Genesee
Robinson
Millport

Schuylkill County
Pottsville
Hazelton
Frackville

Snyder County
Selinsgrove

Somerset County
Casselman
Somerset

Sullivan County
Laporte
Eagles Mere

Susquehanna County
Montrose
Brooklyn
Silver Lake Township

Tioga County
Mansfield
Tioga

Union County
Lewisburg
Milton

Venango County
Rockland Township
Franklin

Warren County
Garland
Sugar Grove
Bear Lake

Washington County
Washington
West Middletown
Centerville

Wayne County
Honesdale

Westmoreland County
Greensburg
Mt. Pleasant

Wyoming County
Factoryville
Dixon

York County
York

Index

Page numbers of illustrations are in **bold**. When surnames of slaves are not known, they are listed by first name only.

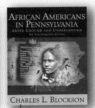

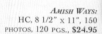

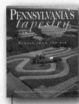